POSTCARD HISTORY SERIES

Fort Payne

On the Front Cover: This well-dressed 1910 family sits in a very nice surrey with fringe on top in front of the DeKalb County Courthouse in Fort Payne. (Courtesy of Collins Kirby.)

On the Back Cover: This postcard shows Fort Payne's Main Street (now First Street) facing west toward the courthouse on a busy day. (Courtesy of Collins Kirby.)

POSTCARD HISTORY SERIES

Fort Payne

John Alexander Dersham

ARCADIA
PUBLISHING

ISBN 978-1-4671-1390-8

Published by Arcadia Publishing
Charleston, South Carolina

Printed in the United States of America

Library of Congress Control Number: 2015958281

For all general information contact Arcadia Publishing at:
Telephone 843-853-2070
Fax 843-853-0044
E-mail sales@arcadiapublishing.com
For customer service and orders:
Toll-Free 1-888-313-2665

Visit us on the Internet at www.arcadiapublishing.com

This publication is dedicated to all the wonderful residents of Fort Payne and surrounding areas who call this area their home. From its rich cultural and historical past to its exciting present and its promising future, this book tells much of our area's story through postcards. For generations, postcards were the way we showed off our vacations, and we collected them to remind ourselves of our good times at home and while traveling.

Contents

ACKNOWLEDGMENTS

Many thanks go to the contributors of information and images. I am grateful for Landmarks of DeKalb County Inc., Collinsville Historical Association, Judy Brown, Dr. Stephen Brewer, Olivia Cox, and Randy Grider for history lessons and input on facts, dates, and miscellaneous historical information. Special thanks are owed to David Rains, Judy Brown, Rosalie and Charles Shipp for contributing postcards for this project. I would like to especially thank Collins Kirby; without his knowledge of Fort Payne history and his vast collection of postcards, this project would not have been possible. Special thanks are also given to Walter Raymond for his donation of valuable O.W. Chase 1889 original glass negatives to Landmarks of DeKalb County Inc., some of which are used in this publication.

Introduction

Fort Payne, Alabama, has a unique history. In the 1880s, New Englanders, mostly from Boston, came to Fort Payne to "boom" the town. This was a common expression at the time, used by wealthy industrialists who would scour the country for unique business opportunities. In the case of Fort Payne, it was to establish an iron and coal industry. The railroad, which was to bring new residents and supplies to build a new town, was complete, and Fort Payne appeared to have all the right ingredients for success. The city of Fort Payne is situated in the beautiful Wills Valley between Sand Mountain to the west and Lookout Mountain to the east. It was pleasing to the eye and seemed plentiful in resources. In 1889, massive construction projects sprang up all over town. Victorian houses, as well as a huge hotel, were being built, downtown buildings and factories were constructed to accommodate the growth, and even an opera house was erected to satisfy the refined, wealthy new citizens of the town. The architecture of Fort Payne is reminiscent of the Northeast, and to this day, a visit to Fort Payne inspires visions of a different time and a different part of the country.

The news of the mineral-rich mountains around Birmingham provided hope that the mountains around Fort Payne would be just as productive. After all, they were not that far apart. Perhaps, Fort Payne could become the "Pittsburgh of the South." The assumption was incorrect, and by 1892, after three years of mining, the local mountains proved not as rich in either coal or iron. The city population plummeted as many returned to the Northeast or went to Birmingham. Of the ones who stayed, their families continue here today, and they have a proud heritage. The population reached 2,900 at its peak in 1890, and when the bust came in 1893–1894, the population plummeted to half; at times, it was as low as a few hundred residents.

Prior to its incorporation in 1889, Fort Payne was a quiet little spot at the foot of Lookout Mountain. In 1780, the area currently known as Fort Payne was called Willstown, after Cherokee chief Will Weber. In the 1820s, Willstown's most famous resident, Sequoyah, created the Cherokee alphabet, providing for the first time a written language for the Cherokee Nation.

The first general use of the name Fort Payne came several years after the Cherokee removal stockades had been abandoned in 1838, and in 1869, Fort Payne became the official name. Not long after, on May 5, 1878, Fort Payne became the county seat of DeKalb County. The town had a small population living off the land, farming, and felling lumber, as well as shops, including a blacksmith and a few retailers, and churches.

After the boom days, Fort Payne struggled to find a new way to survive and to grow again; in 1907, Fort Payne found its answer. That year, on October 16 at 6:30 a.m., the Florence Knitting Company opened for business in a building that was formerly a hardware manufacturing company.

A few years later, in that very same building, the W.B. Davis Hosiery Company opened its doors for business. To this day, this building still stands as a reminder of the boomtown Fort Payne once was and also of the hosiery industry that made Fort Payne the "Sock Capital of the World." At its peak in 2006, Fort Payne had more than 350 sock mills in operation, and just as it peaked, US trade regulations began to favor free market global manufacturing. Lower-cost business arrangements with lower-cost expectations from retailers pushed the sock industry out of Fort Payne to mostly South American countries.

Fort Payne is a very picturesque city of nearly 15,000 (2010 census). It is located at the foot of beautiful Lookout Mountain, made famous by two Civil War battles at Point Park in Chattanooga, Tennessee, and Chickamauga, Georgia. Lookout Mountain is nearly 100 miles long, running south from Chattanooga, Tennessee, through northwest Georgia and ending in Gadsden, Alabama. Lookout Mountain is, and has been since the Civil War, a tourism mountain. After the war, soldiers who were there in battle loved the landscape and began coming back to build hunting lodges, hotels, and summer camps, and ultimately, lands were preserved as state parks by the three states the mountain is located in and by the federal government as Little River Canyon National Preserve. Attractions cropped up all across the mountain, including the famous Rock City and Ruby Falls near Chattanooga. From Chattanooga, you can drive the Lookout Mountain Scenic Parkway all the way to Gadsden, Alabama, with quaint towns, wonderful artisans, and boutique shopping along the way. You can visit Cloudland Canyon State Park in Georgia and DeSoto State Park and Little River Canyon National Preserve on the mountain at Fort Payne. Going south on the parkway, you end up at Noccalula Falls Park near Gadsden. Lookout Mountain is covered in woodlands and waterfalls. It is in climate zone seven, which allows seasonal temperature to support growth of many plant species most typically associated with points farther north and farther south. Fort Payne city limits run from the historical downtown area in Wills Valley up to lands and communities on top of the mountain. Fort Payne is far enough south to enjoy somewhat mild winters compared to points farther north but far enough north to enjoy four distinct seasons and great deciduous forests with fantastic fall color.

In the 1880s, the New Englanders came to Fort Payne to boom the town on the railroad, which is still a main line route from the Northeast all the way south to New Orleans. The beautiful sandstone Alabama Great Southern Railroad depot, now a museum, is located in beautiful downtown Fort Payne across from Fort Payne City Park, which was originally the location of the Victorian-era DeKalb Hotel, built during the boom days. From the Fort Payne City Park or the depot, you look east to Lookout Mountain from the last level ground before you start your ascent.

Many of the scenes in this book look much as they did in 1889 and through the years afterwards. Our history is etched in our culture and in our appearance. Fort Payne does not look like, nor does it have origins similar to, any other city in Alabama, and due to its unique appearance and cultural flavor, Fort Payne and Lookout Mountain have become significant tourist attractions, making tourism the largest nonagricultural business in DeKalb County. Fort Payne's scenic valley location with mountains surrounding it provide a great mix of business and recreational opportunities and is certainly a comfortable place to live from a cost of living and a weather point of view.

One

Greetings from Fort Payne

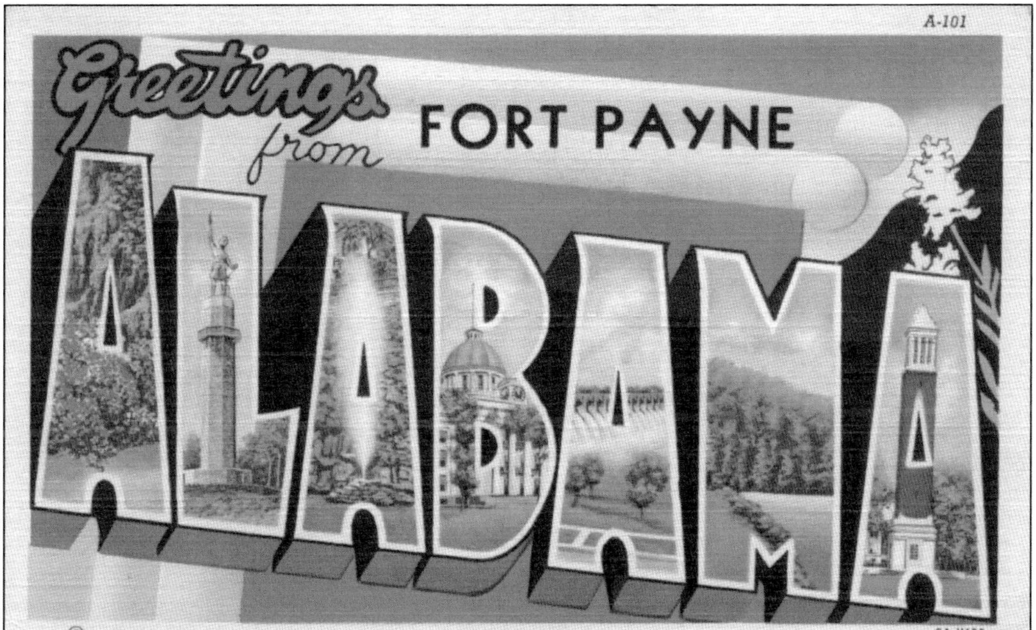

This "large letter" postcard by Curt Teich & Company, published in 1939, is the company's standard Alabama card, which has been overprinted with the town name, as was the practice for small towns. These iconic large letter postcards from Curt Teich & Company, E.C. Kropp, and Tichnor Brothers have been reproduced and parodied for many advertising and promotional purposes over the decades since their initial publication in the 1930s and 1940s. (Courtesy of Collins Kirby.)

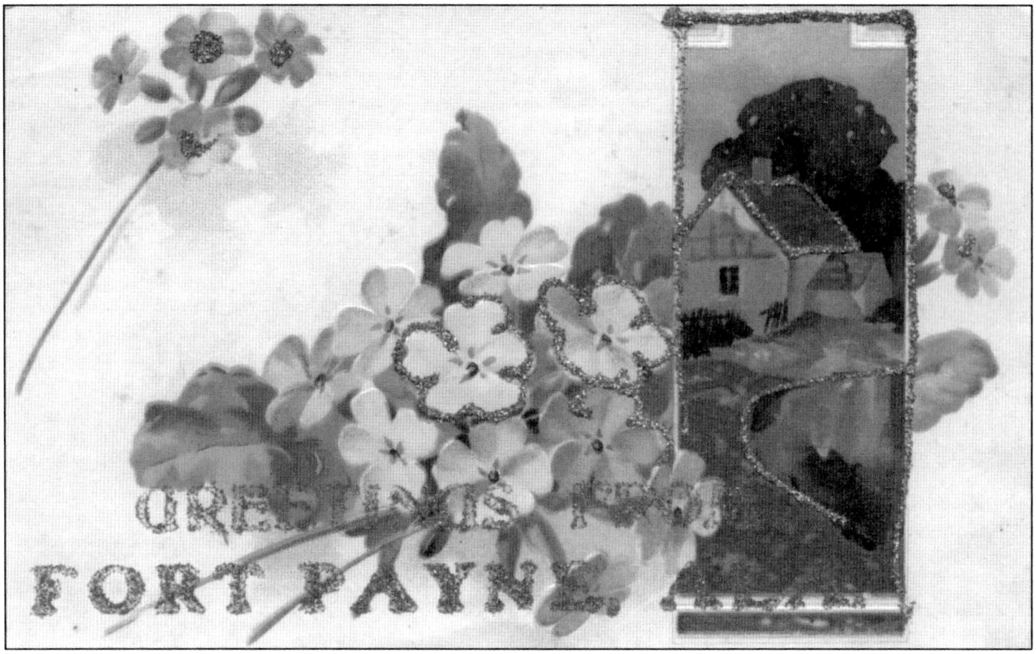

Germany was the world's leader in high-quality printing at the turn of the 20th century, producing embossed postcards in full color. This example, bearing a Fort Payne postmark of 1907, was decorated and localized using glitter, a German invention. It read, "Greetings from Fort Payne, Ala." (Courtesy of Collins Kirby.)

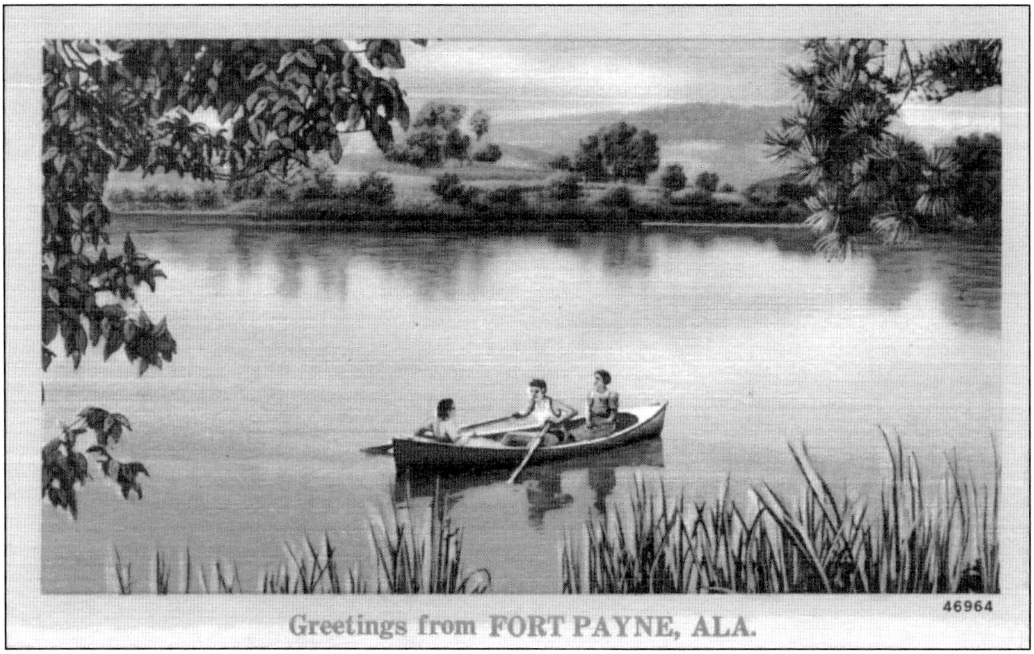

In a fashion similar to the large letter cards, generic scenes like this one were distributed far and wide in the late 1930s, using an overprint to specify the town where it was sold. This linen example from the NYCE Publishing Company is one of several by that company that were distributed in Fort Payne. It bears a 1941 postmark. (Courtesy of Collins Kirby.)

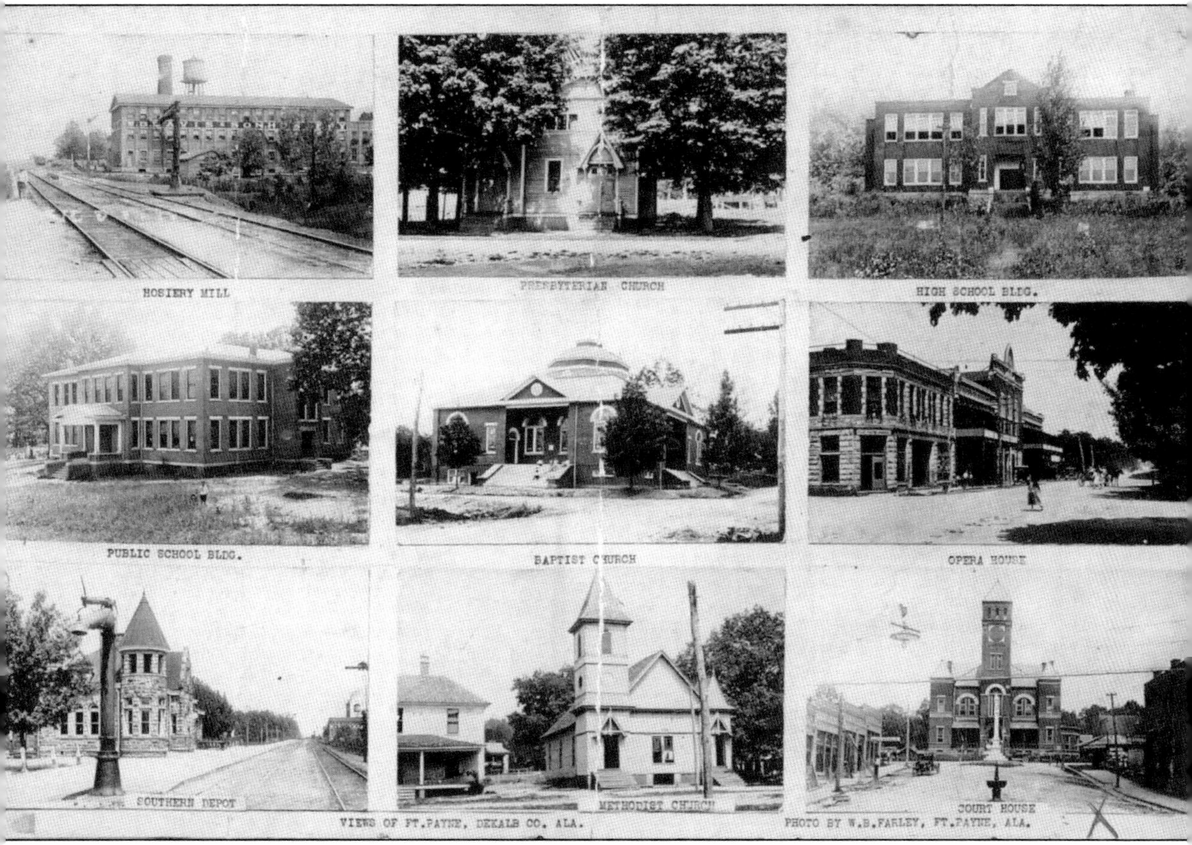

This interesting composite by W.B. Farley was created in the late 1920s by assembling and photographing nine postcards and postcard-size pictures. A typewriter was used to label each one in the margin between pictures. The buildings included are the W.B. Davis Hosiery Mill, Presbyterian church, high school building, public school building, Baptist church, opera house, Alabama Great Southern Railroad depot, Methodist church, and the courthouse. The card is titled "Views of Ft. Payne, DeKalb Co. Ala." (Courtesy of Collins Kirby.)

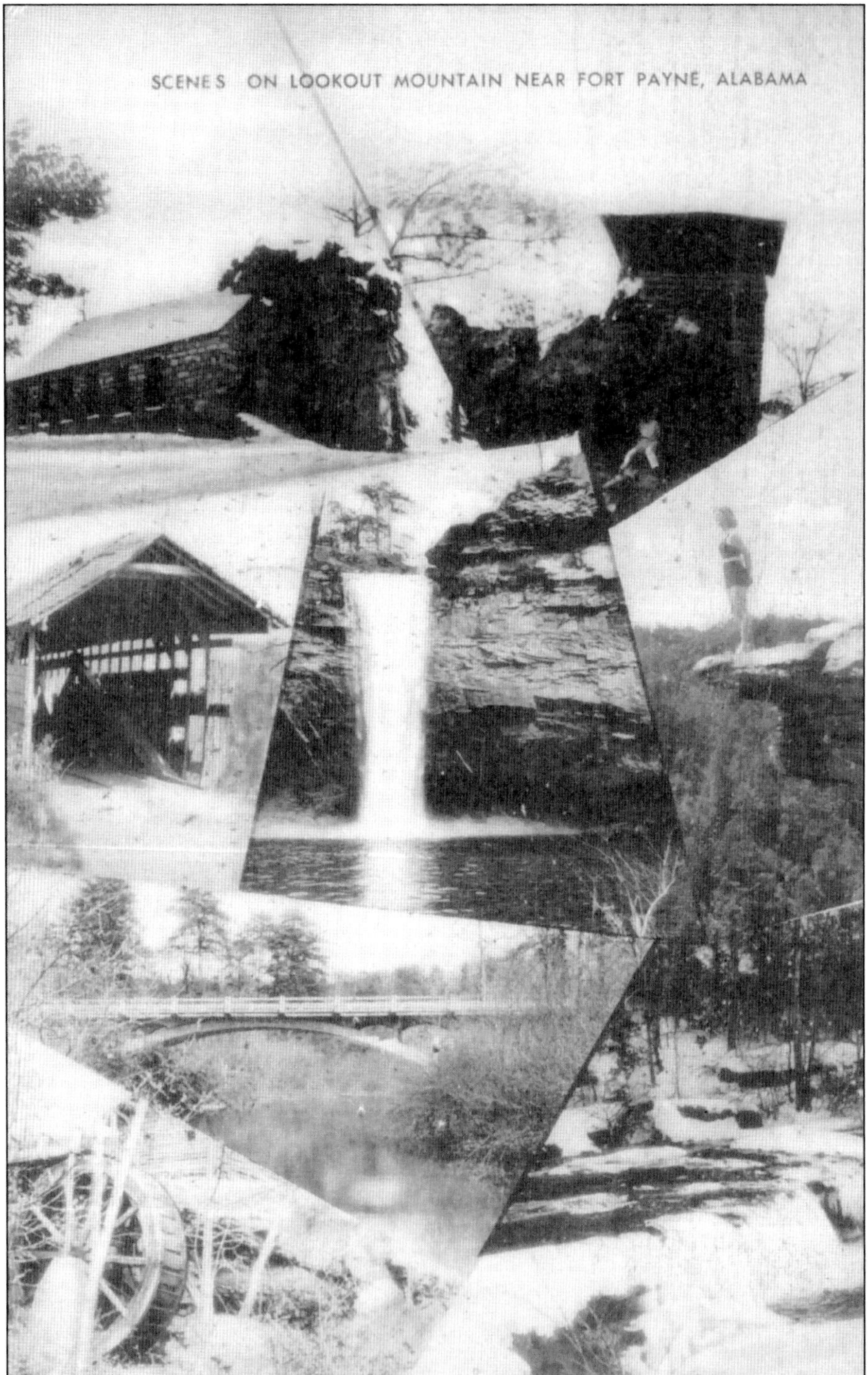

These scenes on Lookout Mountain near Fort Payne, Alabama, create a montage featuring pictures of DeSoto Falls, Howard's Chapel, the gristmill at Alpine Dam, a high diver, and a covered bridge in Mentone, Alabama, among others. It was published by Mayrose Company of New York and is postmarked 1941. (Courtesy of Collins Kirby.)

Two

BIRDS-EYE VIEWS

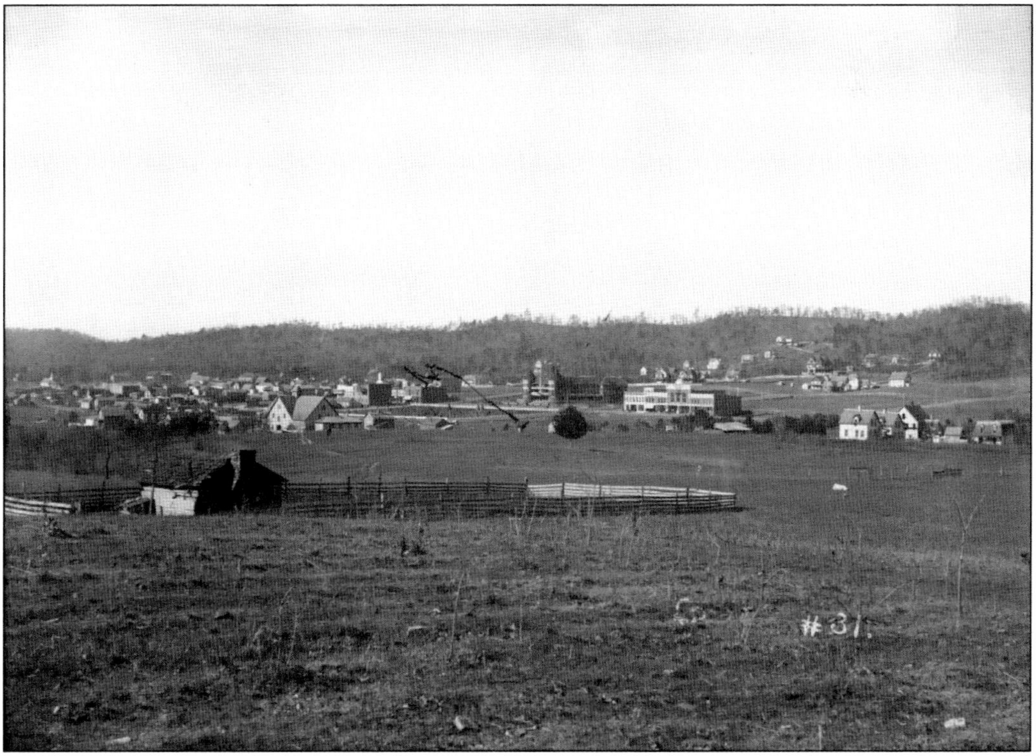

This amazing photograph by O.W. Chase, taken in 1889, shows the new DeKalb Hotel, the Fort Payne Coal and Iron Company office, and the completed opera block. O.W. Chase's work is described as primarily having been done in 1889, but it is the author's opinion in looking at construction projects underway or not yet underway in various pictures that Chase's work was likely to have been done over several years from 1888 through 1891. The beautiful sandstone Alabama Great Southern Railroad depot was built in 1891, and none of Chase's images include it, lending to the theory that he was done with his commercial images of Fort Payne prior to 1891. This image would show the depot if it were built or under construction. (Author's collection.)

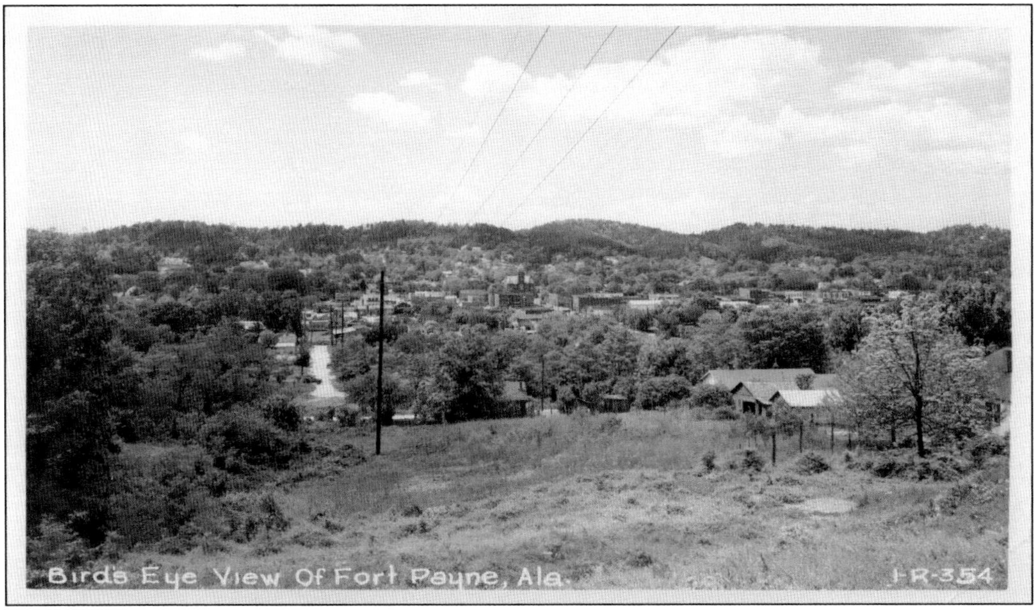

This wonderful real-photo postcard by Walter Cline from the early 1940s was taken from the side of Lookout Mountain looking west toward downtown from Third Street South. Under close examination, the courthouse and some downtown buildings on First Street are visible. Postcards that were printed on real-photo paper can be scanned and enlarged to any size. Commercially printed, non-photo postcards pick up the dot matrix of the printing process and make enlarged viewing more difficult. By the 1950s, real-photo postcards became rare. (Courtesy of Collins Kirby.)

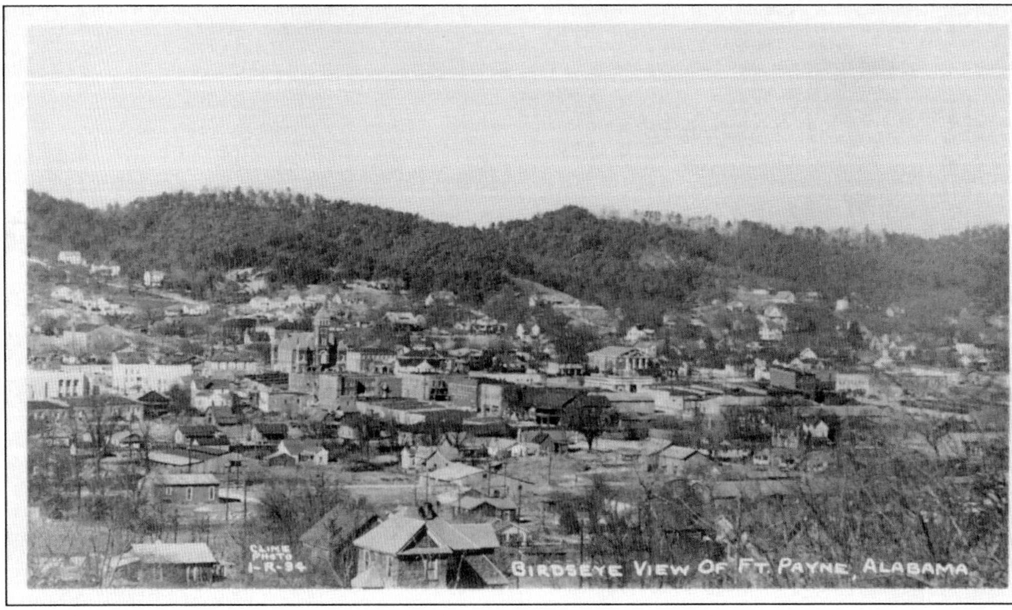

Another Cline real-photo postcard from the early 1940s shows a beautiful distant portrait of downtown Fort Payne. This card shows a winter scene, which provides better visibility of the downtown than the prior summertime one. They are close in location. This one moves slightly north of the last image but still shows the courthouse, downtown buildings, and churches. It is shot with a longer lens (telephoto), which enlarges the viewpoint. (Courtesy of Collins Kirby.)

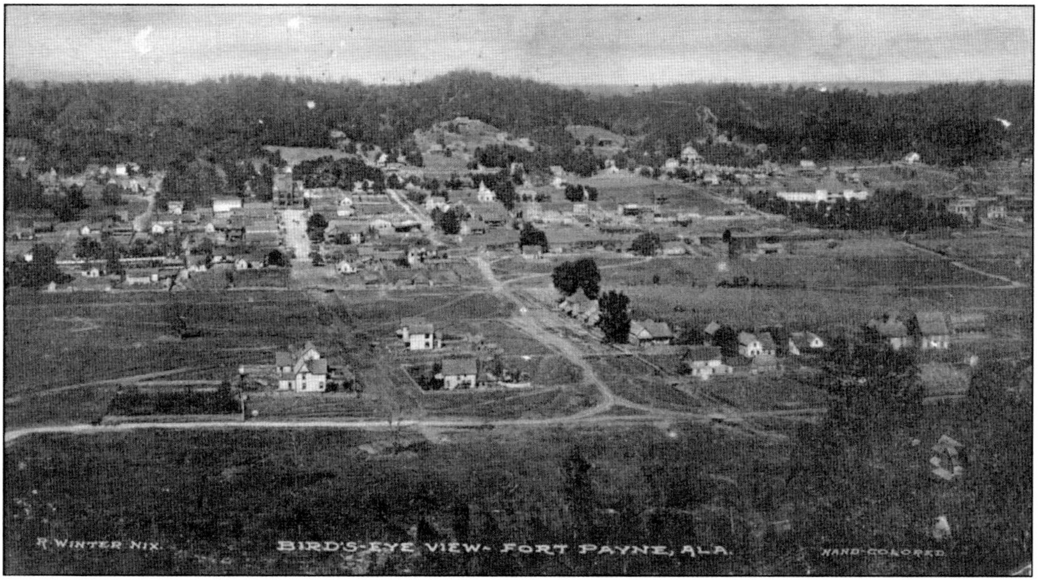

This is another view like the last two, but this one was taken a little farther north, almost looking west straight down First Street. This card by R. Winter Nix is hand colored and is from the early 1900s, but pre-1910. The amazing difference here is the lack of trees in the view. Most of the trees on Lookout Mountain and in the valley had been cleared for construction lumber and farming. From the time of this scene until now, the woodlands have been mostly left intact around the developed areas. There is no view from this location today due to reforestation. (Courtesy of Collins Kirby.)

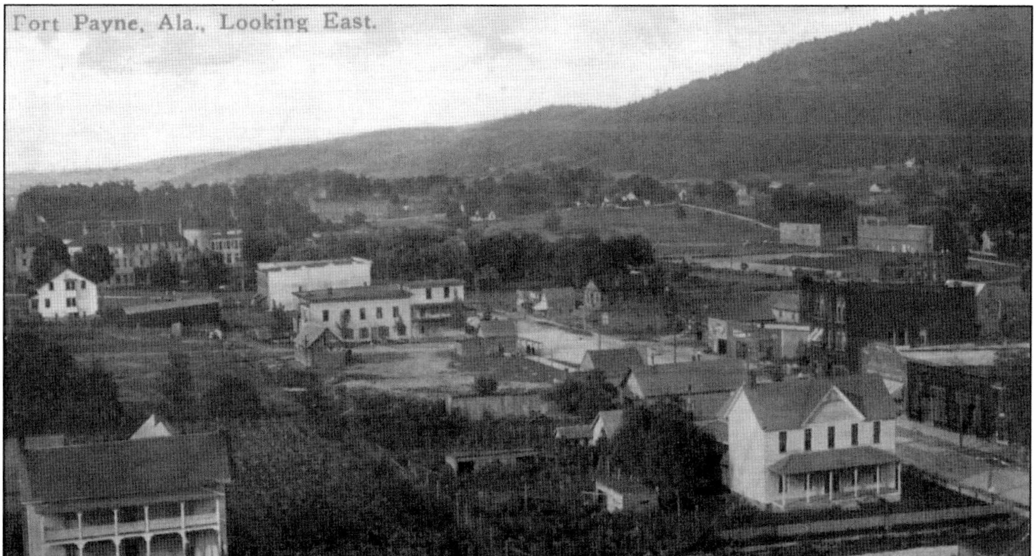

Published for W.L. Haralson of Fort Payne, this card, postmarked April 8, 1913, shows Gault Avenue running to the north. The DeKalb Hotel is at center left, and the W.B. Davis Hosiery Mill is at top center to the right of the hotel. This view provides a pretty scene of Lookout Mountain. Lookout Mountain runs 100 miles from Chattanooga, Tennessee, to Gadsden, Alabama, and is filled with lovely canyons, fluctuations in altitude, and beauty the entire 100 miles. (Courtesy of Collins Kirby.)

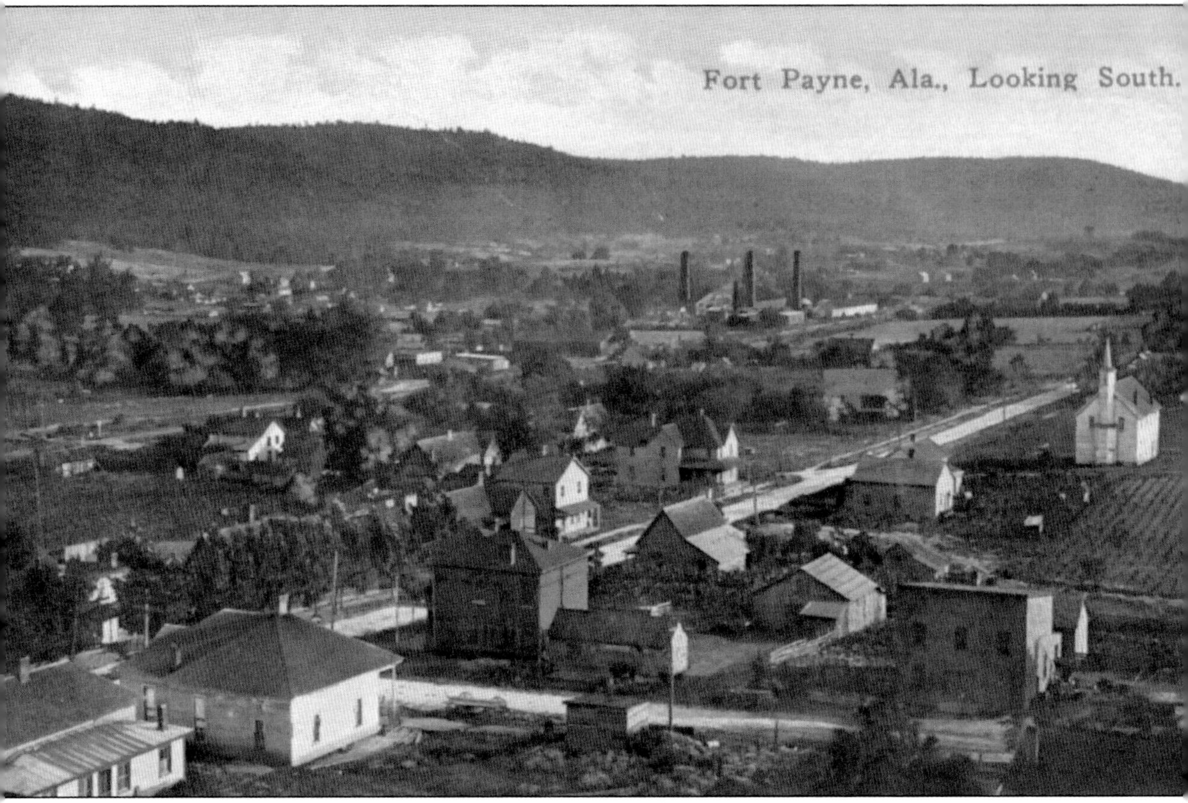

Also published for W.L. Haralson in 1913, this postcard looks south from Alabama Avenue. The Fort Payne Fire and Clay Works can be seen at upper left. (Courtesy of Collins Kirby.)

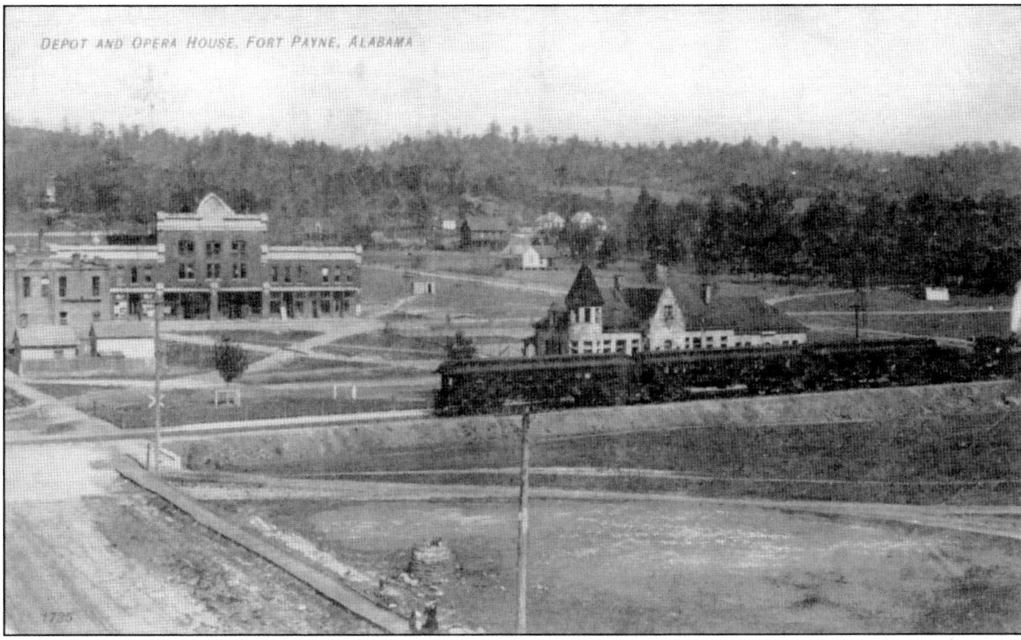

Postmarked November 16, 1908, this card shows the Alabama Great Southern Railroad depot with a historic steam train on the track and the opera house behind it. To the far left is Fifth Street Northeast; in front of the track is a tributary of Wills Creek; the c. 1906 sidewalk bridge, slightly left of center, is still used today. The area in front of the track is the current location of the Alabama Walking Park and the Rotary Pavilion. At this time, Fort Payne was a quieter town than it was in the late 1880s. This scene shows very little activity and no construction. Everything in the picture was built by 1889, with the Alabama Great Southern Railroad depot being the last completed in early 1891. Below is the back of the postcard. (Both, courtesy of Collins Kirby.)

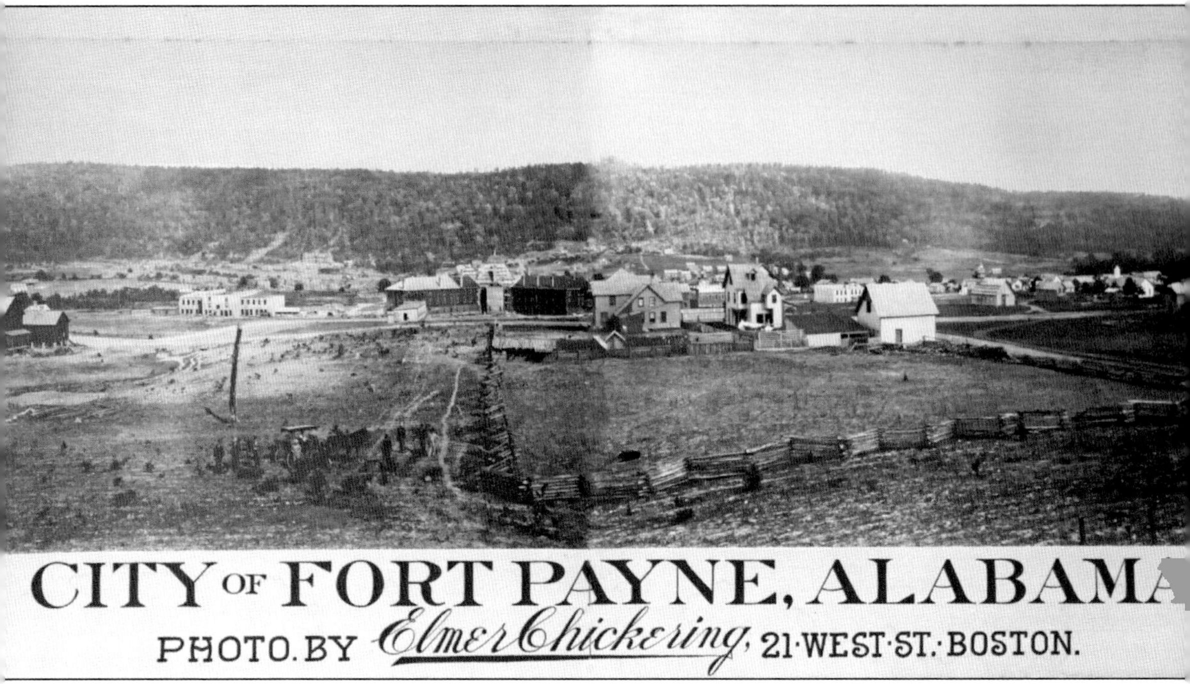

Elmer Chickering was a well-known commercial photographer from Boston. He visited Fort Payne in 1889 and shot this panoramic image. It is actually two separate photographs pieced together. (Courtesy of Landmarks of DeKalb County.)

Three

Government Buildings

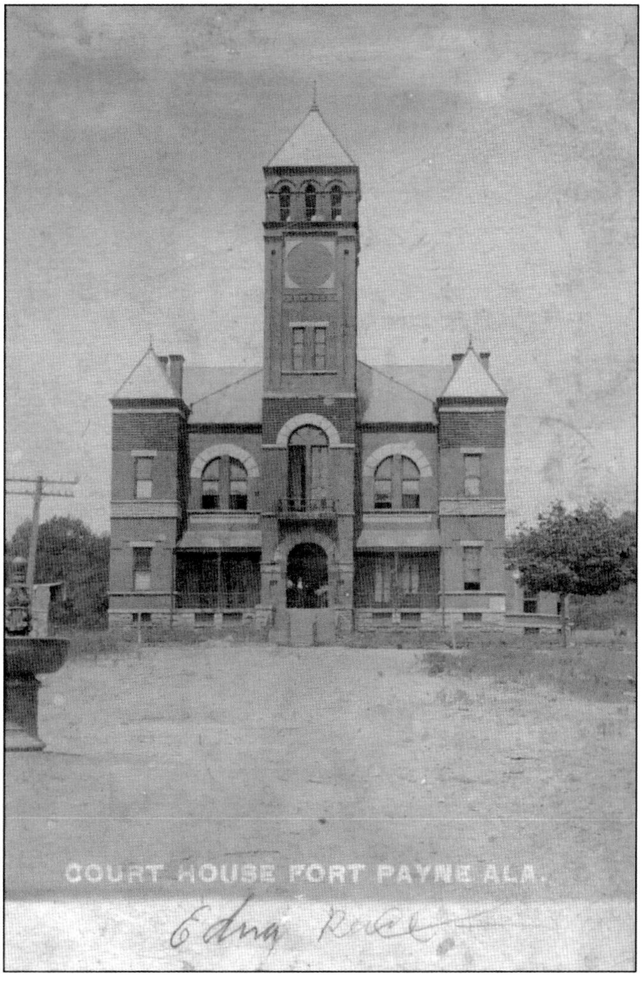

Fort Payne became the county seat in 1878, and a small, two-story courthouse was erected at the intersection of what is now First Street West and Grand Avenue. In 1891, at the height of the boomtown, that original building was dismantled and replaced by the imposing edifice seen in this real-photo postcard, postmarked 1907. The magnificent clock tower was not fitted with a clock until 1925. Two adults and two children can be seen standing beneath the entrance arch. The horse-watering fountain is partially visible at left in the foreground. (Courtesy of Collins Kirby.)

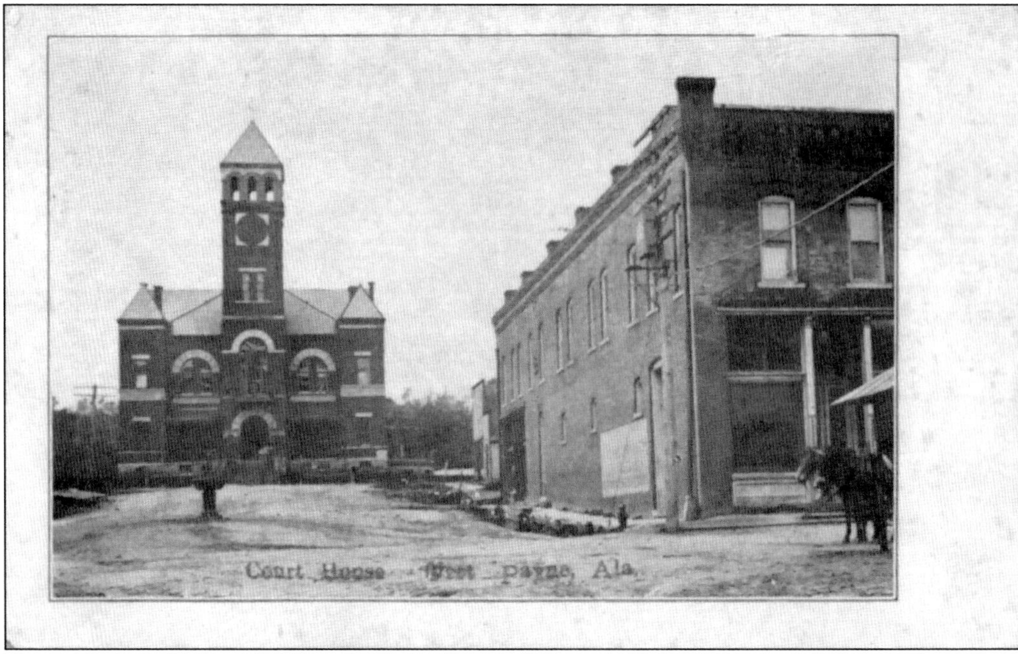

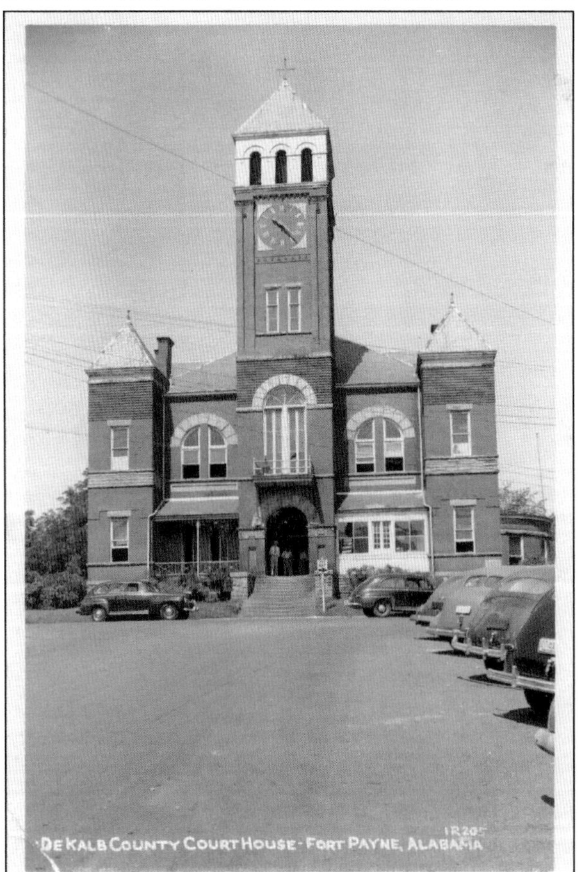

This c. 1910 printed card depicts the massive, two-story mercantile building at the northwest corner of Gault Avenue and First Street. The adjacent sidewalk is lined with rather large stones used to scotch the wheels of wagons parked on the hill. (Courtesy of Collins Kirby.)

Walter Cline's card from the mid-1940s plainly shows the 10-foot diameter Seth Thomas clock, which was installed by A.A. Miller of the Fort Payne Light and Power Company. Three men in summer attire are seen beneath the arch. The sandstone front steps are visibly worn from 50 years of use. (Courtesy of Collins Kirby.)

This 1945 Curt Teich & Company postcard is beautifully retouched and plainly shows the clock. (Courtesy of Collin Kirby.)

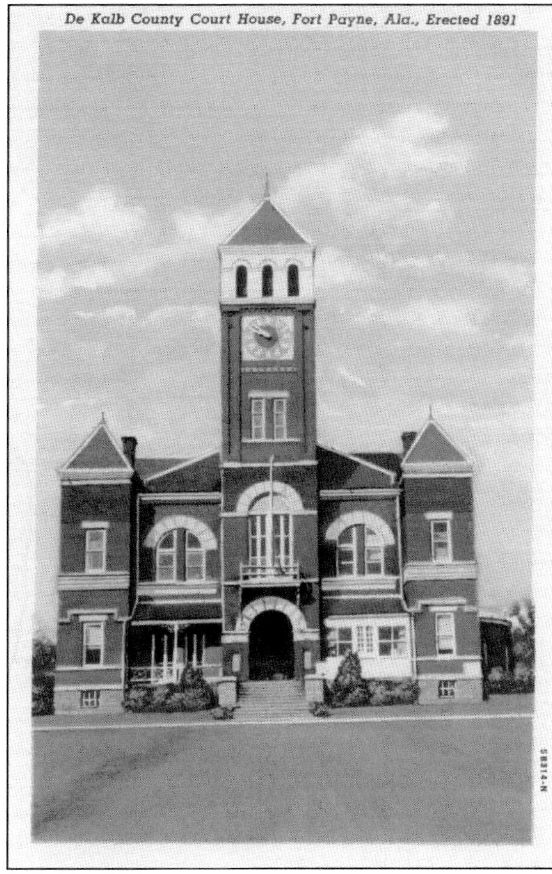

The DeKalb County Commission erected Fort Payne's third courthouse beginning in 1949 on Grand Avenue west of the intersection at Third Street Southwest. The county jail was on the fourth floor. This Cline postcard from 1951 was published before the landscaping was completed. (Courtesy of Collins Kirby.)

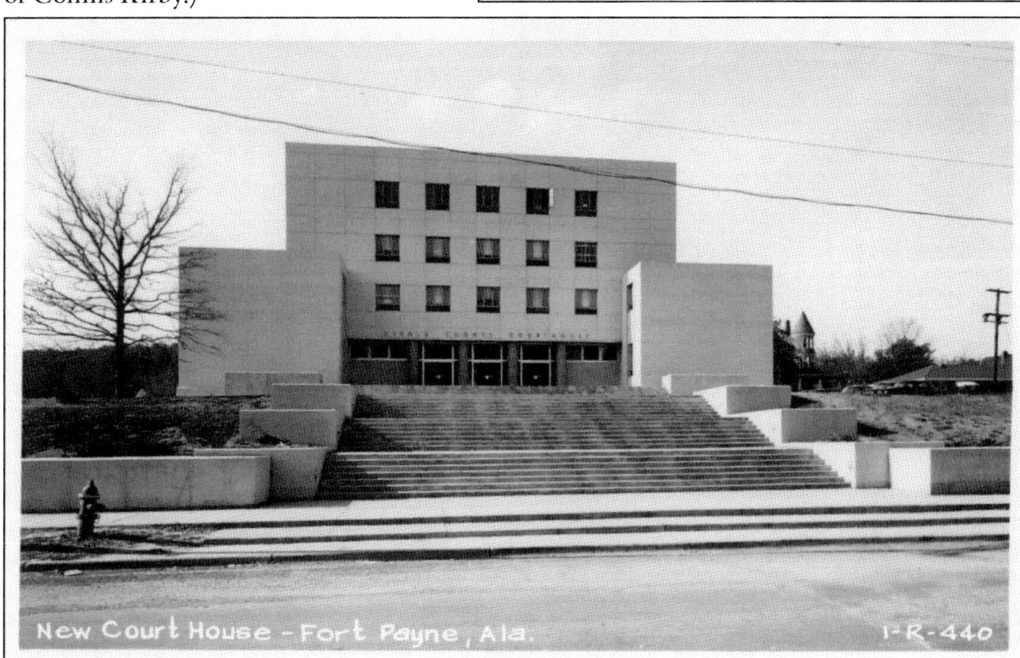

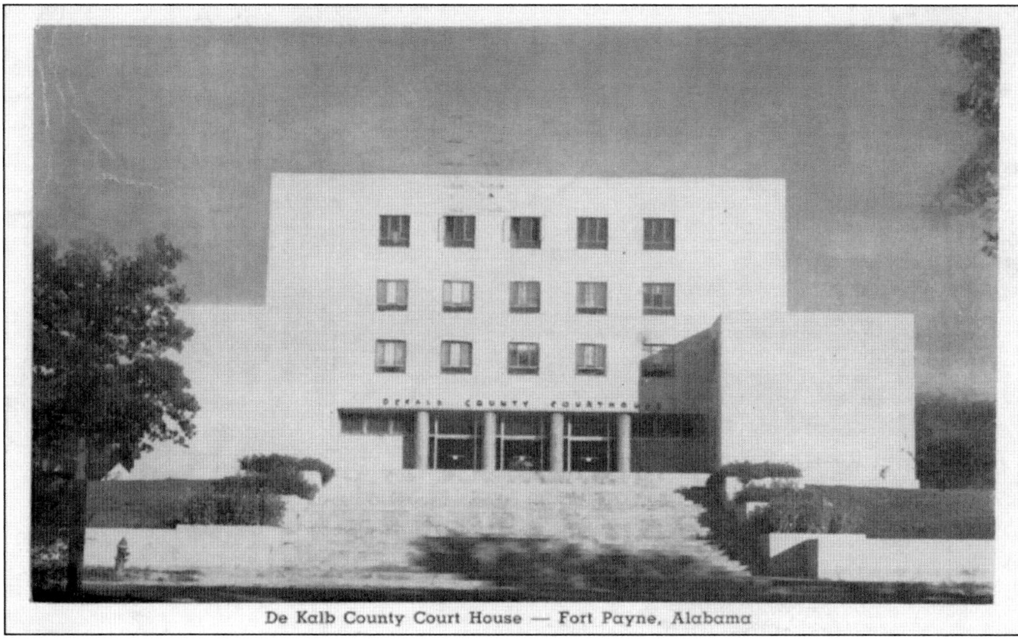

Postmarked 1952, this printed card by an unknown publisher shows that the shrubbery had been installed in the huge planters along the broad steps. (Courtesy of Collins Kirby.)

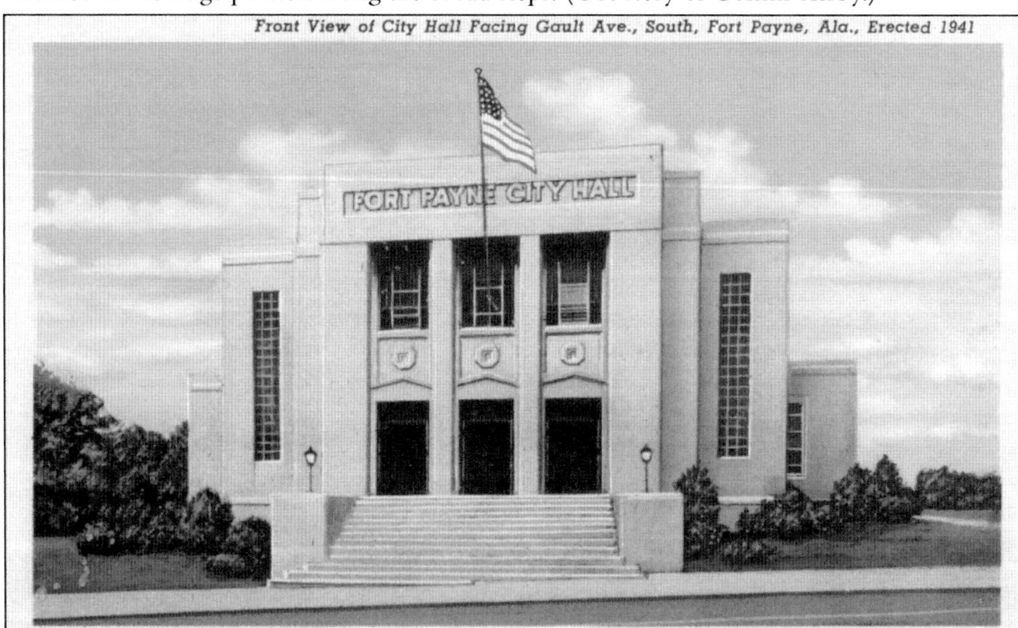

Fort Payne City Hall, erected in 1941 on the site of the previous brick city hall building, is a sturdy two-story structure in the Art Moderne architectural style, and originally housed all of the various offices of the city, like the police and fire departments, utilities offices, and, in the basement, the DeKalb County Library. Over the years, the electric and water boards moved to larger facilities, and the library moved to its new building in 1995. In 2006, the former Forest Avenue School buildings were repurposed as the new city hall, allowing the police department to expand into the entirety of this building. (Courtesy of Collins Kirby.)

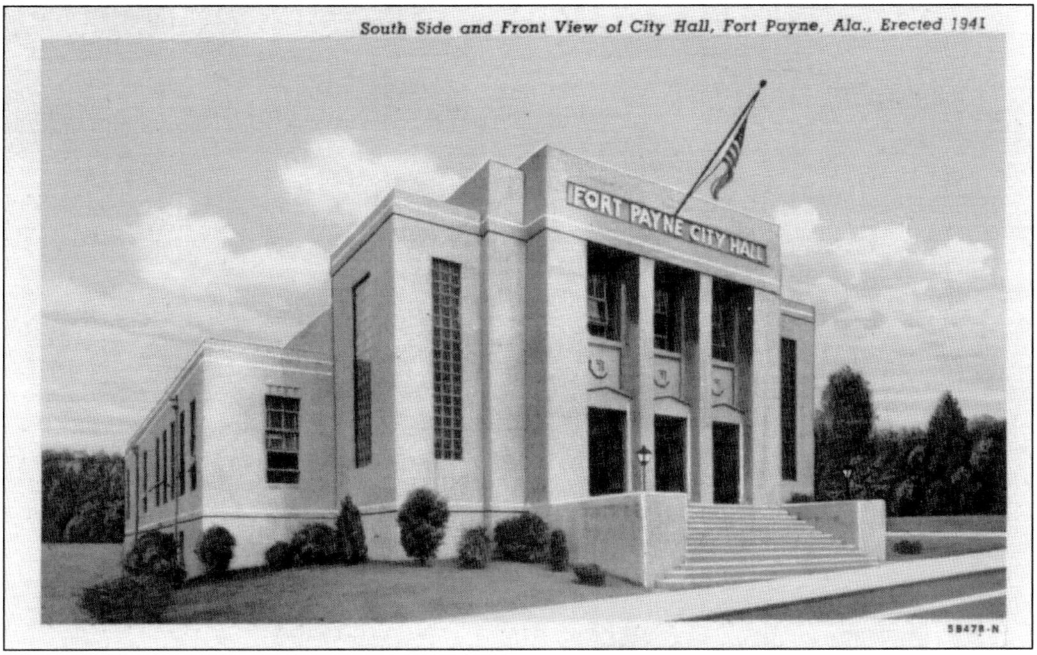

Another postcard in the Curt Teich & Company series of 1945 looks north from a dramatic angle. This picture shows a very pretty city hall with nice landscaping. (Courtesy of Collins Kirby.)

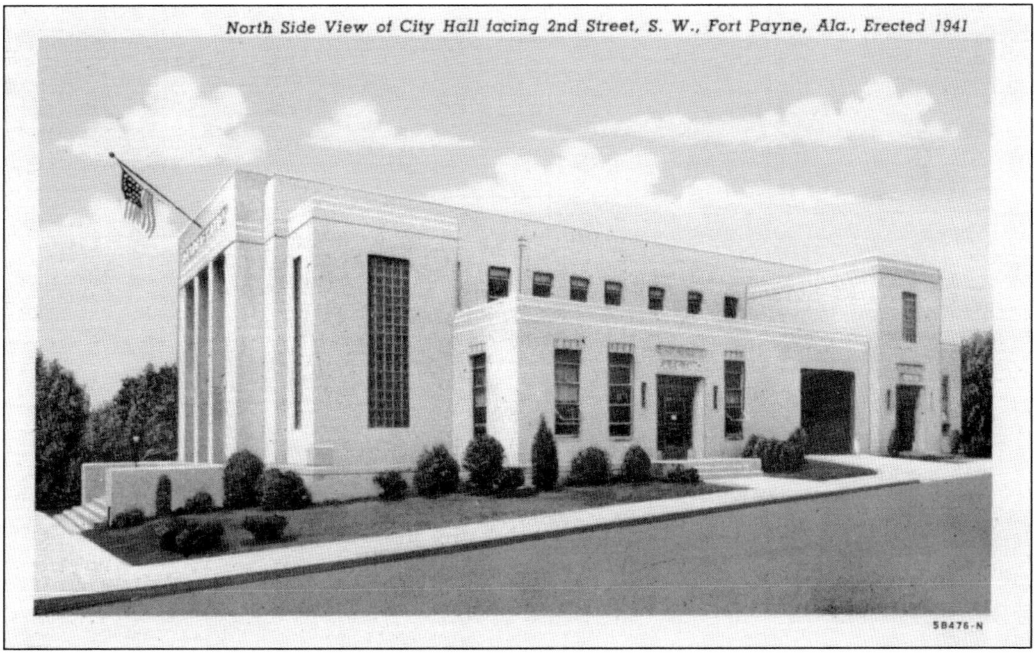

This Curt Teich & Company side view of city hall shows the Second Street South entrance for the electric board, whose offices were used later by the water board; the roll-up door for the fire truck's bay; and the entrance to the police station and city jail. (Courtesy of Collins Kirby.)

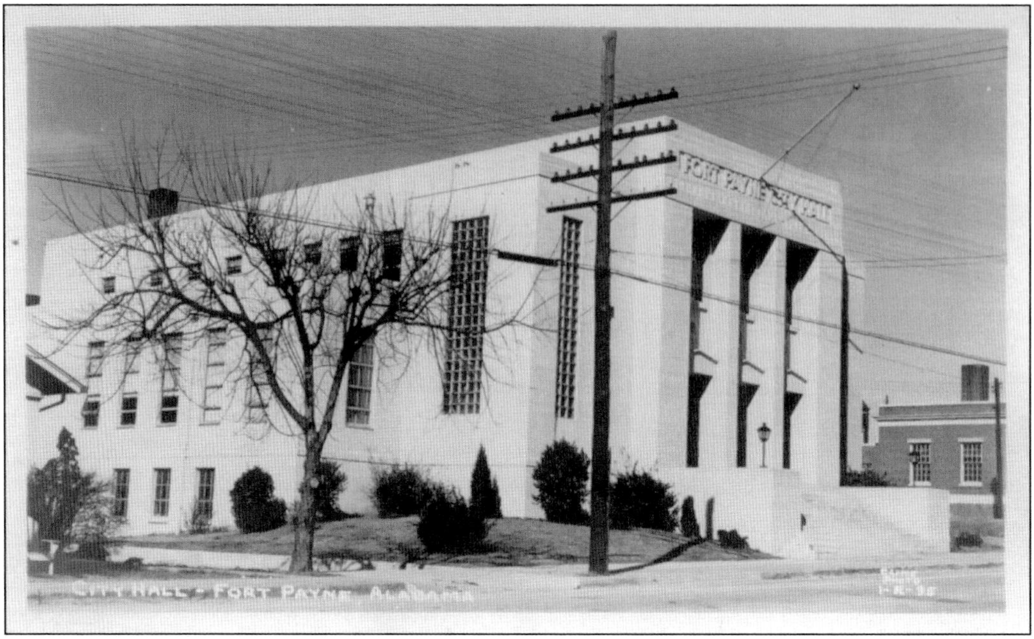

Bearing a 1946 postmark, Cline's real-photo postcard, looking north, has a glimpse of the post office at far right. The image quality of this card is good enough to enlarge to very large sizes. (Courtesy of Collins Kirby.)

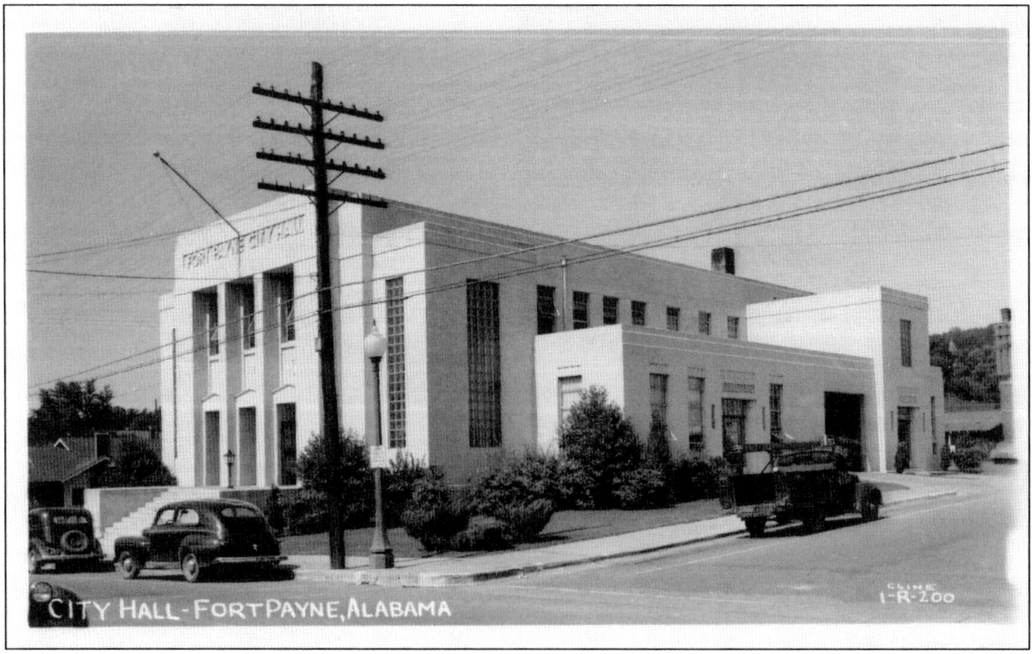

This late 1940s Cline image, looking west, gives a tiny view of the corner of Fort Payne's first county jail at far right. (Courtesy of Collins Kirby.)

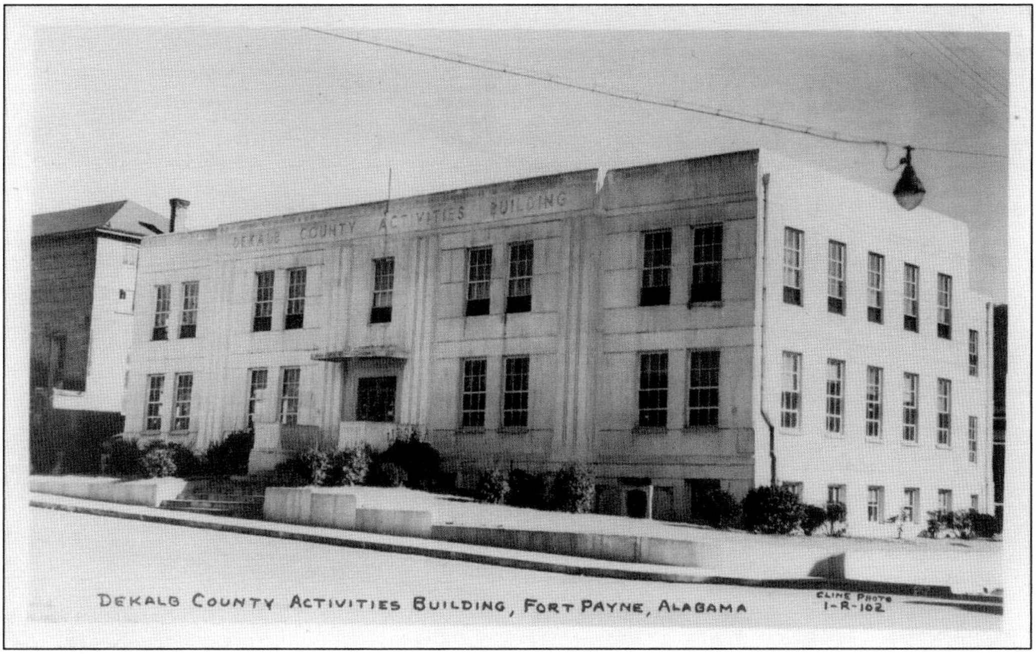

The DeKalb County Activities Building, erected in 1940, shares the Art Moderne style with the 1941 city hall and has, over the years, housed offices of the county's agricultural and forestry agencies, the Red Cross, Civil Defense, the health department, the welfare department, Social Security, the county commission, the board of education, the county 911 emergency center, and others. (Courtesy of Collins Kirby.)

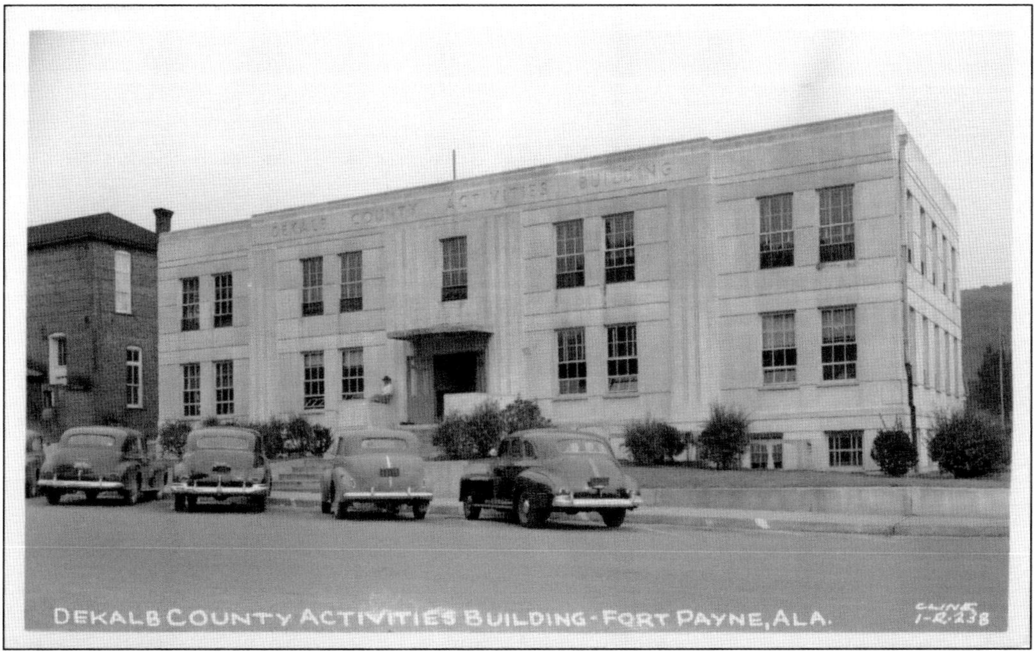

Cline's late 1940s postcard of the activities building shows several sedans from the era and a casual visitor on the stoop. (Courtesy of Collins Kirby.)

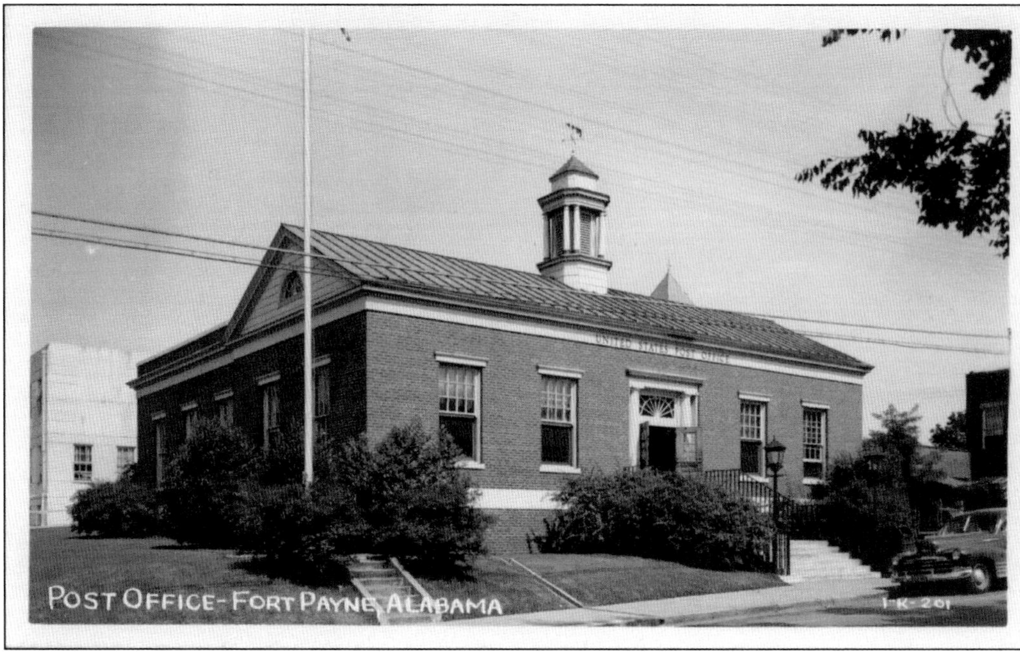

Cline's real-photo postcard of the post office was taken around 1950 and reveals a portion of the rear of the activities building in the left background. (Courtesy of Collins Kirby.)

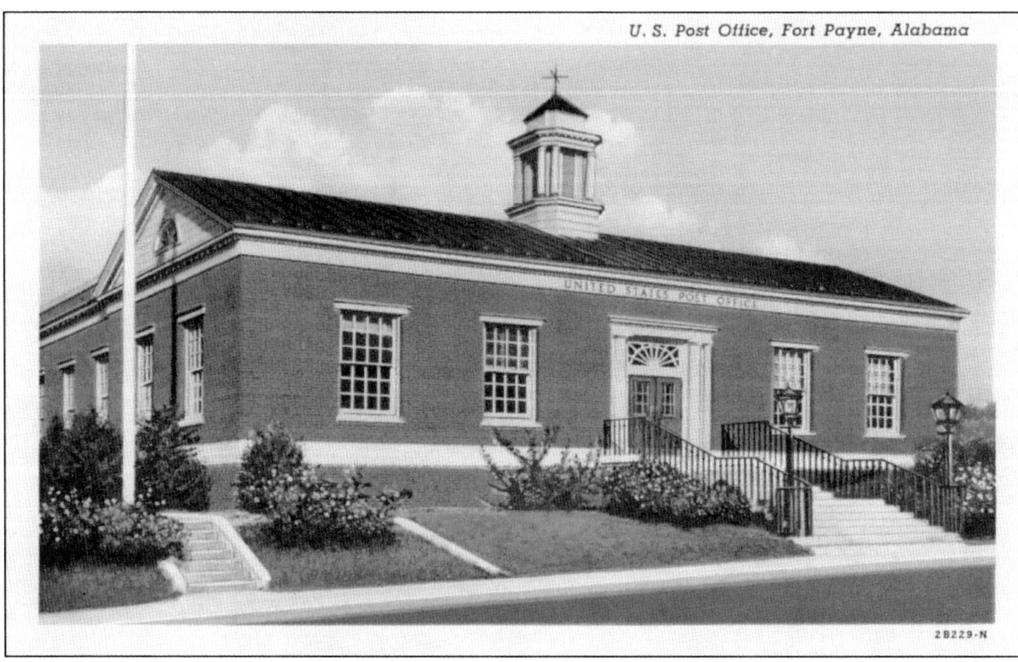

This 1942 Curt Teich & Company card of the post office depicts the beauty of the spring blossoms along the front of the building. This building remains today and looks much the same. When the Jimmy Carter Post Office was built on First Street in 1980, the old post office was used as a career center but now sits empty. (Courtesy of Collins Kirby.)

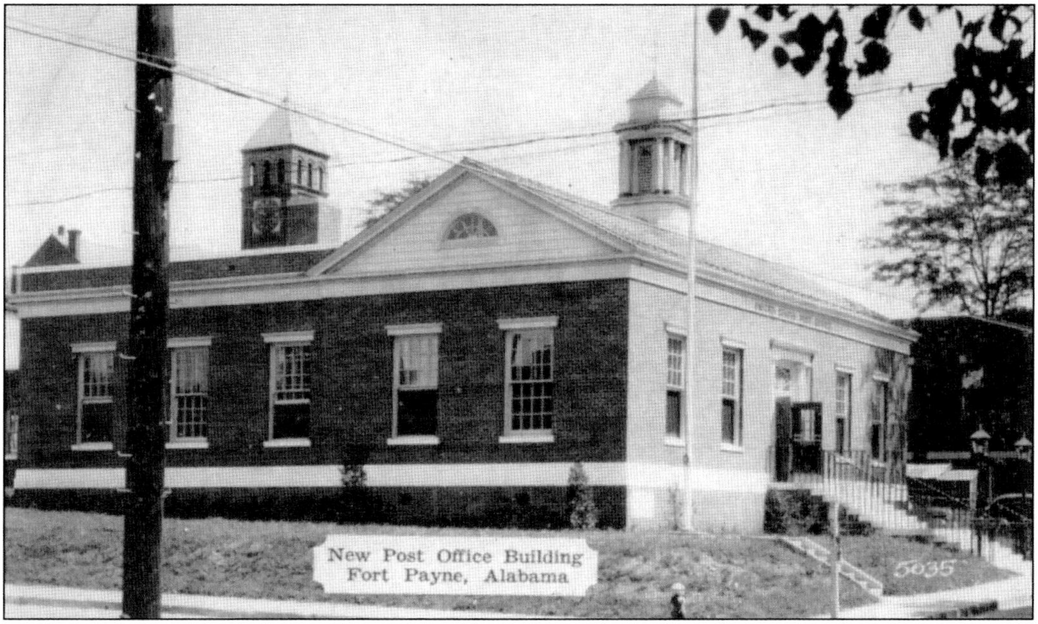

This c. 1940 postcard by Dexter Press shows the Fort Payne Post Office in warm weather, with doors and windows open to provide ventilation. Built by the Public Works Administration in 1936 in the Classical Revival style, it is typical of post offices of that era. A rare view of the south face of the courthouse's clock tower is visible above the roofline. (Courtesy of Collins Kirby.)

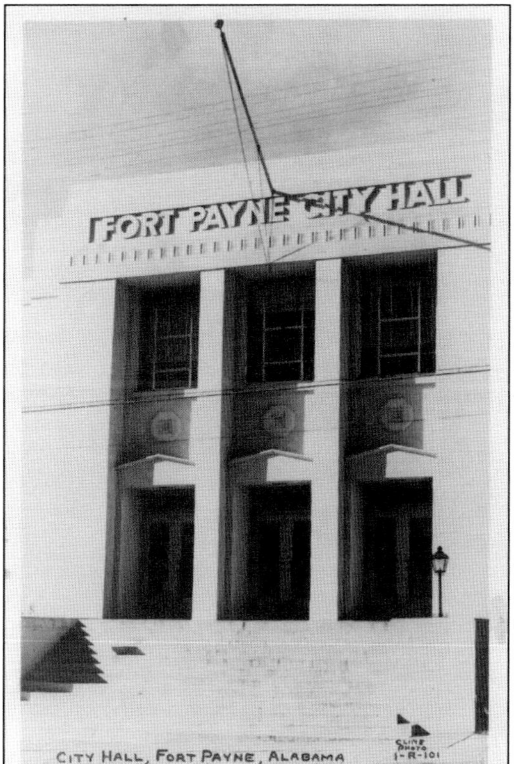

Walter Cline was a great postcard photographer. For years, he used real-photo paper for his cards, which was more expensive, but higher quality. He did this because he owned his own large photo processing lab in Chattanooga. Cline not only took photographs for postcards throughout most of the Southeast and beyond, but also processed film for customers taking their own photographs. In the 1970s, his lab was sold to Fox Photo, a major nationwide wholesale photofinisher. Fox Photo later merged with Colorcraft Corp., and soon Colorcraft Corp. merged with Kodak Labs to become Qualex, a subsidiary of Eastman Kodak Company. Cline's Chattanooga lab closed in 1999 as digital photography was gaining market share and Kodak began reducing the number of large wholesale labs it operated. Prior to digital, most large discount department stores, drugstores, camera stores, and grocery stores used large wholesale photofinishers to process customers' film. It was a profitable business. (Author's collection.)

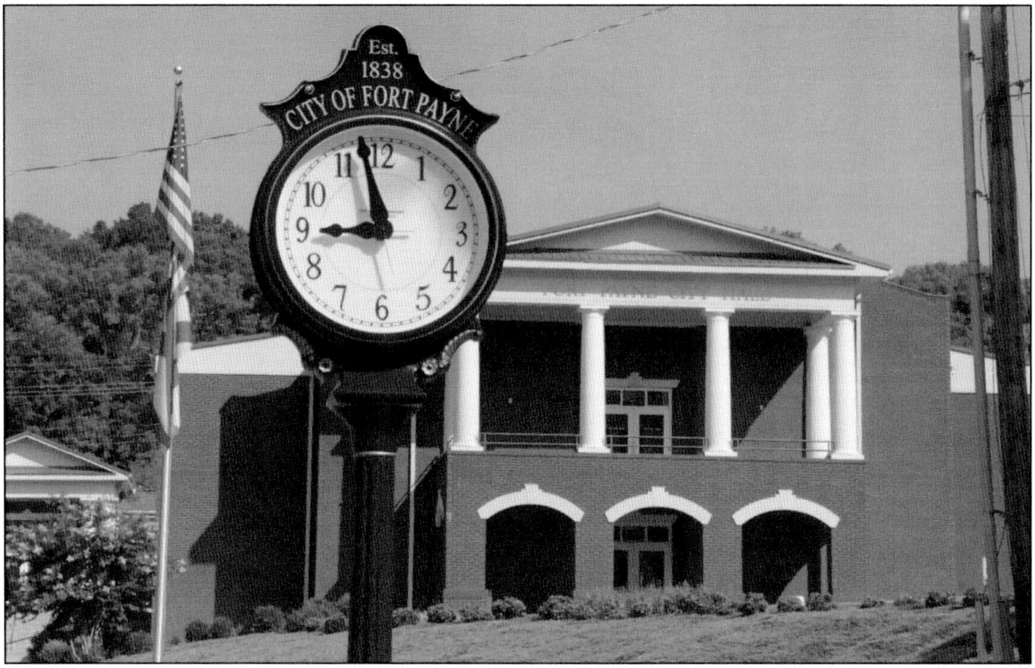

The new Fort Payne City Hall building, opened in 2006, occupies the former Fort Payne City School (formerly the Forest Avenue School), which was the only elementary and middle school in town. The school's gym and auditorium building is now the Fort Payne Municipal Auditorium. This photograph was taken not long after city officials moved their offices to this building. (Author photograph.)

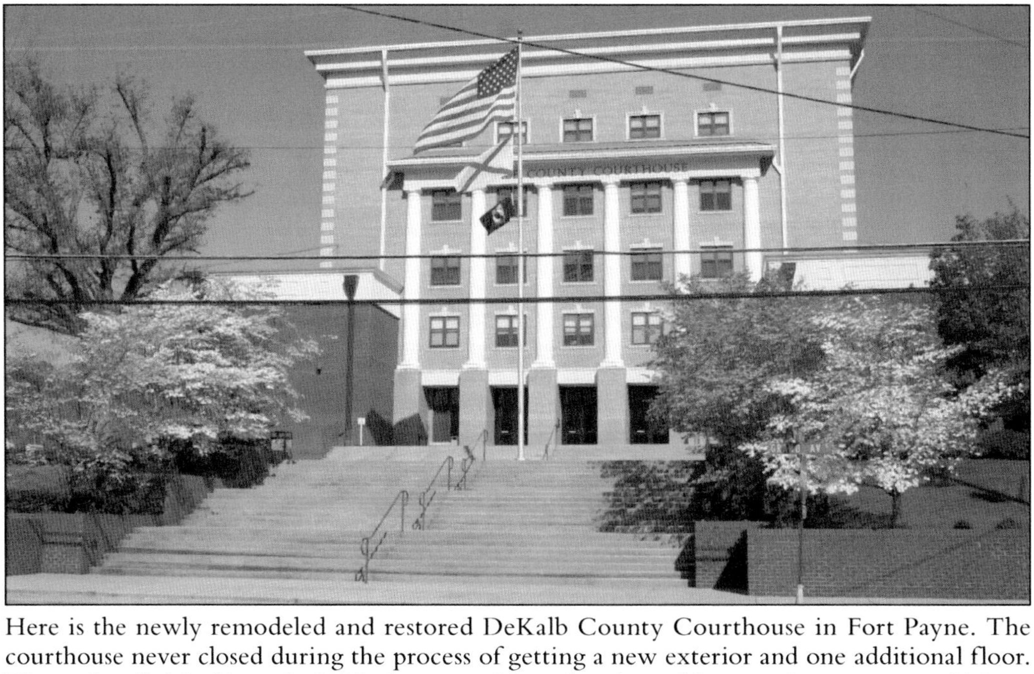

Here is the newly remodeled and restored DeKalb County Courthouse in Fort Payne. The courthouse never closed during the process of getting a new exterior and one additional floor. The project finished in early 2003. Compare this to the view of the courthouse on page 21 from just after it opened in 1951. (Author photograph.)

Four

The Opera Block and Train Depot

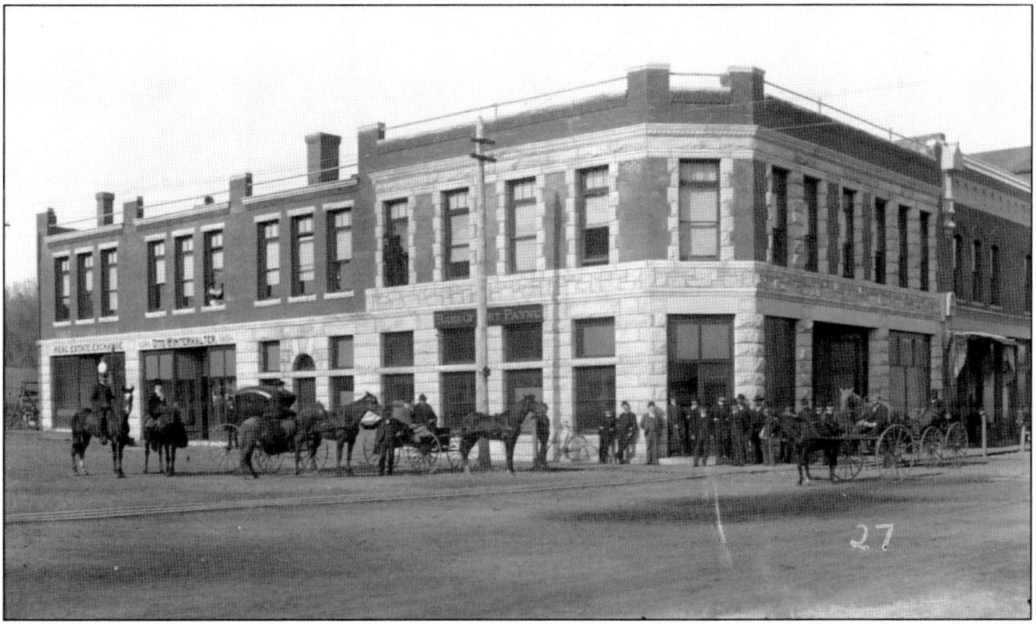

This grand photograph by professional photographer O.W. Chase was taken in front of the Fort Payne Coal and Iron Company building at the corner of Gault Avenue and Fifth Street Northwest. It shows the building completed with proud boomtown pioneers in front, ready to develop the iron and coal industry. Speculation is that this photograph was taken during a grand opening event. At the time, O.W. Chase was contracted to do the photography that would be used in a brochure to promote Fort Payne to New Englanders in hopes of getting more people to invest in the Fort Payne Coal and Iron Company in the late 1880s. (Author's collection.)

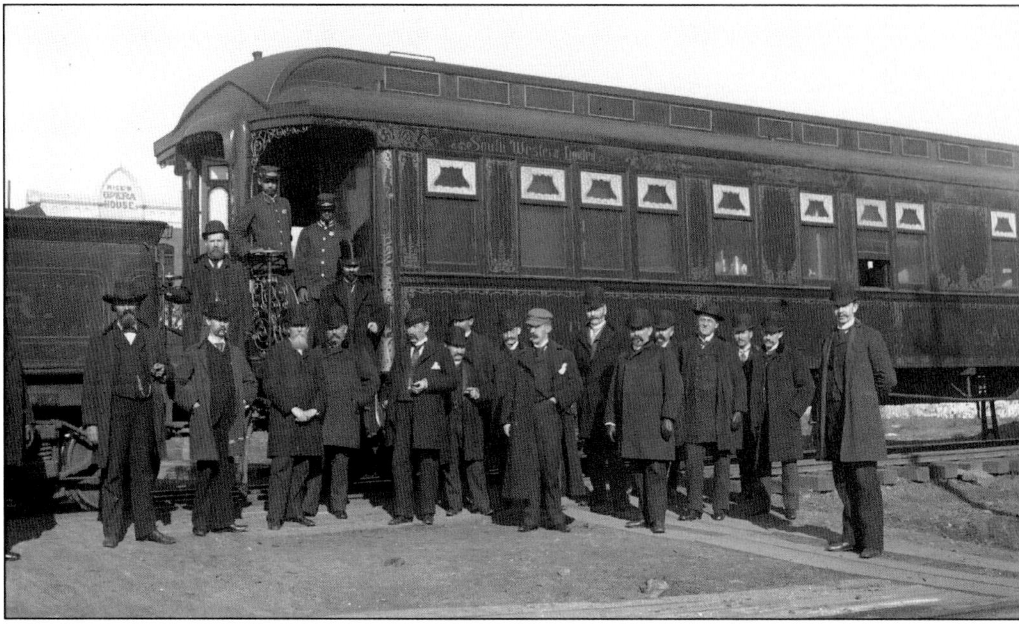

Most likely, this photograph was taken by O.W. Chase the same day as the one prior, as it contains some of the same people. It was taken just a block east of the last picture, at the railroad. At one time, the Fort Payne Coal and Iron Company had its own railroad cars and track going up Lookout Mountain to the mines. The opera house can be seen in the background, located in the same block as the Coal and Iron Company office. (Author's collection.)

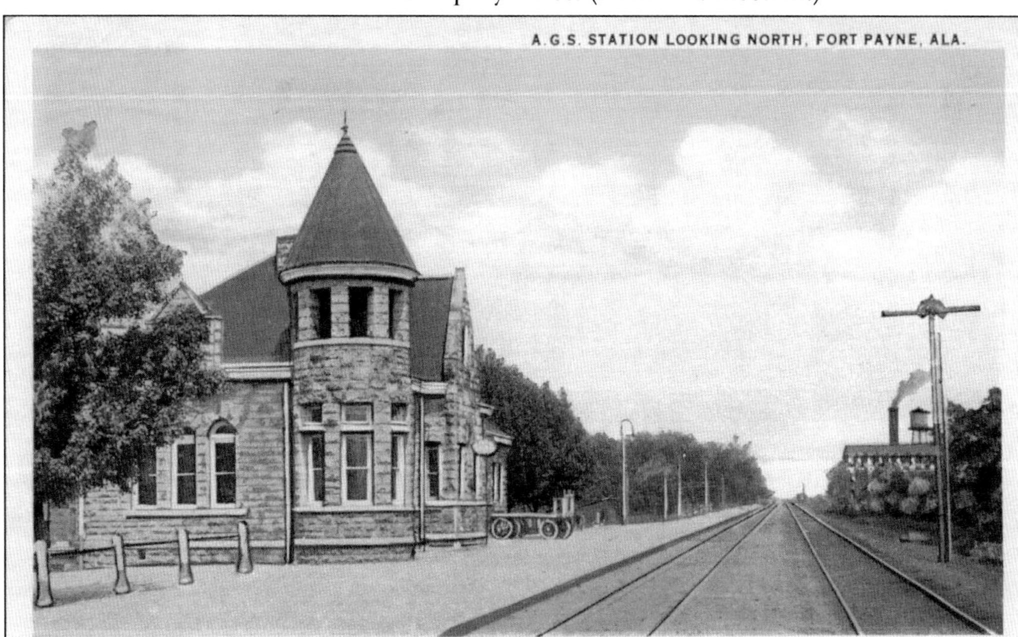

This 1930s postcard shows the Alabama Great Southern Railroad depot and to the right, the W.B. Davis Hosiery Mill. Many commercially printed postcards from this era, like this one, were printed on high-quality, acid-free paper that did not yellow with age. At this time, many postcards were still printed on real-photo paper, which provided the best quality available. (Courtesy of Collins Kirby.)

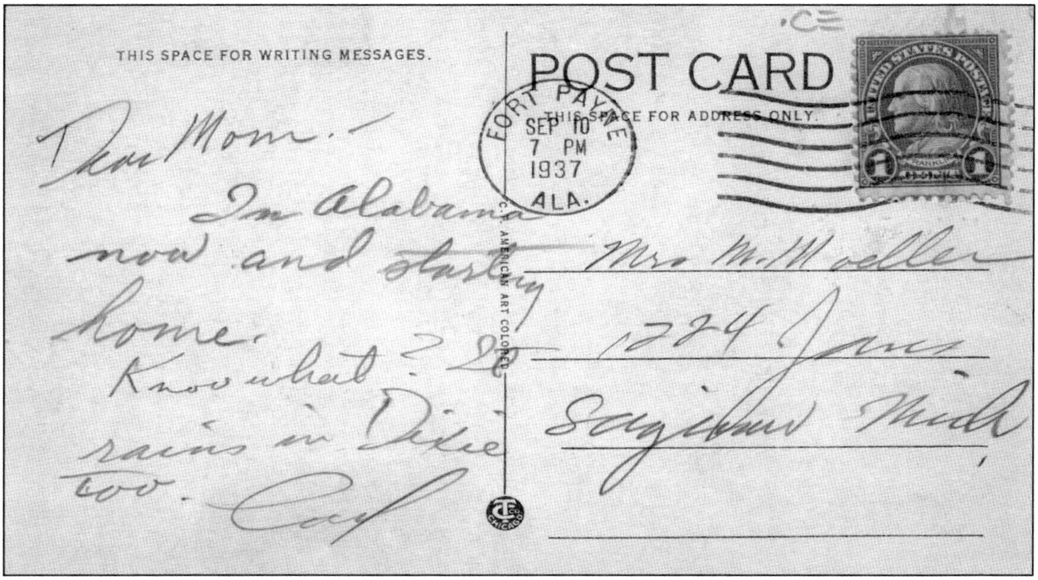

This is the back of the previous card, postmarked September 10, 1937. Many people collected postcards from everywhere they traveled, and used them while traveling to stay in touch with the people at home who also looked forward to hearing from friends and family. This is why postcards from all eras are still easy to find. The traveler and the receiver always held on to their cards. (Courtesy of Collins Kirby.)

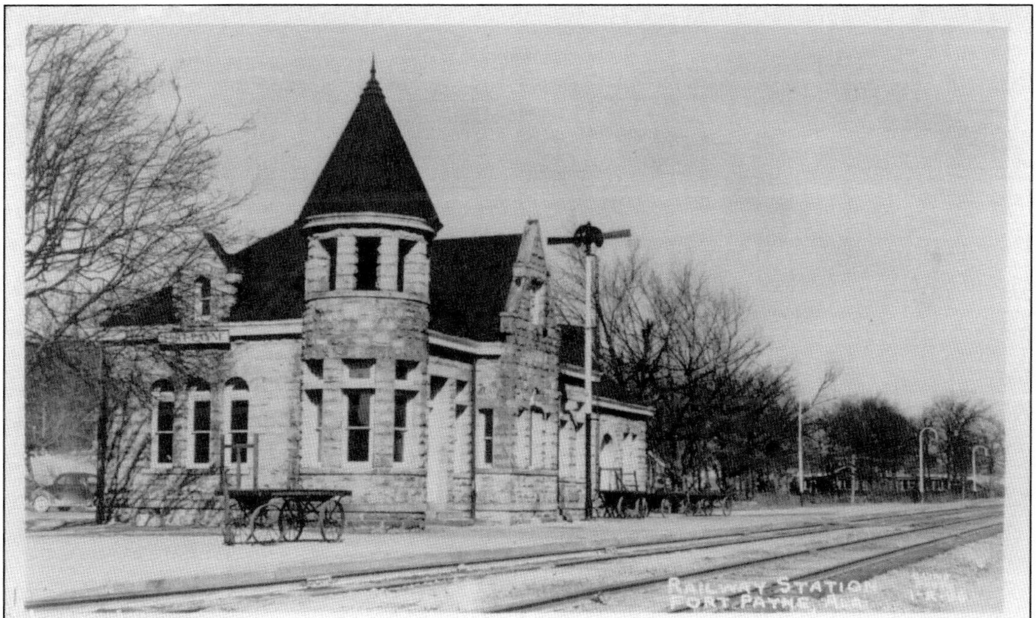

This real-photo postcard by Walter Cline from the 1940s shows the Alabama Great Southern Railroad depot, with the double track. In later years, the passenger track was removed; there is one track today. The current line is for freight, and the depot is now a local history museum. A few times a year, a scenic passenger tour, starting in Chattanooga, goes south through Fort Payne and turns back at Attalla, Alabama. It is a historic steam locomotive, and a crowd always gathers at the depot to watch it pass. (Courtesy of Collins Kirby.)

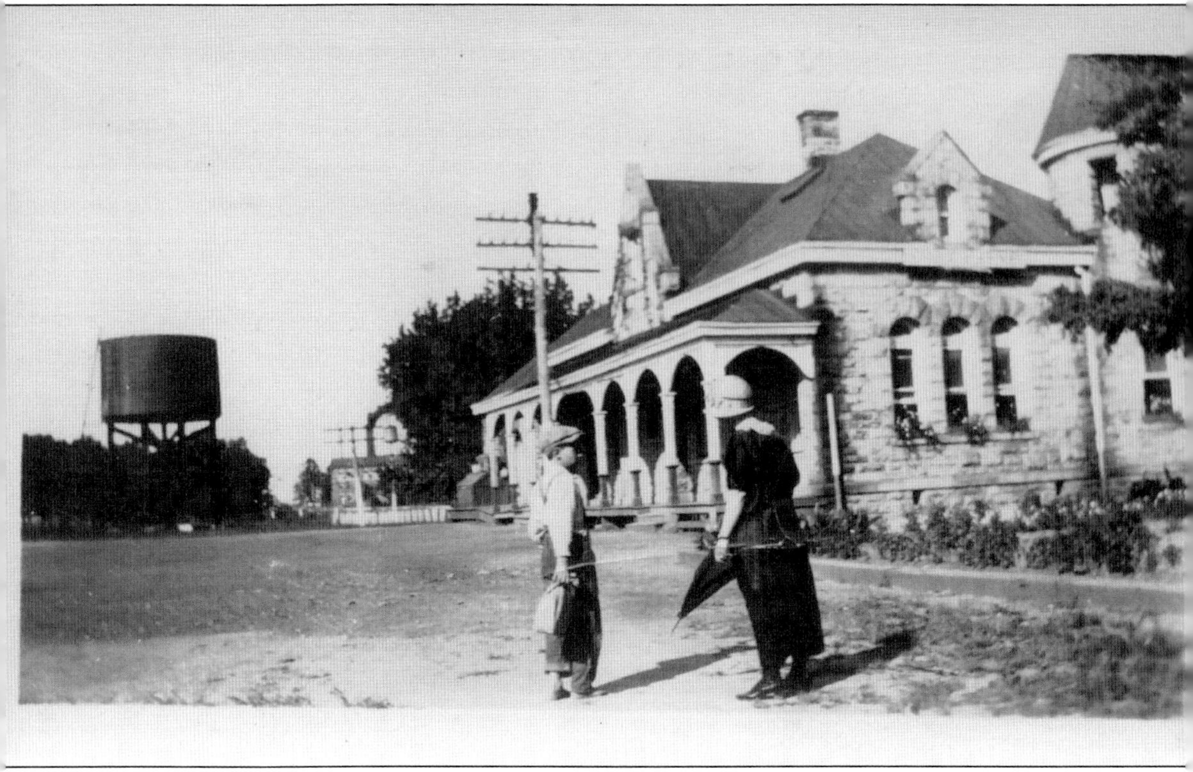

This rare view of the depot from the front shows a porch, which is no longer there. Many older residents do not remember the porch being there in their lifetime, and they are, in fact, surprised by this picture. In the back, the W.B. Davis Hosiery Mill is visible. (Courtesy of Collins Kirby.)

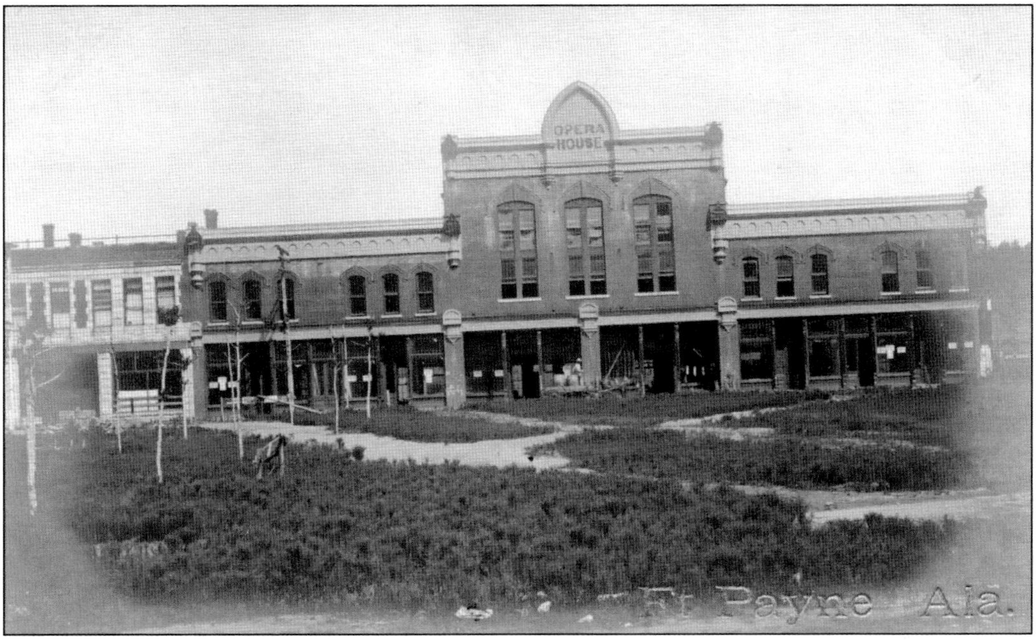

This real-photo postcard is from 1889. It clearly shows the opera house and the entire block still under construction. This view faces west, with the railroad tracks directly behind the photographer. (Courtesy of Collins Kirby.)

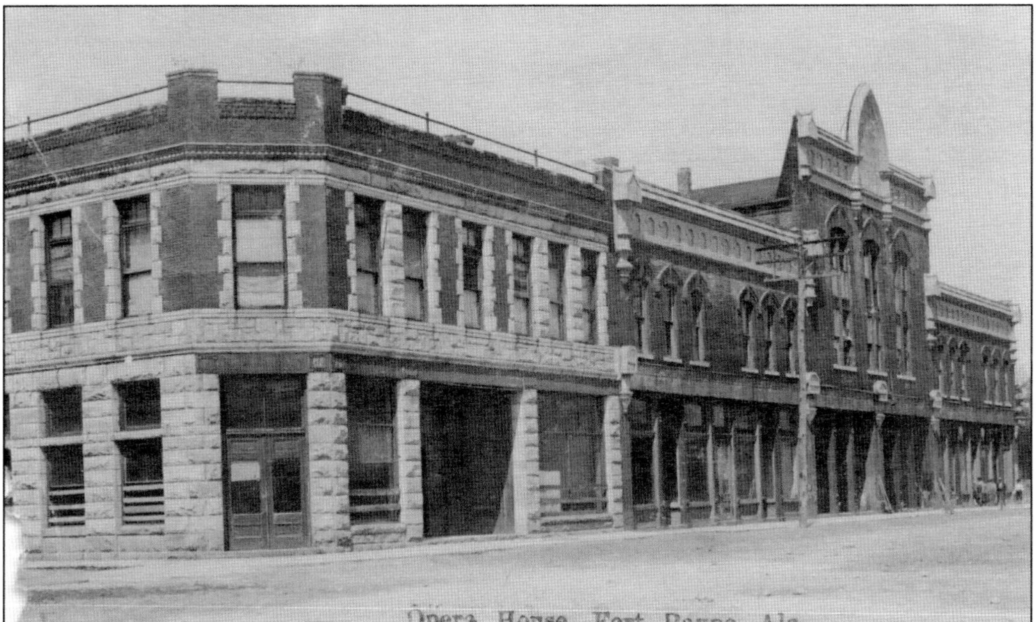

Taken at the same time as the prior view, this postcard shows the Fort Payne Coal and Iron Company building and the opera block under construction. These two photographs were most likely taken minutes apart and are both printed on sepia-toned real-photo paper. (Courtesy of Collins Kirby.)

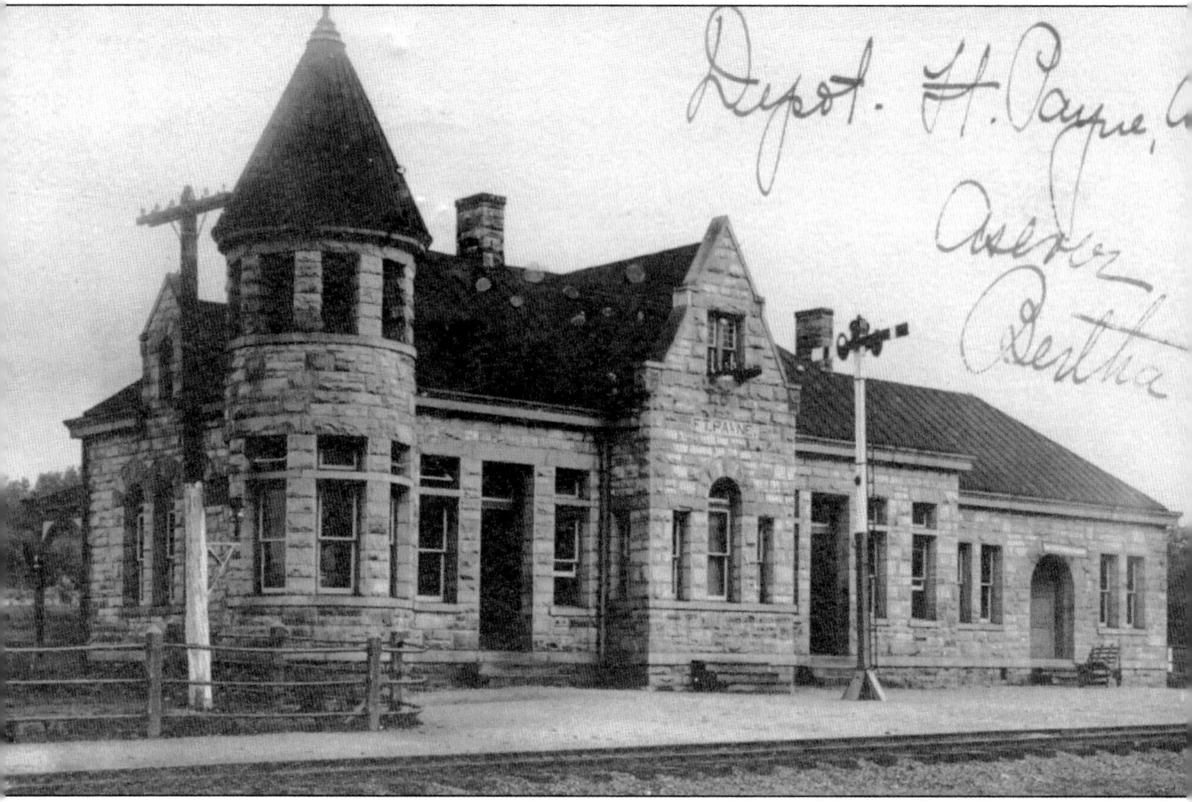

The Alabama Great Southern Railroad depot opened in 1891. It is made of locally quarried sandstone and was extremely well built and is still beautiful today. In the 1970s, a local group of concerned citizens, headed by Marjorie Ferguson, Emma Jordon, and others, saved the depot from demolition. At the time, the railroad was removing unused stations without soliciting the communities. It is a beautiful building in a great location in downtown Fort Payne. The Fort Payne Depot Museum, which currently occupies it, has the best collection of the area's boomtown artifacts. The museum also has a collection of Cherokee Indian baskets and pottery, military uniforms, dioramas by Steve Fiora, and other interesting items. (Courtesy of Collins Kirby.)

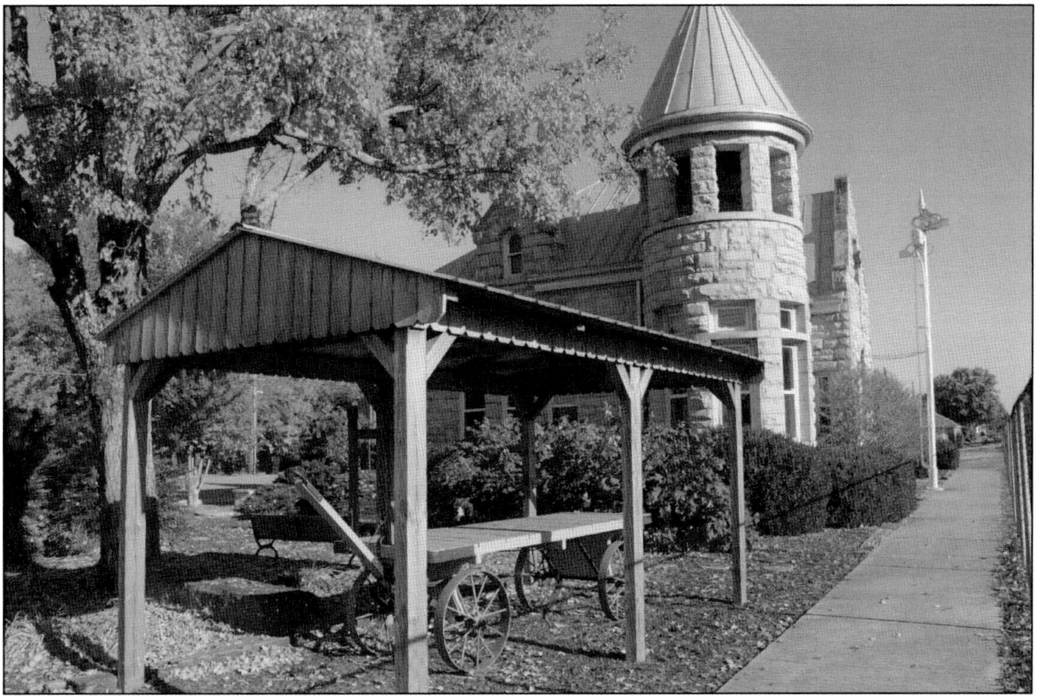

This photograph of the Fort Payne Depot Museum was taken in 2008. The first-class local museum features a finely preserved look back in time at the early pioneers in Fort Payne as well as the area's Native American cultures. (Author photograph.)

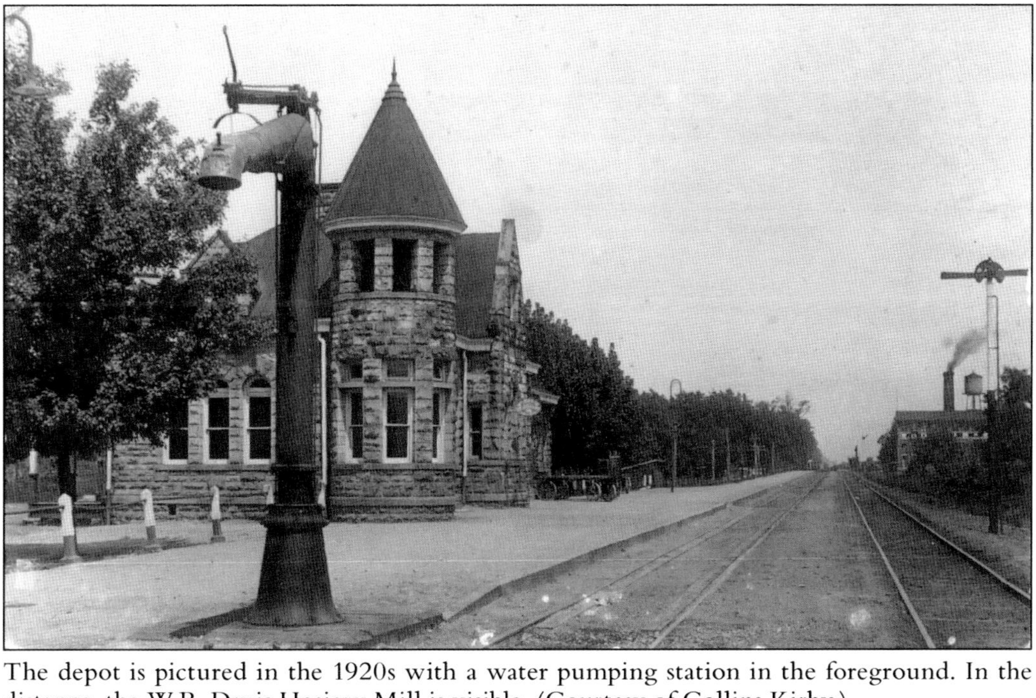

The depot is pictured in the 1920s with a water pumping station in the foreground. In the distance, the W.B. Davis Hosiery Mill is visible. (Courtesy of Collins Kirby.)

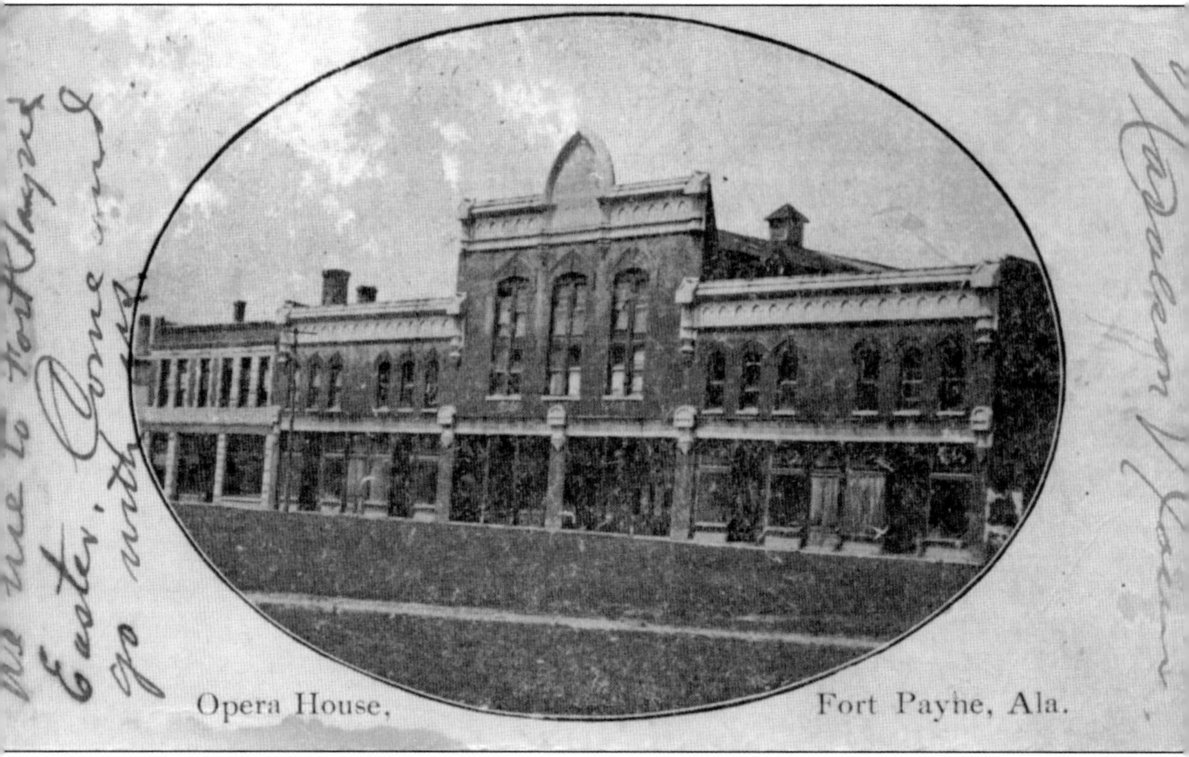

Pictured is the opera block before 1907. Prior to that year, postcard senders were not allowed to write on the backs of postcards, which were reserved for the recipient's address. This is why writing is often found on the fronts of postcards from this era. (Courtesy of Collins Kirby.)

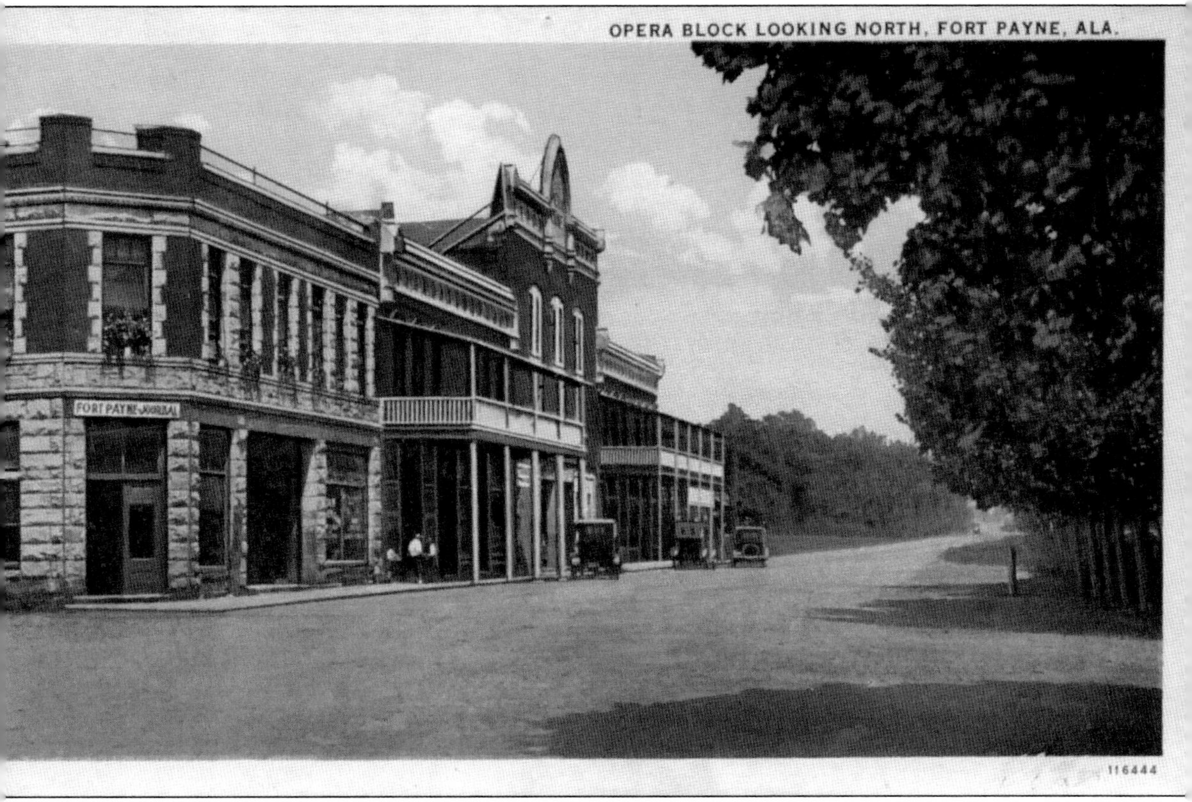

This linen, hand-colored postcard from the 1920s provides a very peaceful view of the Fort Payne Coal and Iron Company building and opera block. At the time of this card, the *Fort Payne Journal* occupied the Coal and Iron Company building. This newspaper is still in business, operating as the *Fort Payne Times Journal*. To the right, behind the trees, is the Rainey Hotel (not visible). Note that at this time, there is no continuing development along Gault Avenue. Though it appears to be the northernmost end of town, there are houses and factories well beyond this point. (Author's collection.)

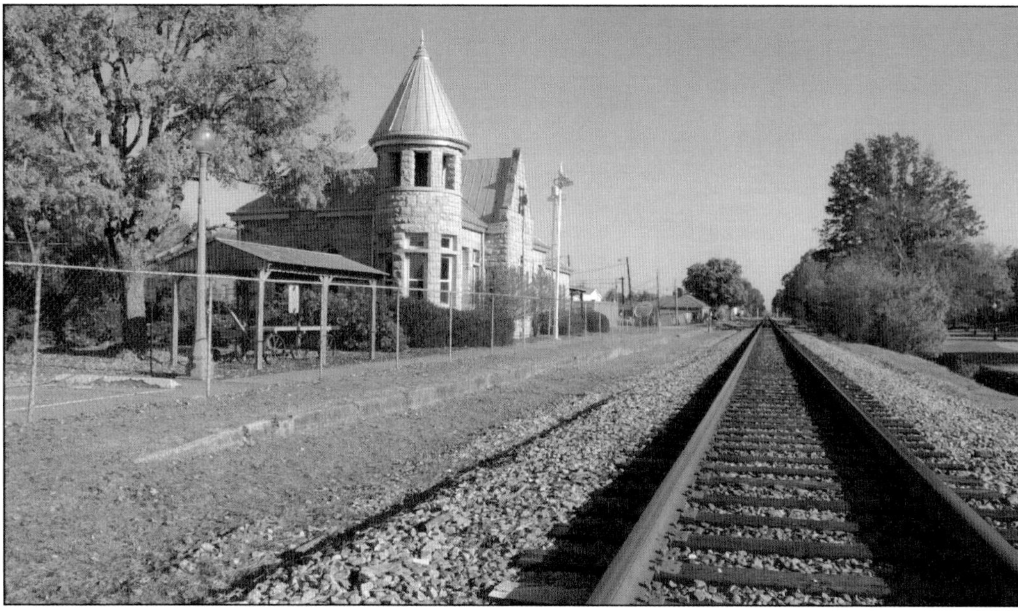

Here is the current single track running by the depot. This 2008 image shows the original curb next to the station. As one can tell from this scene, the old passenger track, which was closer to the depot, was the track that was removed. The passenger line was discontinued on August 24, 1970. Freight continued to be picked up at this station for a few years, but by the mid-1970s, freight vacated, and the depot sat unused until 1986, when the building became the Fort Payne Depot Museum. (Author photograph.)

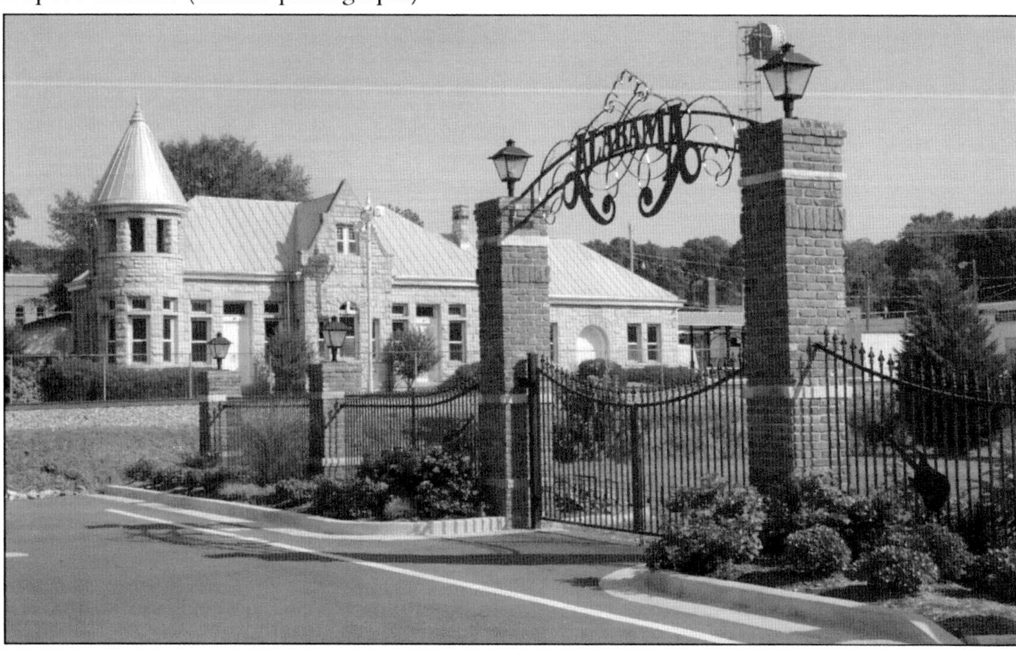

The depot and the Alabama Walking Park entrance are seen here. The arch was made using the band Alabama's logo. The city named the park after the group to honor the highly successful band members who still call Fort Payne their home. This park is part of a complex of parks in the historic district of downtown Fort Payne. (Author photograph.)

Five

Residences

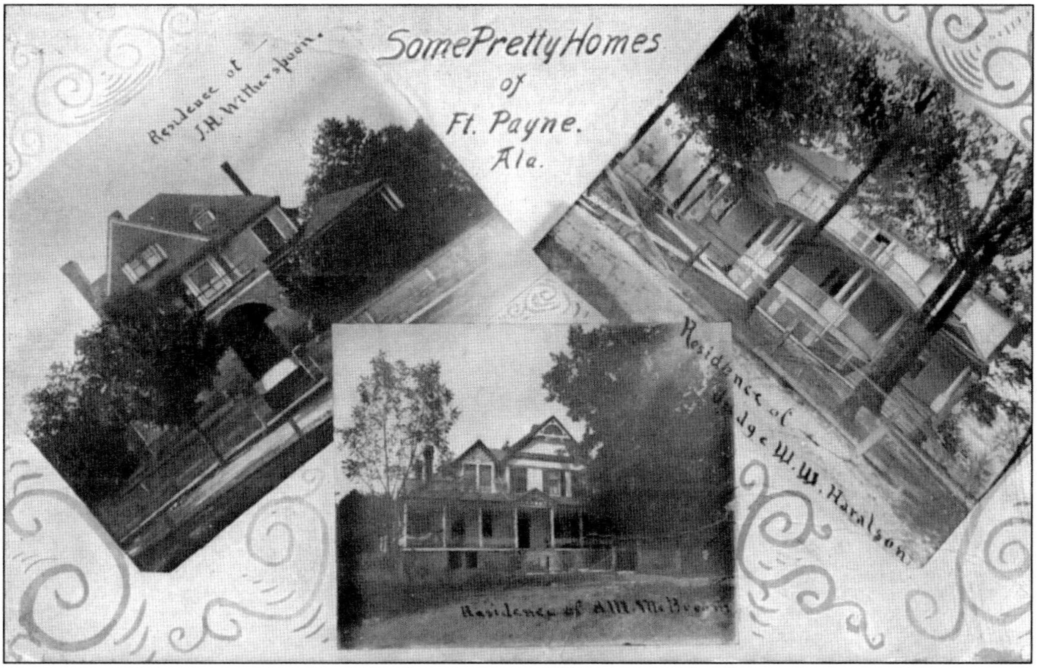

This card, with a Chattanooga & Meridian Railway Post Office postmark of 1914, features "Some Pretty Homes of Fort Payne." The three residences pictured are, from left to right, J.H. Witherspoon, A.M. McBroom, and Judge W.W. Haralson. The Witherspoon house, at 404 Forest Avenue North, was built by W.P. Rice and had previously been owned by Fort Payne's first mayor, C.O. Godfrey. The McBroom residence at 808 Alabama Avenue was built by Col. William H.H. Minot. The W.W. Haralson home, named "The Oaks," at 250 Forest Avenue North, predates the boomtown and remained in the Haralson family for four generations. (Courtesy of Collins Kirby.)

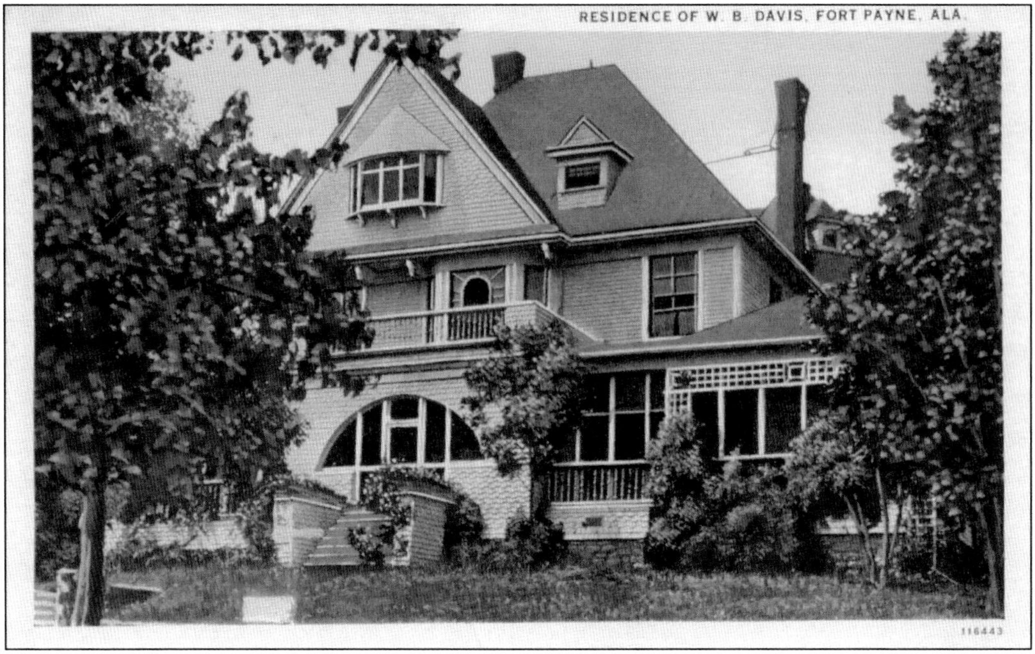

By the time this postcard was published in 1927, this house belonged to hosiery manufacturer W.B. Davis, Fort Payne's leading industrialist during the first half of the 20th century. Noticeable are the landscaping improvements and the screening of the porch. (Courtesy of Collins Kirby.)

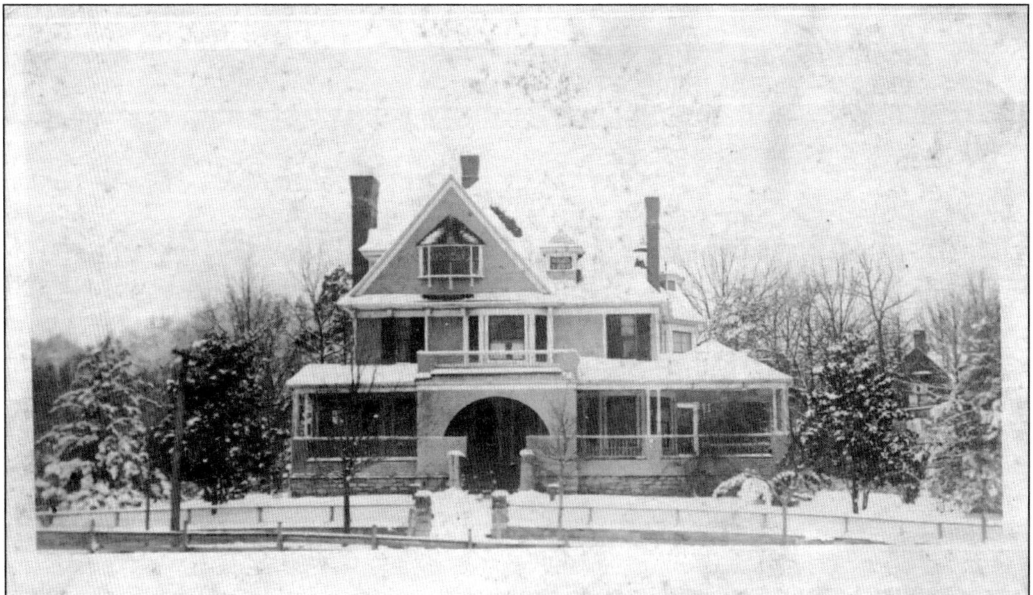

This pre-1920s real-photo postcard depicts a snow-covered Rice-Godfrey-Witherspoon house and grounds. (Courtesy of Collins Kirby.)

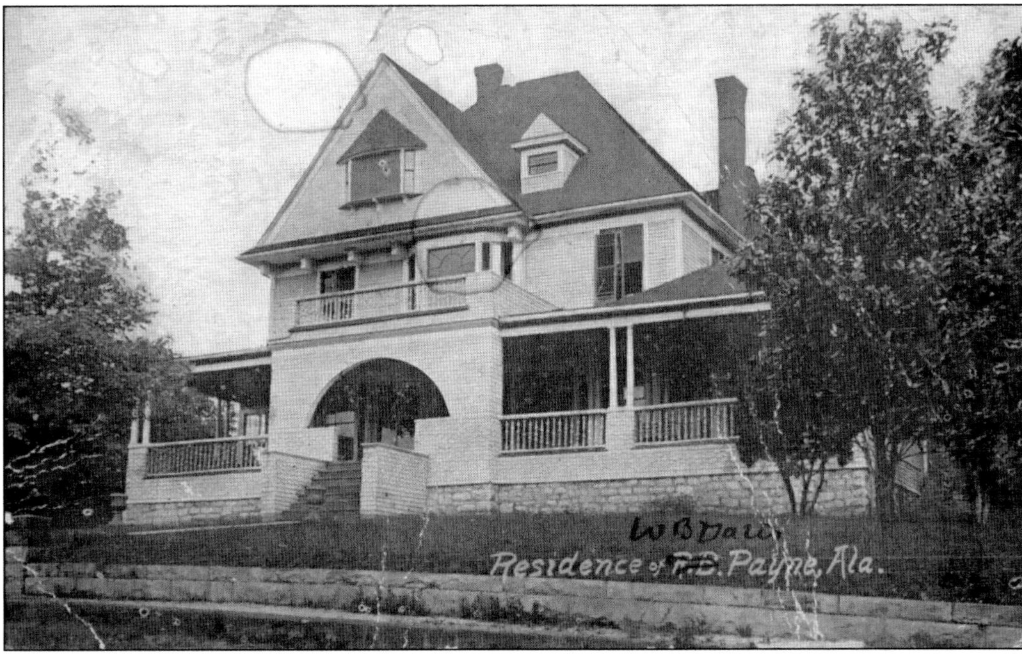

A card postmarked in Fort Payne in 1920 offers another view of the same home, and the message on the reverse mentions the opening of the W.B. Davis Clubhouse. (Courtesy of Collins Kirby.)

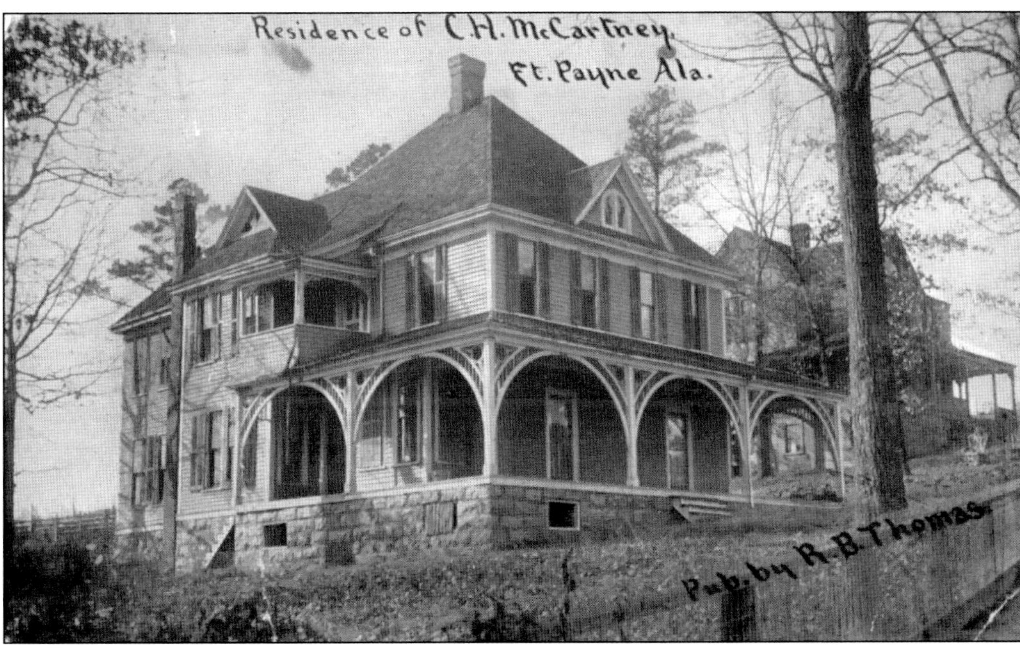

The beautiful late Victorian structure pictured here was the residence of C.H. McCartney in the 1910s, when R.B. Thomas published this hand-colored postcard. The house was built at the beginning of the boom era by attorney True P. Pierce, who was an officer of the Fort Payne Investment Company and a director of Southern Banking Company. It was purchased by US congressman Col. Milford W. Howard in 1899; he lived there until 1905. It was destroyed by fire in 1954. (Courtesy of Collins Kirby.)

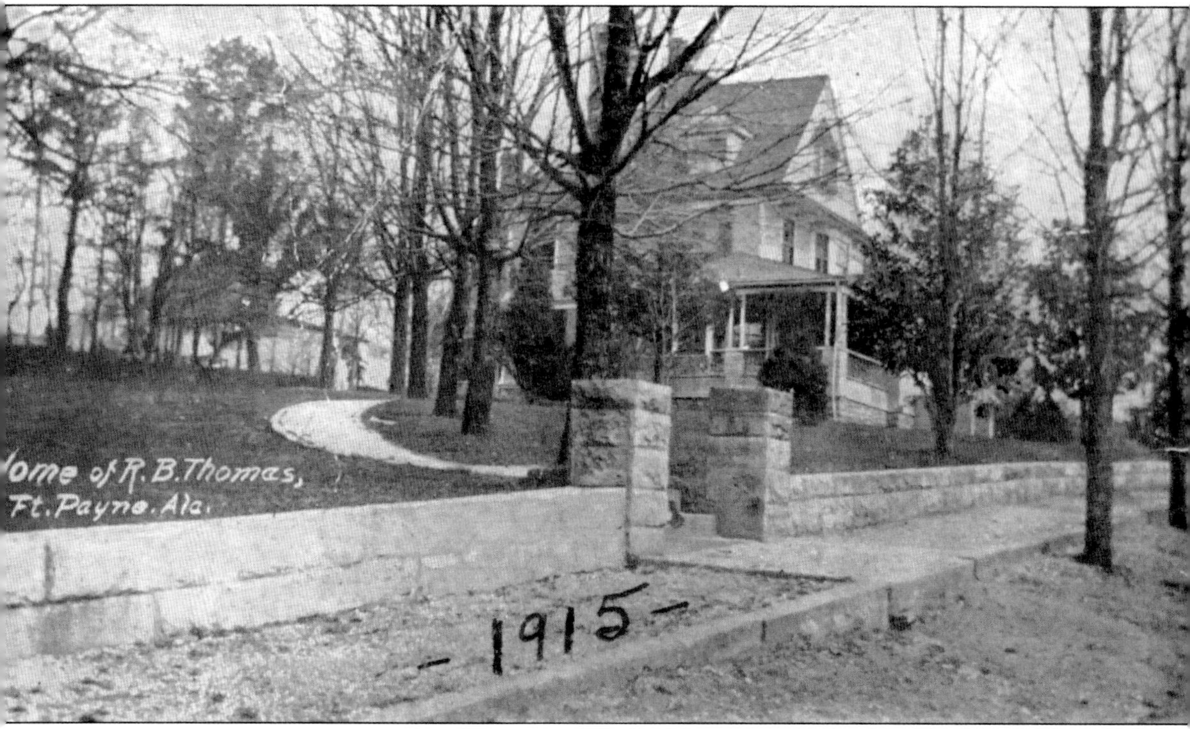

Around 1915, R.B. Thomas is listed as the owner of the often-traded residence pictured on this postcard. The card was hand-dated 1915 and presents the house from a viewpoint facing north. (Courtesy of Collins Kirby.)

Six

Street Scenes

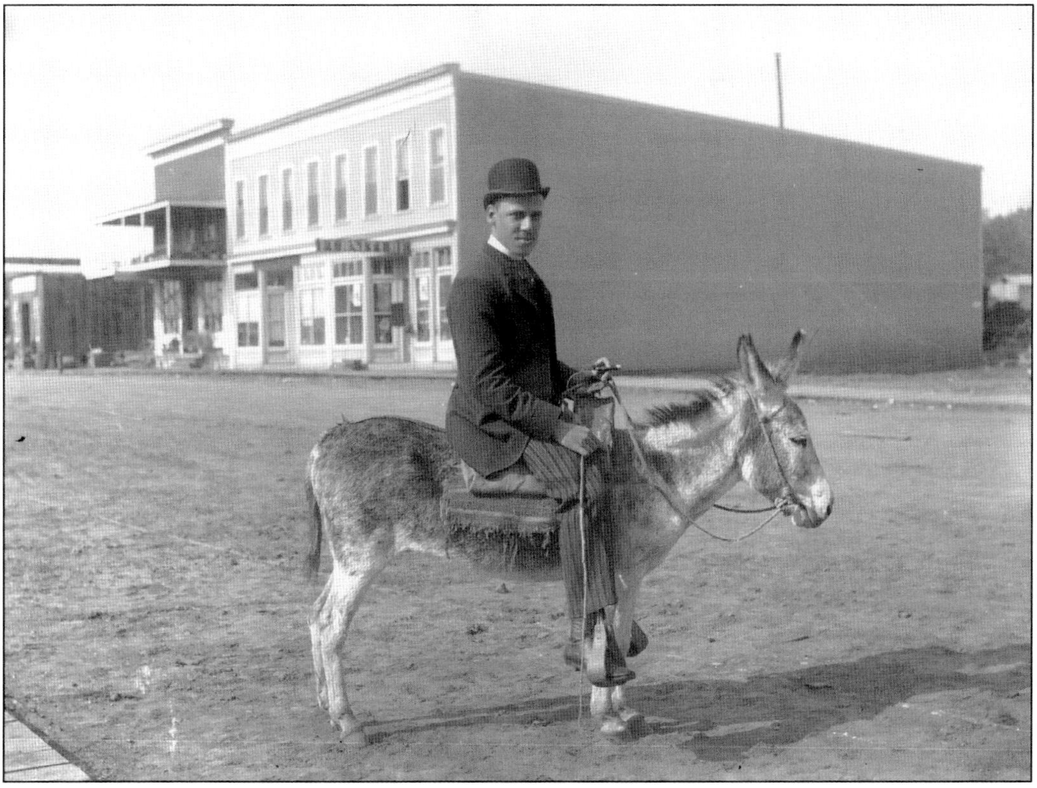

This photograph by O.W. Chase is a bit comical. Several views by Chase show portraits of people who seem too big for the animal they are riding. In a couple of his pictures, a man's hat lies to the side with other props, which suggest that Chase was setting up some shots. This one was taken on Gault Avenue, probably in 1889 or soon thereafter. (Author's collection.)

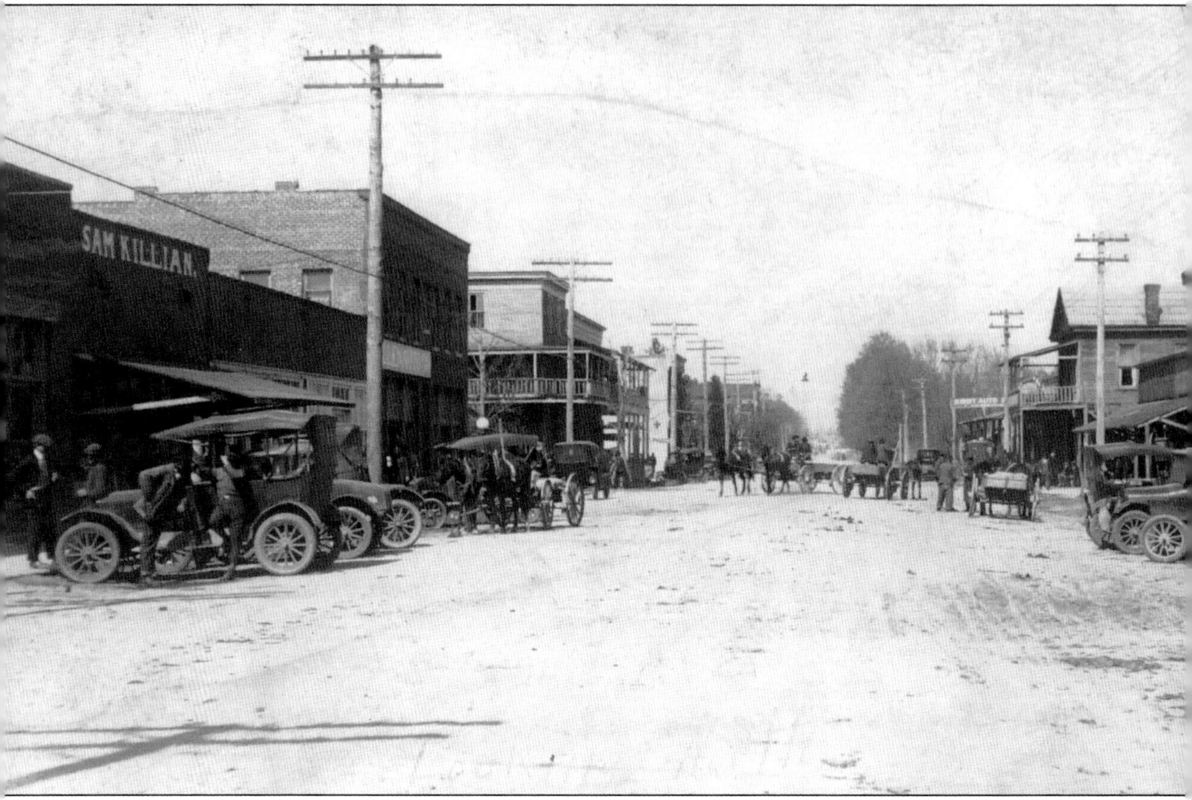

This 1920 photograph was taken from the middle of the 200 block north of Gault Avenue. The Sam Killian Store and Allen Auto Company are visible along the left side of the street. Across Third Street North, a two-story wooden building is seen with a rickety wraparound balcony. Also visible but barely readable is a sign for Farley Photographer's Studio. On the right side of Gault Avenue, at far right, is a Texaco filling station that sold Firestone Tires. Farther north on that side, a Kirby Auto Shop sign hangs over the sidewalk. A.C. Kirby Sr., the proprietor, was the grandfather of Collins Kirby. (Courtesy of Collins Kirby.)

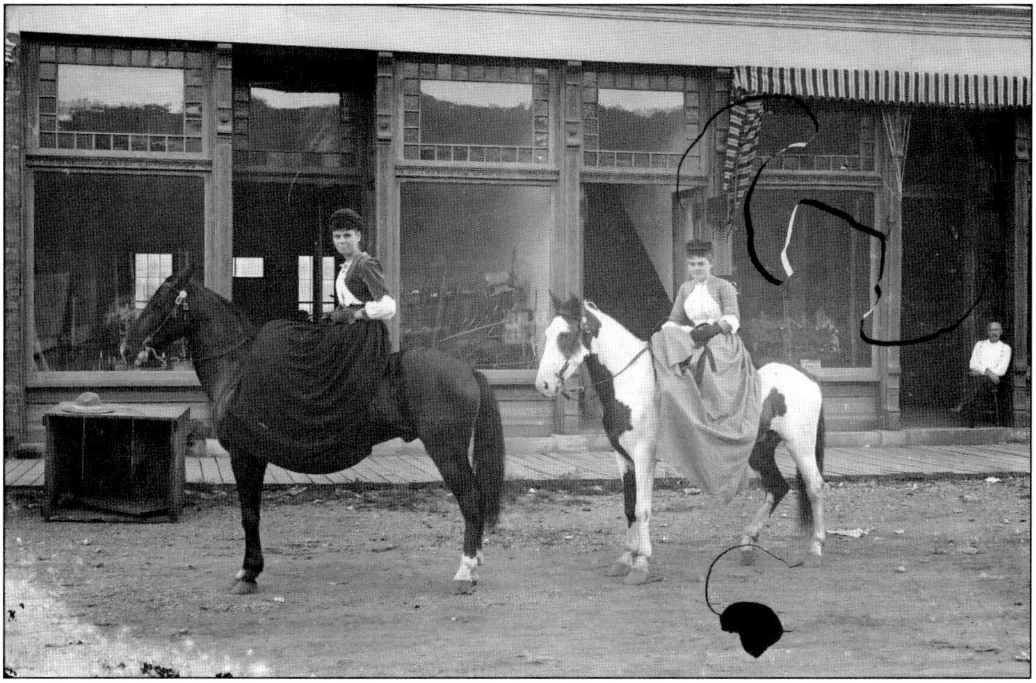

This O.W. Chase image appears to be a posed portrait of two young women taken in 1889 or later. The opera block sits behind the ladies, and the store is stacked full of chairs. Although this building should only be a year or less old, it appears to be in some disrepair, which means it could have been taken later. The wooden sidewalk does not look new. Most of O.W. Chase's photographs show construction in progress, which helps to date them. (Author's collection.)

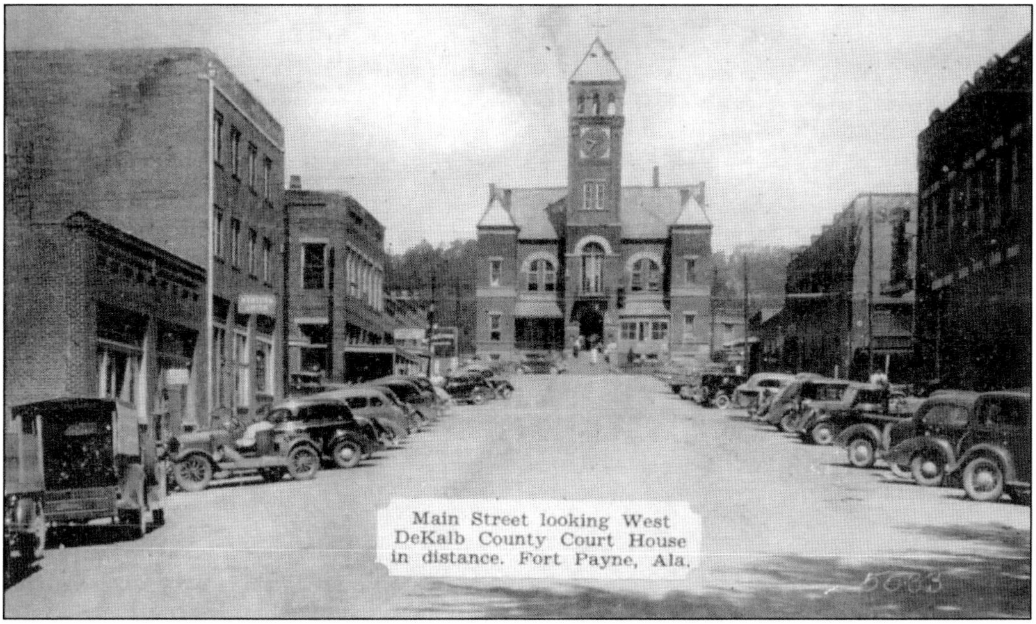

Dexter Press published "Main Street Looking West" around 1940. At left is Western Union in the Quin Hotel Building. At right are Owen Hardware and Southern Hardware. The courthouse rises above it all. (Courtesy of Collins Kirby.)

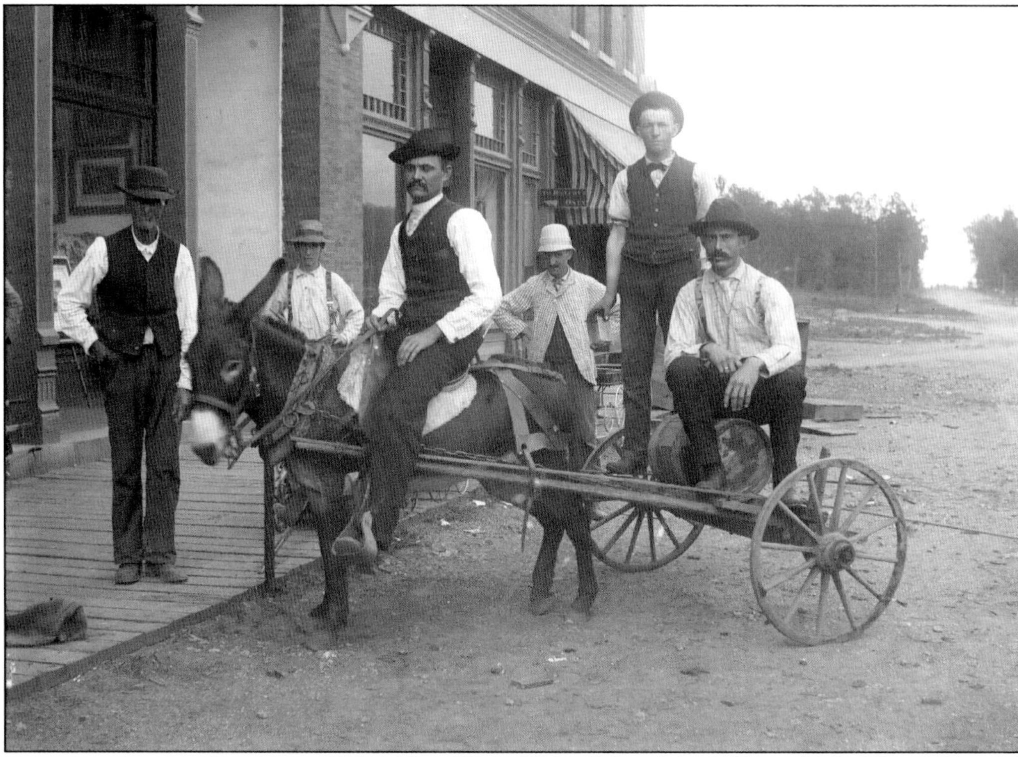

Here is another posed image by O.W. Chase in front of the opera block. These were all shot with a professional camera taking 6½-by-8½-inch glass negatives. The image quality is incredible even by today's standards. (Author's collection.)

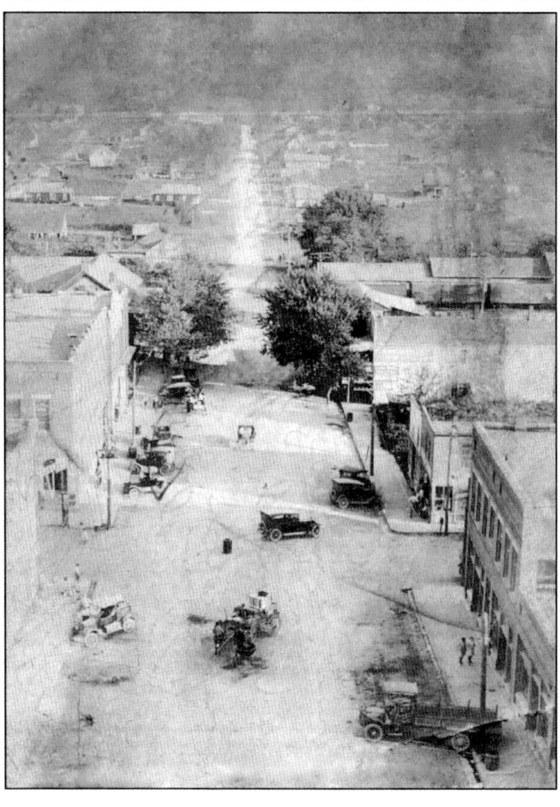

This real-photo postcard from the mid-1920s was taken from the courthouse clock tower. The view looks east down First Street toward Lookout Mountain. (Courtesy of Judy Brown.)

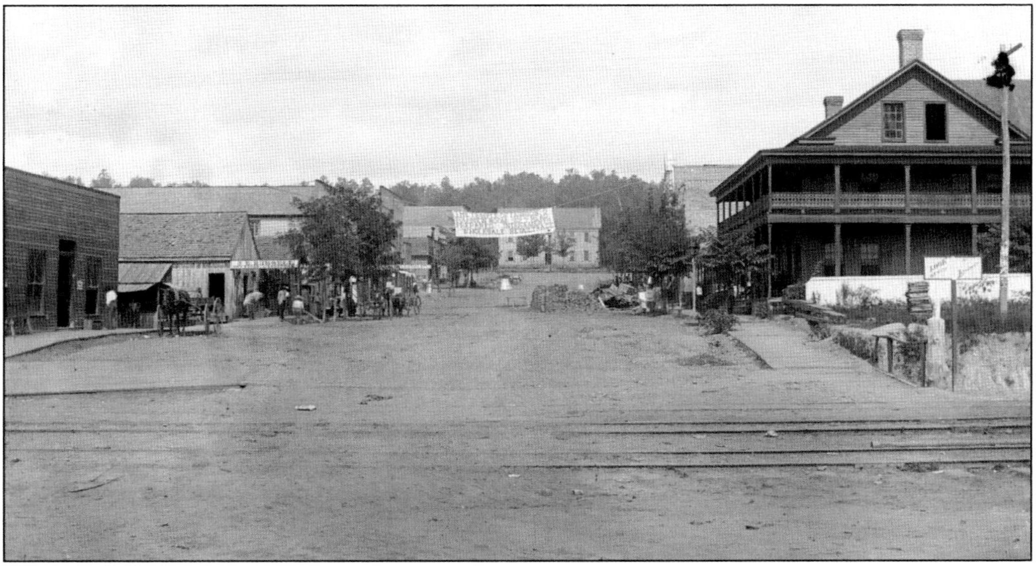

This boomtown image by O.W. Chase shows the first courthouse (1878) in Fort Payne at the end of First Street when Fort Payne became the county seat. This view, looking west from the railroad tracks, shows three sets of tracks at this location. The third track enabled trains to pass. The May Hotel can be seen on the right, and the banner over the road reads, "The temple of fashion will occupy four new rooms Sept 1st ready and prepared to offer inducements to the wholesale as well as retail trade." (Author's collection.)

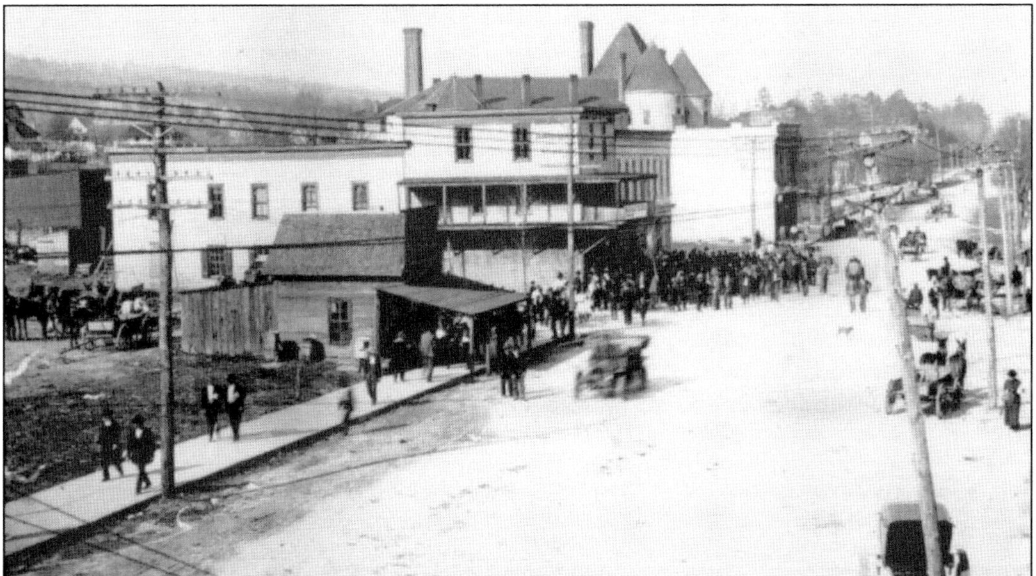

This early 1900s postcard shows a mix of horse-drawn transportation along with cars and trucks. The view is of Gault Avenue looking north. Note the crowd in the street; there is no record of the occasion. The DeKalb Hotel's classic roofline is visible at top. By the time of this image, the boom was over, and the town had gone from approximately 3,000 to an estimated 1,000 or less residents. The Florence Hosiery Mill was the first to open in Fort Payne beginning in 1907. It became the W.B. Davis Hosiery Mill in 1915; gradually other mills opened, and Fort Payne began to grow again for the first time since the boom. (Author's collection.)

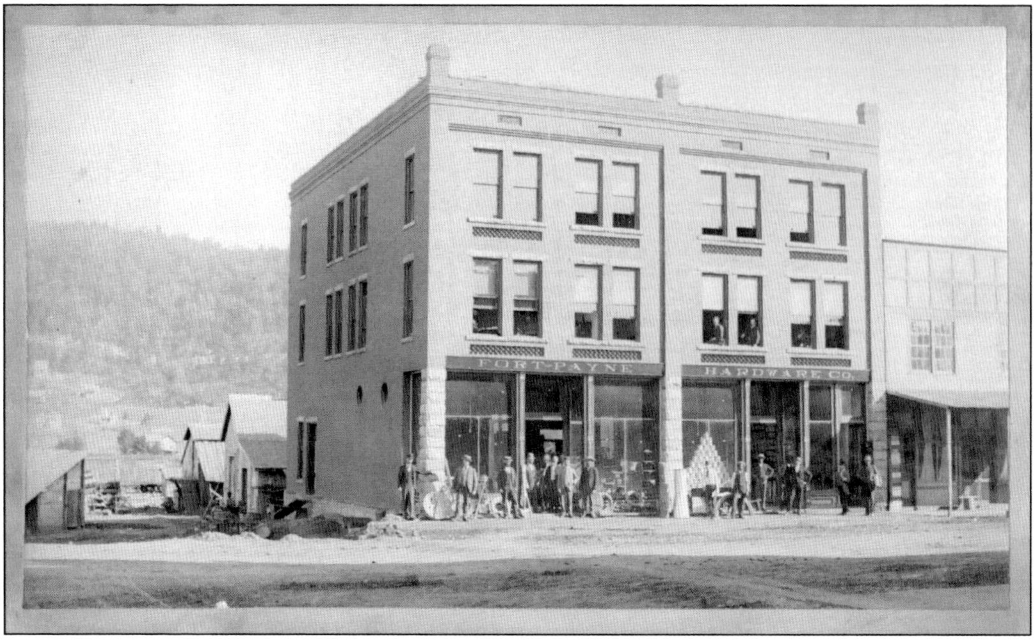

This early 1900s real-photo postcard shows Fort Payne Hardware on Gault Avenue with offices above. Having a picture taken in those days was a big thrill. Note the eager people in the windows posing for the photograph. (Courtesy of Collins Kirby.)

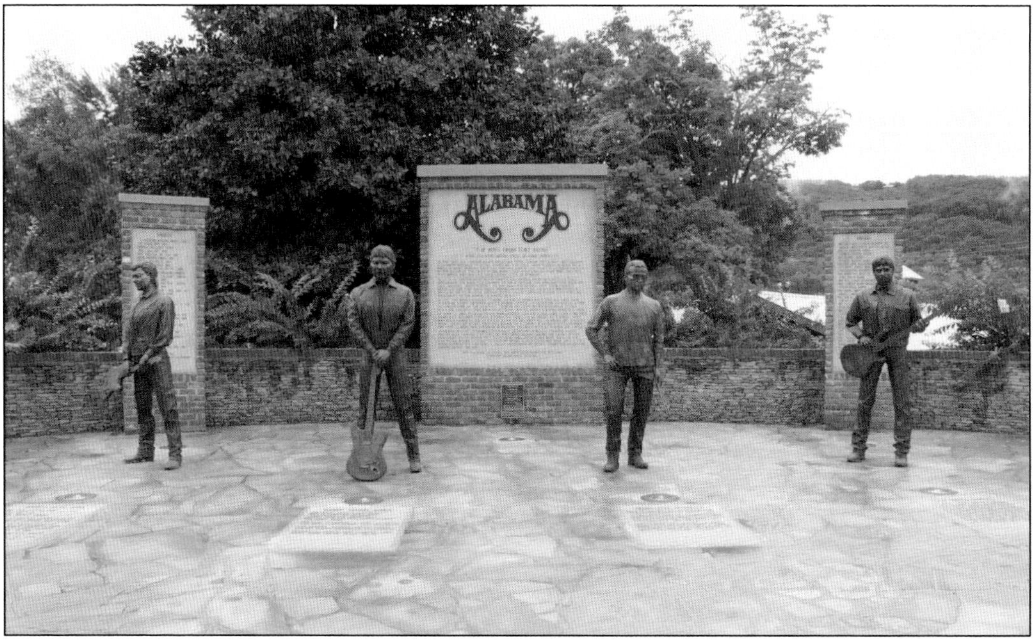

In 2008, the city of Fort Payne unveiled statues of the members of the band Alabama. The bigger-than-life-size bronze statues are by Paula Devereaux of Santa Fe, New Mexico. The statues are on the Fourth Street corner of the Fort Payne City Park. Every day, visitors and fans stop to have their pictures taken with these Country Music Hall of Fame legends, all of whom live in the Fort Payne area. The three cousins, Randy Owen, Teddy Gentry, and Jeff Cook, were born and raised here. (Author photograph.)

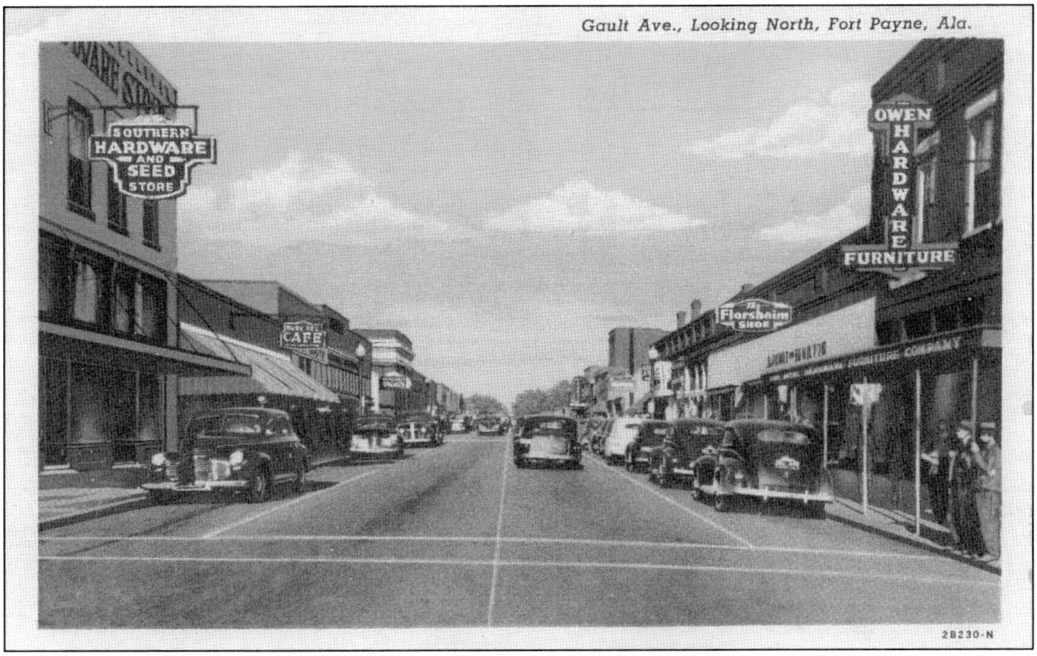

Visible businesses in this 1942 Curt Teich & Company view of First Street and Gault Avenue, looking north, include (at left) Southern Hardware, Busy Bee Café, Haralson's Drugs, and First National Bank. At right are Owen Hardware and Jacoway & Hamilton Clothing Store. (Courtesy of Collins Kirby.)

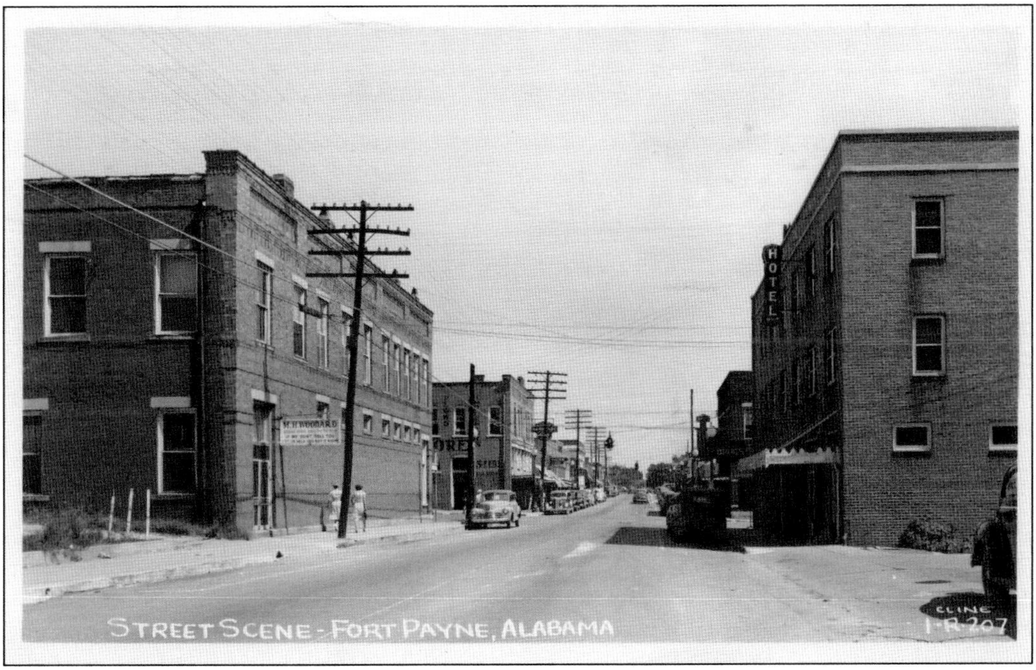

The stores seen in this photograph are M.H. Woodard, Southern Hardware, Hicks Shoe Store, J.C. Penney, V.J. Elmore five-and-dime, Haralson Drugs, First National Bank, Quin Hotel, Owen Hardware, and Joe's Army Store. (Courtesy of Collins Kirby.)

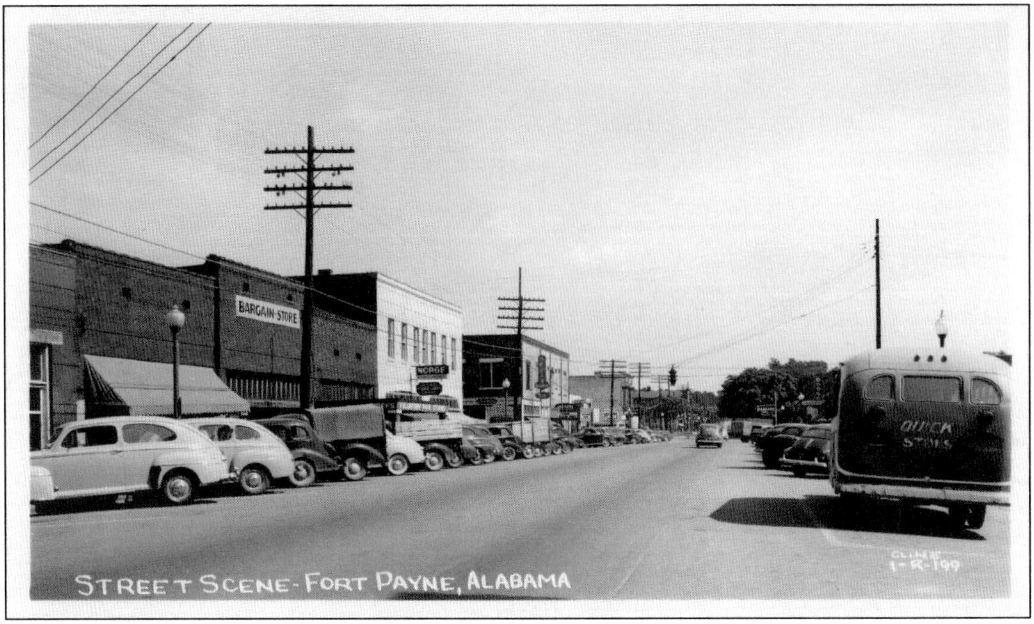

This Cline photograph shows an interesting update to the previous image. This one, from the late 1940s, shows, at left, the Bargain Store, Volunteer Food Store, DeKalb Furniture Company, Stallworth Drug and the DeKalb Theatre in a remodeled structure, the Sawyer Building, signs for Gulf and Texaco stations, and the roof of the opera house. At right are the Sterling Motors Dodge-Plymouth (in a newer building at the former location of Kirby Auto Shop), the Belmont Café, and a Standard Oil sign. (Courtesy of Collins Kirby.)

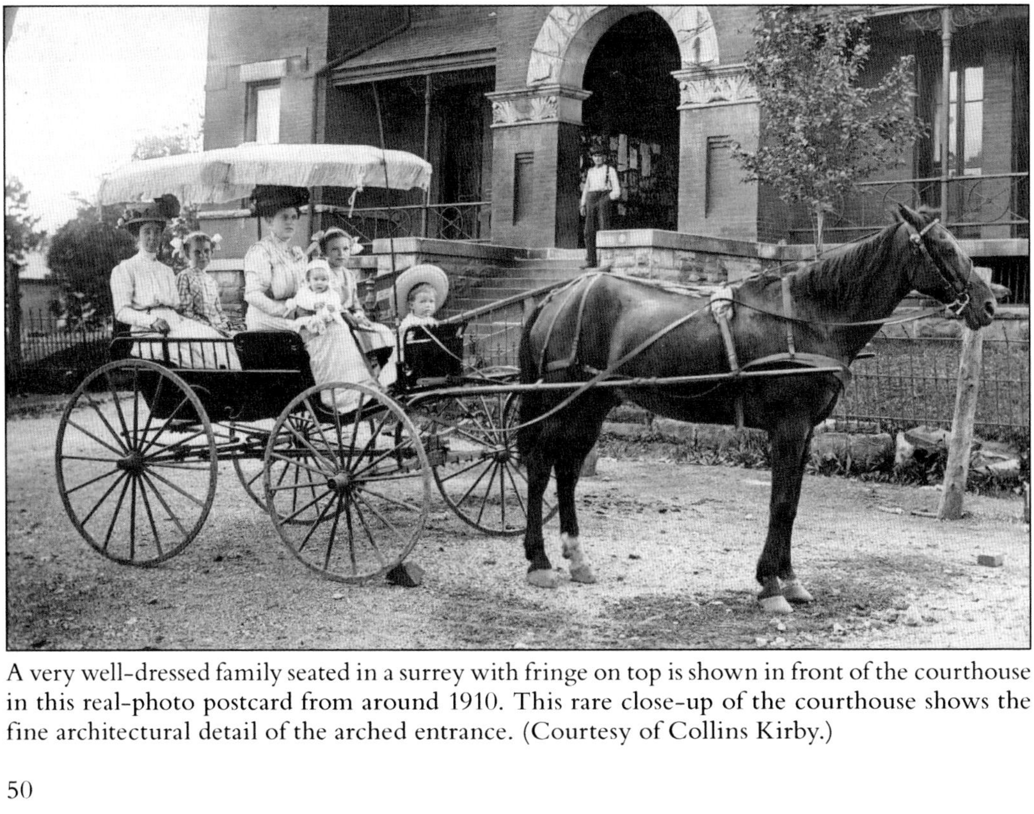

A very well-dressed family seated in a surrey with fringe on top is shown in front of the courthouse in this real-photo postcard from around 1910. This rare close-up of the courthouse shows the fine architectural detail of the arched entrance. (Courtesy of Collins Kirby.)

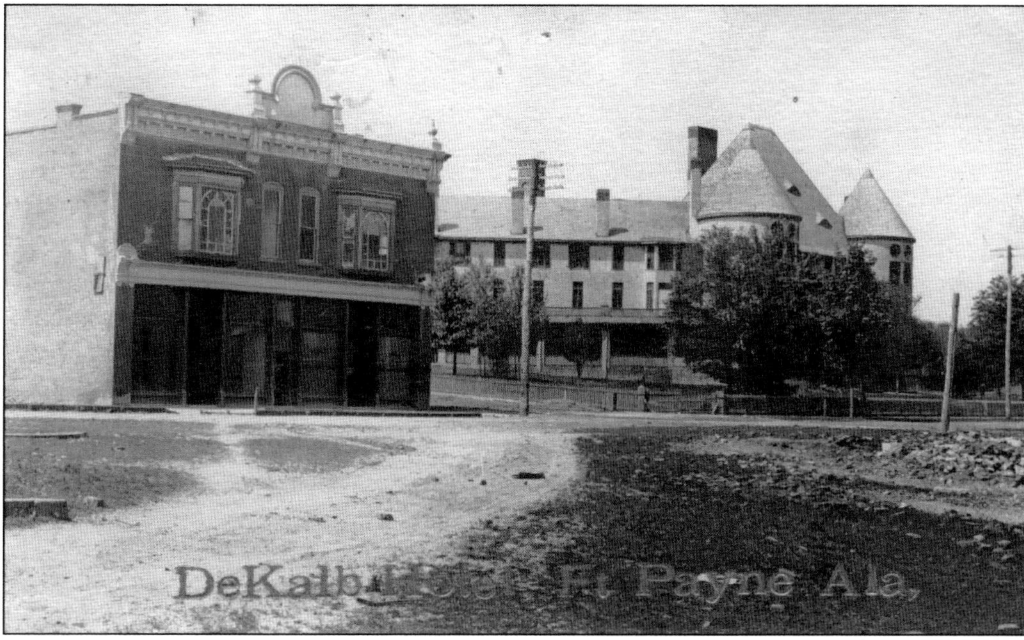

This postcard, postmarked January 12, 1908, shows a very quiet Gault Avenue with the Sawyer Building on the left and the DeKalb Hotel on the right. Around the time this postcard was mailed, new industry had just gotten started in town, and over the next 100 years, Fort Payne became a world leader in the sock manufacturing business, becoming known as the "Sock Capital of the World." Ten years later, in 1918, the DeKalb Hotel on the right burned to the ground due to a chimney fire that caught the wood shingle roof on fire. Local folklore says that if firemen could have gotten to the roof just a few minutes faster, the hotel could have been saved. Below is the back of the postcard, showing the style of the day. (Both, courtesy of Collins Kirby.)

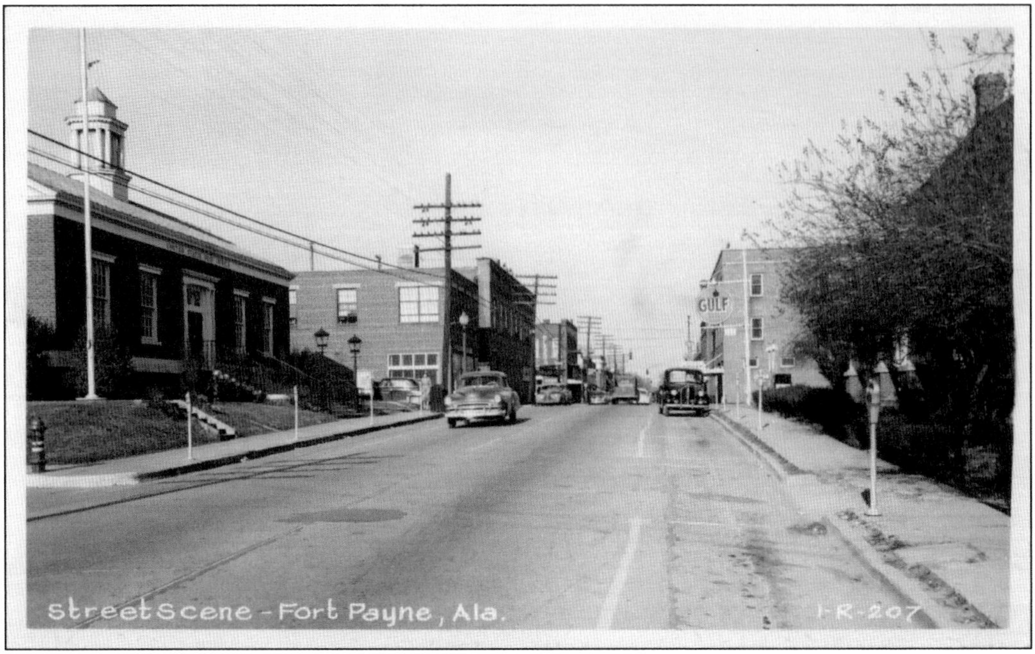

This Cline real-photo postcard is a high-quality image. Is is razor sharp and printed extremely well. Cards like this are a major contributor to the historical record. At the left are the post office, Fort Payne Bank, and Fort Payne Drug. At right are a Gulf station, Quin Hotel, and Owen Hardware. (Courtesy of Collins Kirby.)

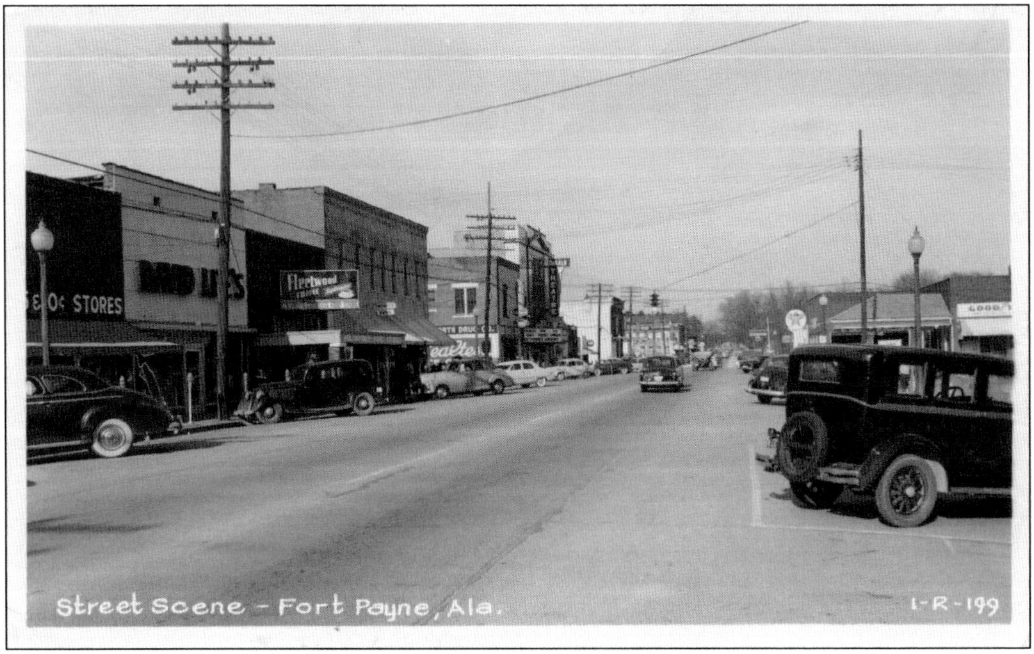

This Cline view from the early 1950s indicates some changes, with the addition of a five-and-dime store, David Lee's, Prewett Bros., and, most interestingly, a totally refreshed DeKalb Theatre, with its higher roof and beautiful Art Deco facade. (Courtesy of Collins Kirby.)

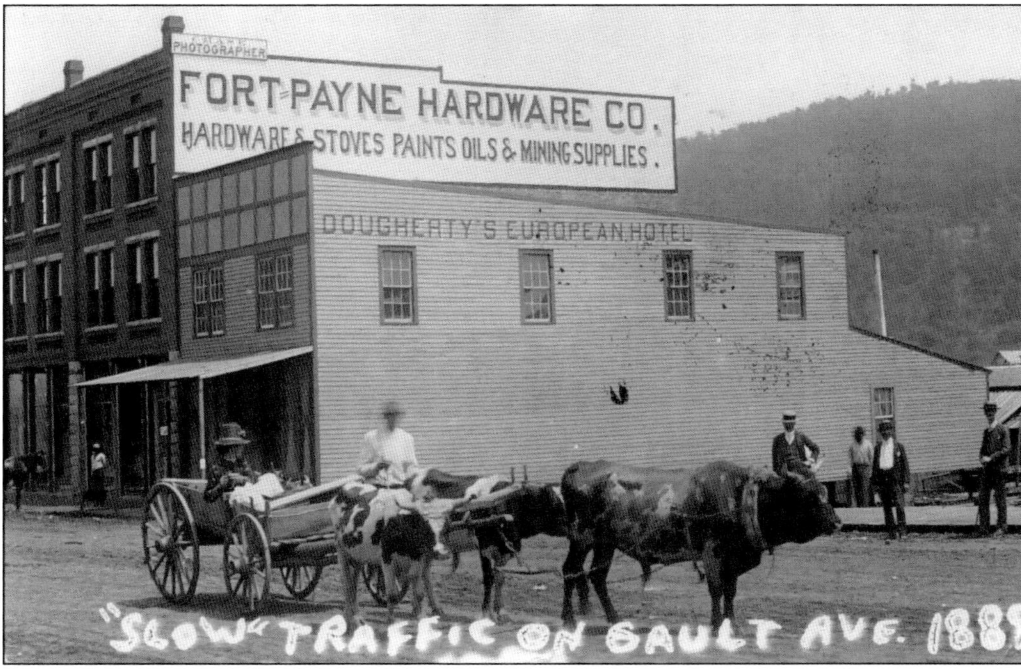

This early 1890s postcard shows "slow traffic on Gault Ave." This fine image shows Fort Payne Hardware and Dougherty's European Hotel. Note the sign for Chase Photographer above the hardware store's sign. (Courtesy of Collins Kirby.)

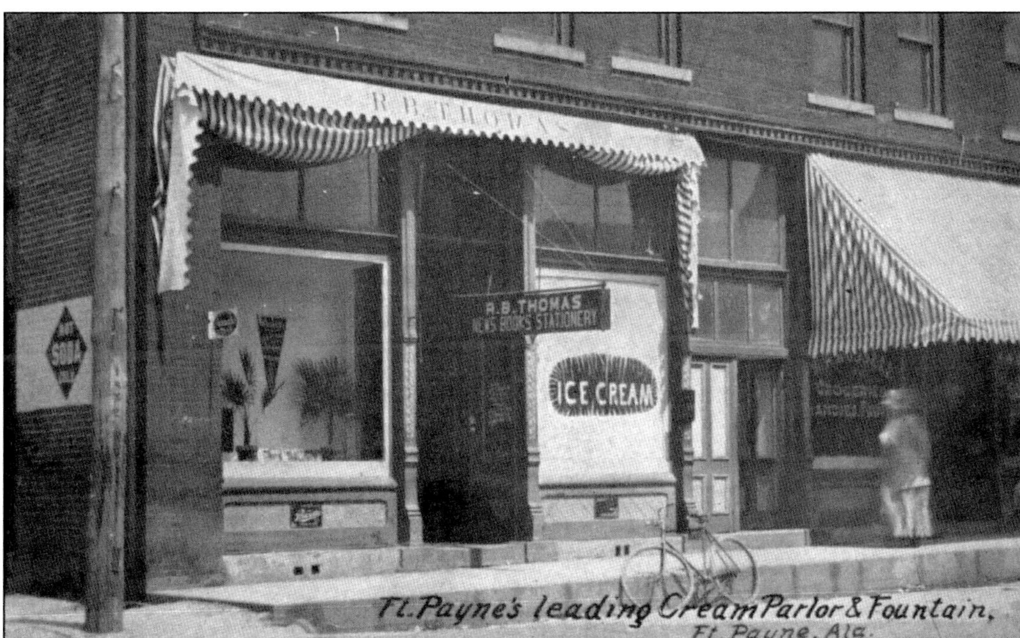

R.B. Thomas Ice Cream Parlor is seen here in the late 1890s. R.B. Thomas was a prominent businessman in town at the time and is responsible for producing a few of the postcards in this publication. (Courtesy of David Rains.)

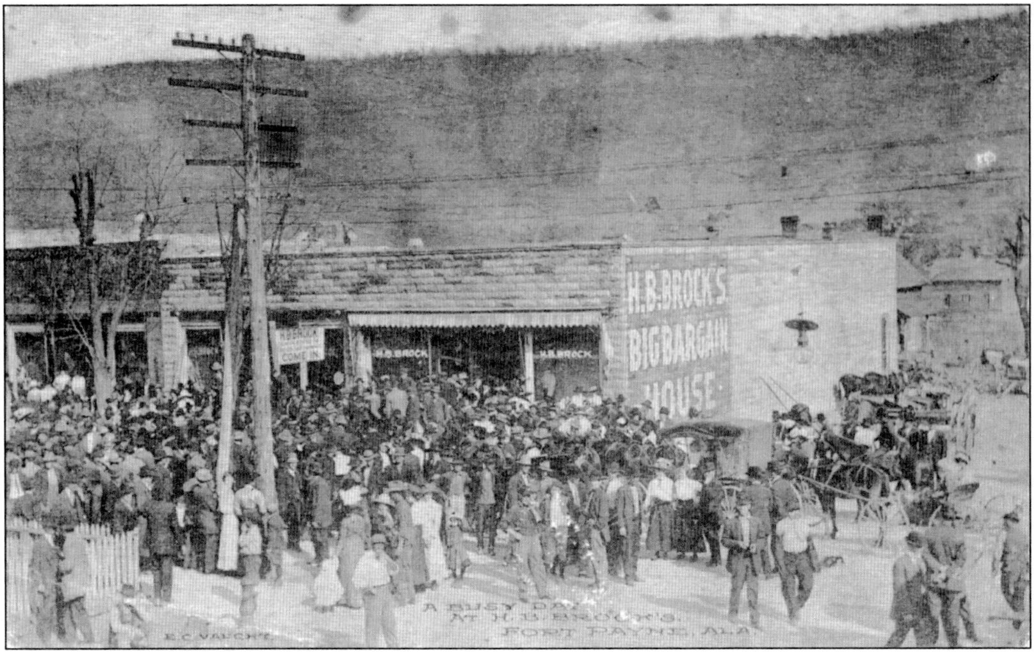

Pictured is a very busy day at H.B. Brock's Bargain House in the late 1890s. There is no record of what was happening to bring out the crowd, but most retailers would have loved to see it. (Courtesy of David Rains.)

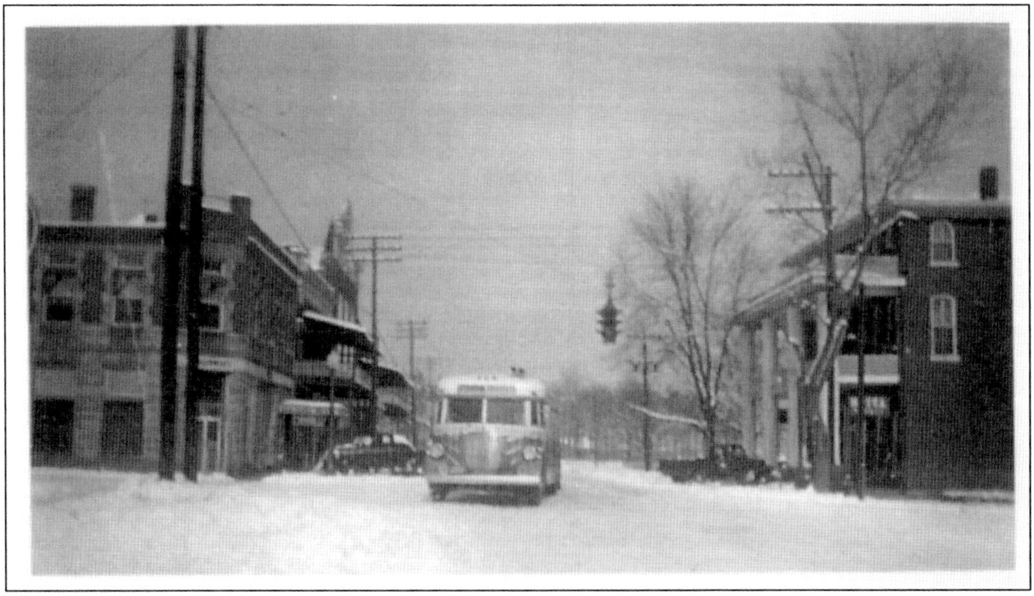

This 1940s view is of Gault Avenue at the intersection of Fifth Street. A bus is arriving, and the Rainey Hotel is visible on the right, with the Fort Payne Coal and Iron Company building on the left. (Author's collection.)

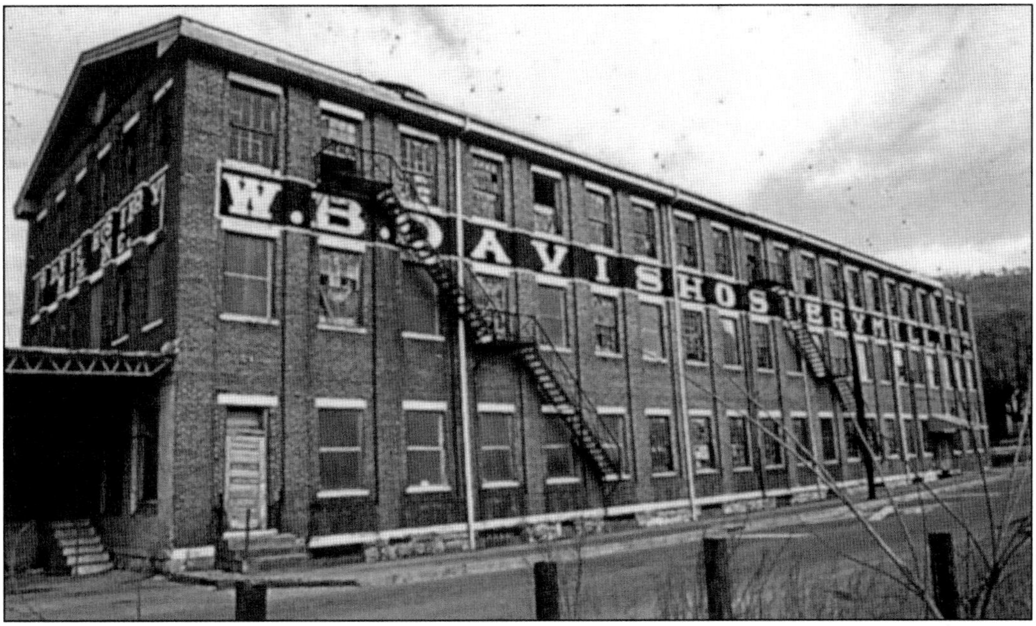

W.B. Davis Hosiery Mill is seen here in the 1960s. The Davis family sold the mill in 1948 and it continued to operate as a hosiery mill until 1973. Even after the mill closed, the building retains the name W.B. Davis Hosiery Mill. Its name, painted boldly on the front and side walls, remains clearly visible today. (Author's collection.)

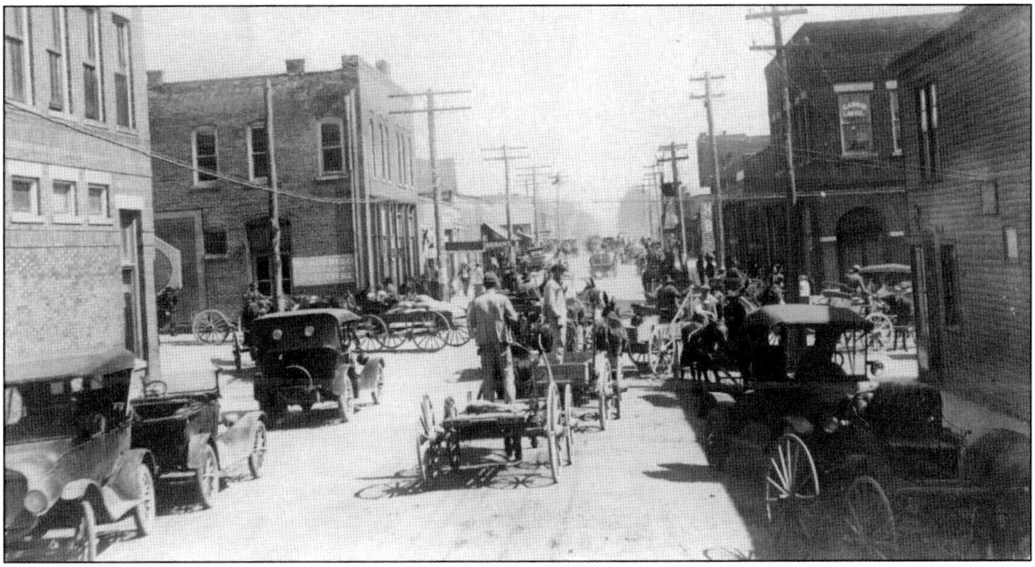

Wagons jockey for position at the intersection of First Street in this real-photo postcard that dates to the early 1920s. Early automobiles are parked along the sidewalk. The original wooden building, which housed Quin Drugs, is at far right. Along that side of the street, and farther north, the second-story law office of C.A. Wolfes can be seen in the W.W. Haralson Building. The H.B. Brock Bargain Store is at the corner of Second Street North, and the third floor of the Masonic building is visible just beyond. On the left side of Gault Avenue are M.L. Mount Outfitters and a restaurant. Part of a very large Chero-Cola sign is visible on the south wall of the M.L. Mount store at far left. Wagons in the distance are loaded with bales of cotton. (Courtesy of Collins Kirby.)

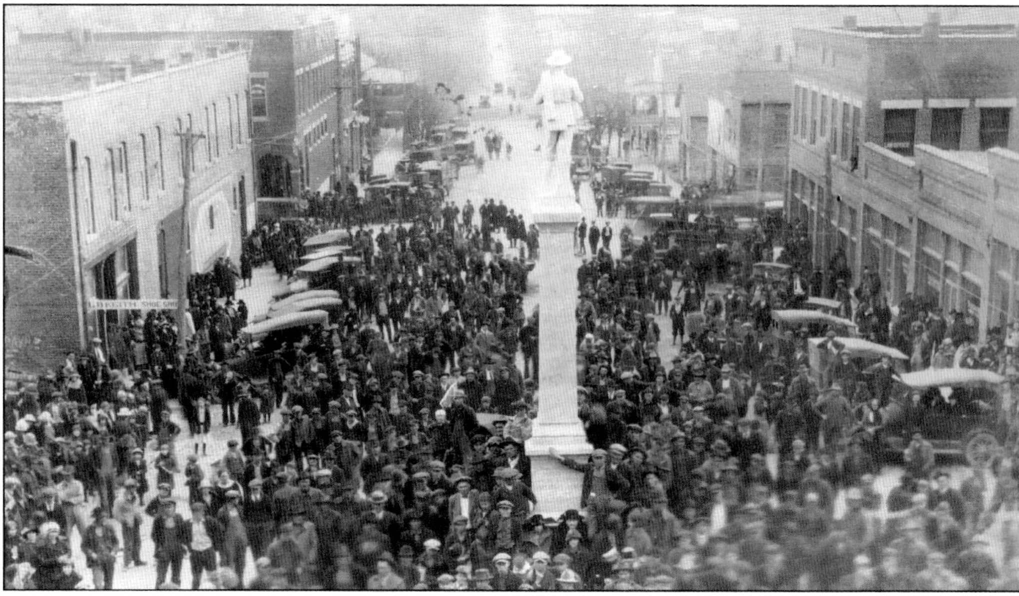

This amazing scene was shot from the second-floor balcony of the courthouse and captures hundreds of citizens gathered on First Street Northwest. Col. C.A. Wolfes's handwritten message on the reverse reads, in part, "The day Fort Payne merchants turned the turkeys loose from the Court House tower, this was part of the crowd." Also handwritten is the date "1/7/24." Visible from left to right are the L.B. Keith Shoe Shop in the rear of the Dobbs Building, the Chero-Cola sign, the W.W. Haralson Building, and the Milford W. Howard Building. The Confederate Monument was erected in front of the courthouse in 1913, and remained until the late 1930s, when it was moved to Union Park, at which time the city council changed the name to City Park. To the right of the statue are Robert L. Wright Jewelry Store (in the far distance), the wooden Quin Drugs Building, and the E.S. Killian Building. (Courtesy of David Rains.)

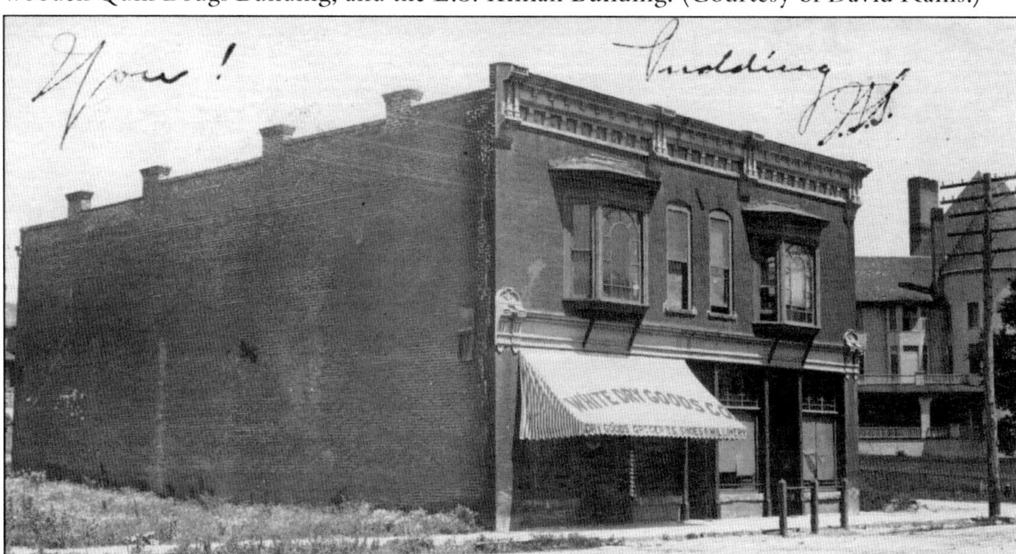

White Dry Goods was located in the c. 1976 Sawyer Building. This pre-1909 postcard shows the DeKalb Hotel to the right. This is another pre-1909 card where only the address could be on the back, so the front had to be used for the message. (Courtesy of Collins Kirby.)

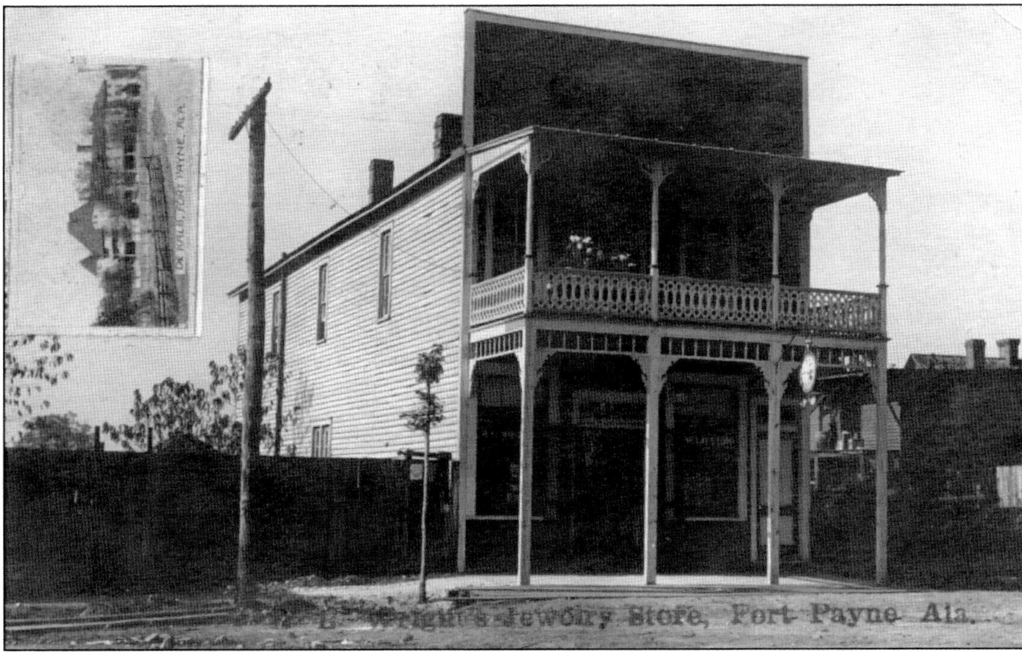

R.L. Wright's Jewelry Store on Gault Avenue is seen in 1908. This is a real-photo postcard, and was created in the same style and era as the real-photo Fort Payne postcards shown earlier in this book. The gold-toned writing can be viewed on other cards showing the opera block from this same time. (Courtesy of Collins Kirby.)

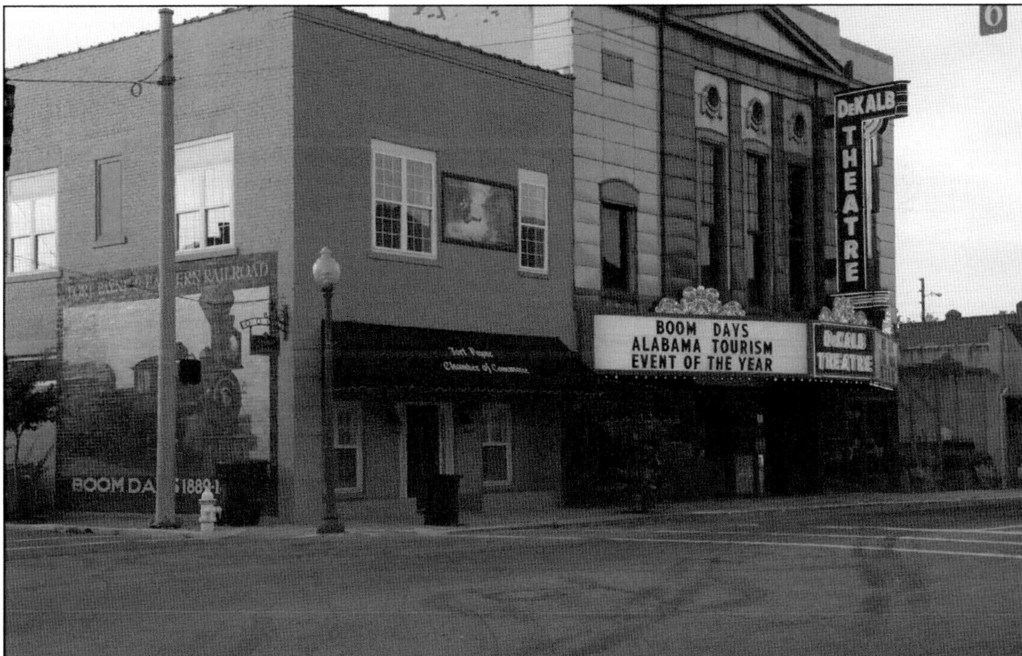

This 2015 view shows the DeKalb Theatre and the Fort Payne Chamber of Commerce. The building is graced with a mural in honor of Fort Payne boom days, painted by Penny Fant. (Author photograph.)

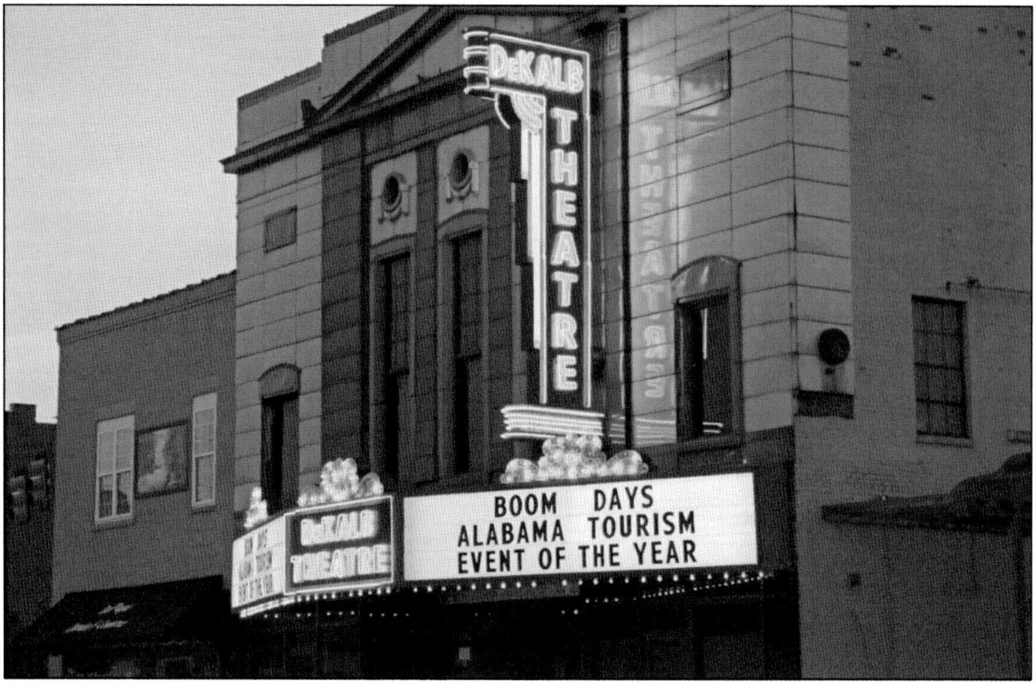

The DeKalb Theatre, built during the boom days, was given its current facade and marquee in 1950. Boom Days Heritage Celebration is the third Saturday in September; it celebrates the boom days era of Fort Payne's history. This photograph was taken after Boom Days won the Alabama State Tourism Event of the Year award in 2015. (Author photograph.)

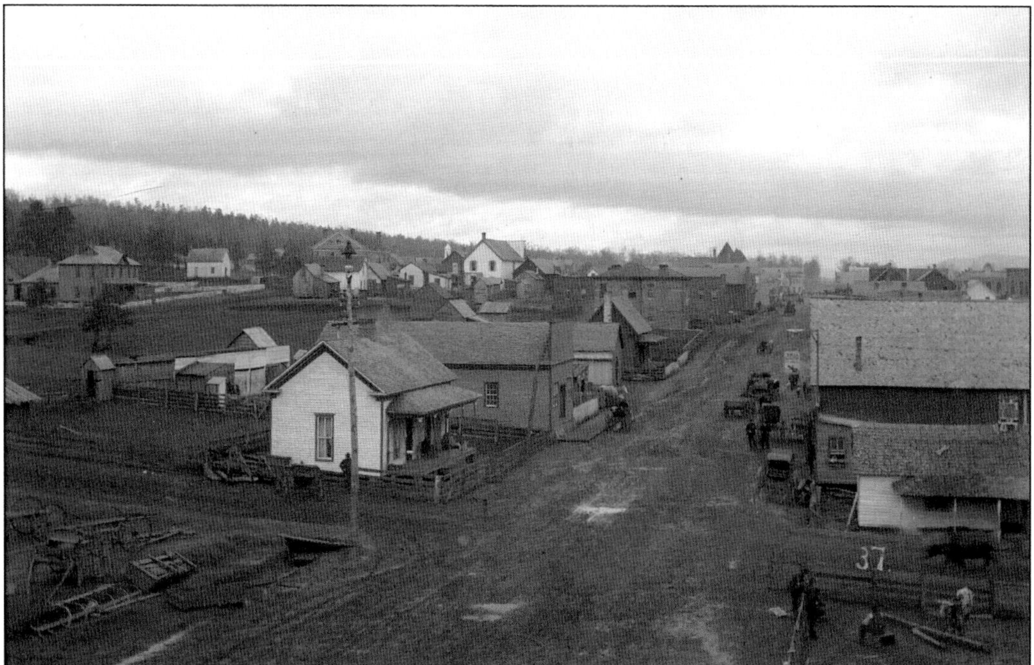

Looking to the north on Gault Avenue, the DeKalb Hotel can be seen in the distance. This scene, taken by O.W. Chase, dates to the late 1880s or early 1890s. (Author's collection.)

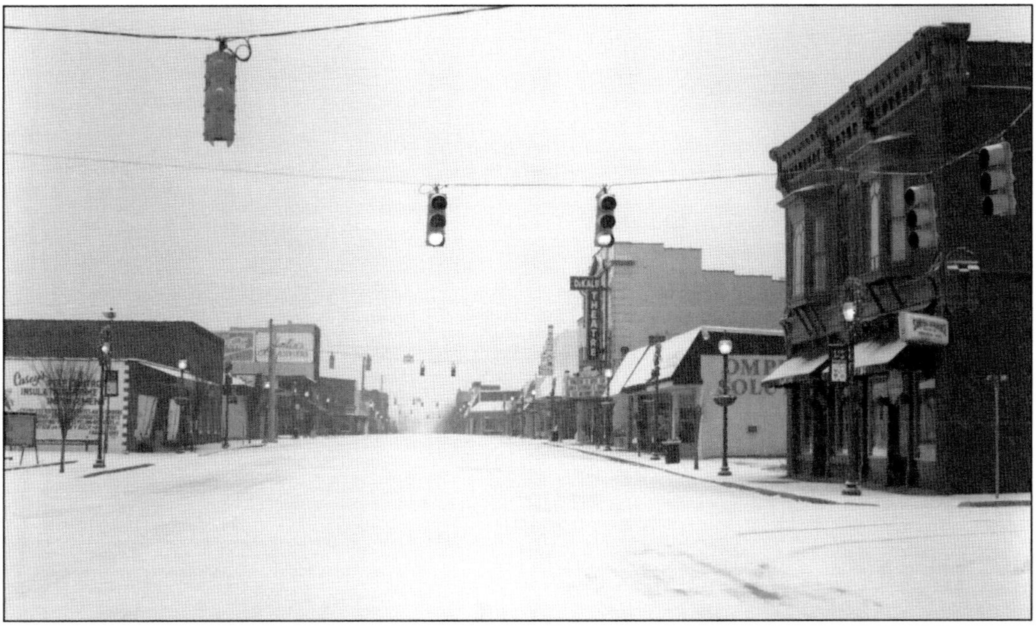

This photograph was taken on January 1, 2001, at 7:00 a.m. It snowed overnight on New Year's Eve, and on this New Year's Day, no one was out nor needed to be on this holiday. This view looking south on Gault Avenue shows the Sawyer Building on the right. The photograph was taken on the block between Fourth and Fifth Streets where the DeKalb Hotel was located. (Author photograph.)

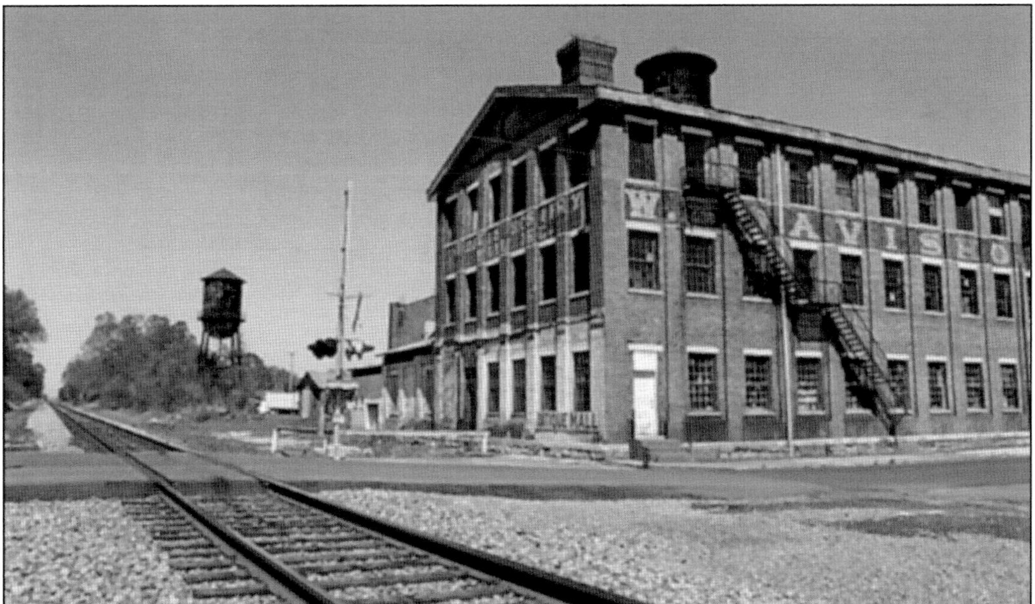

This is a recent postcard of the W.B. Davis Hosiery Mill. By this time, it was the Big Mill Co. Artisans & Antiques and the Vintage 1889 Restaurant and Bar, which offers live music in the concert hall and in the restaurant and bar area. There is a courtyard, as well as a deck, for outdoor seating. The property is currently owned by Dr. Stephen and Lynn Brewer. They have kept the original integrity of this property, preserving its original look and feel. It is an amazing historic piece of boomtown property. (Author's collection.)

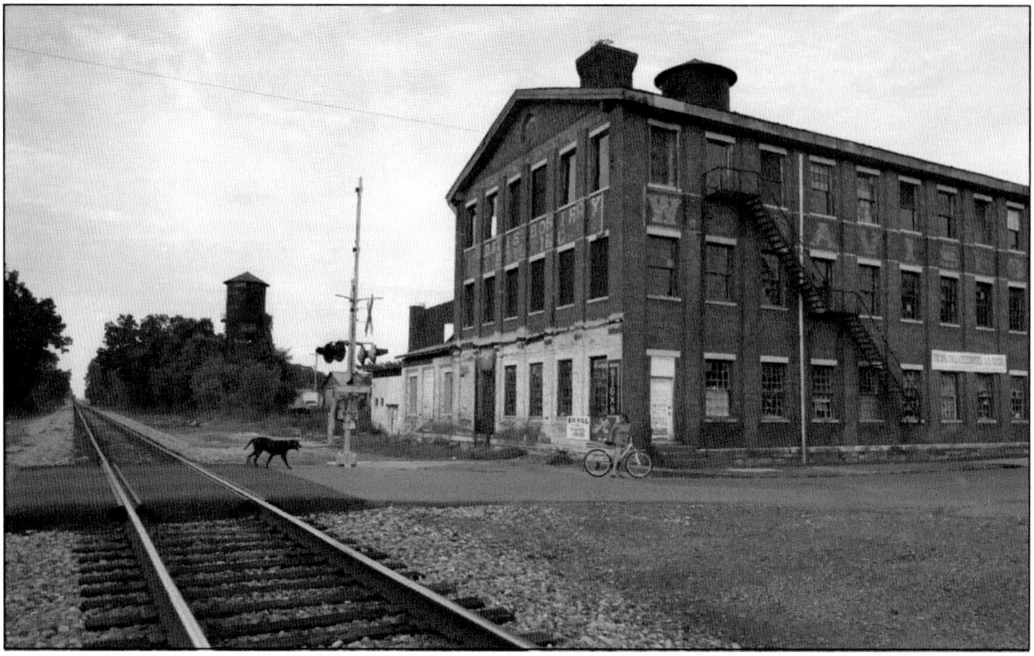

This 2014 photograph mimics the previous image. The image quality and the subject appear much as they would have in 1889 and thereafter. This boom days–era building first opened in 1889 as the Alabama Builders Hardware and Manufacturing Company. The company made hardware, such as brass hinges and other metal hardware for houses and commercial buildings, for the construction industry. In 1907, it became Florence Hosiery Mill, the first hosiery mill in Fort Payne. (Author photograph.)

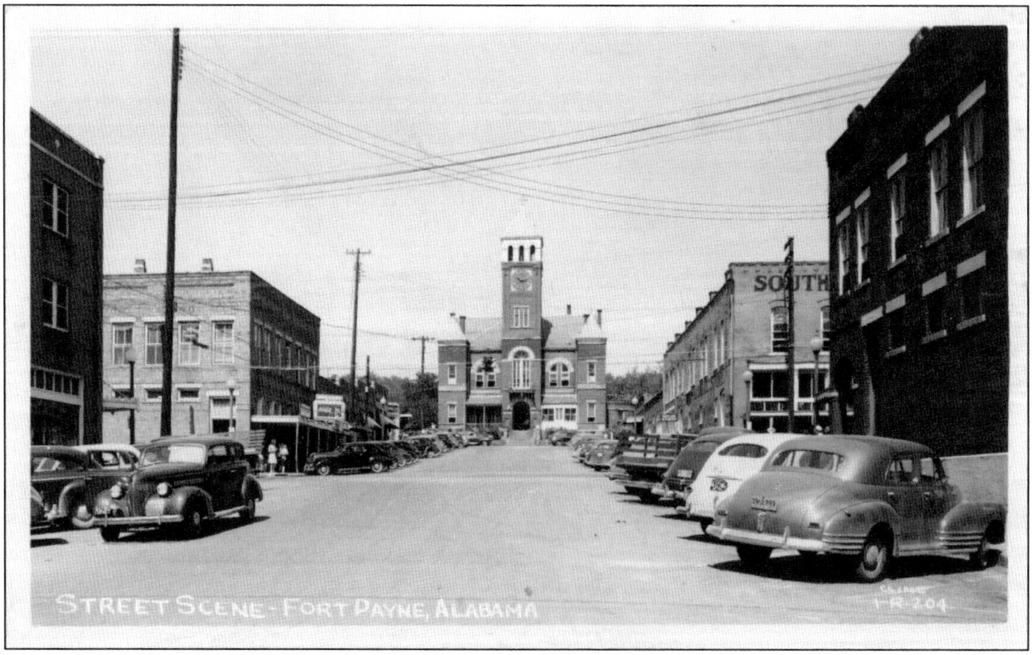

This 1940s Cline real-photo postcard shows a very busy Main Street (now First Street). (Courtesy of Collins Kirby.)

Seven

Schools and Churches

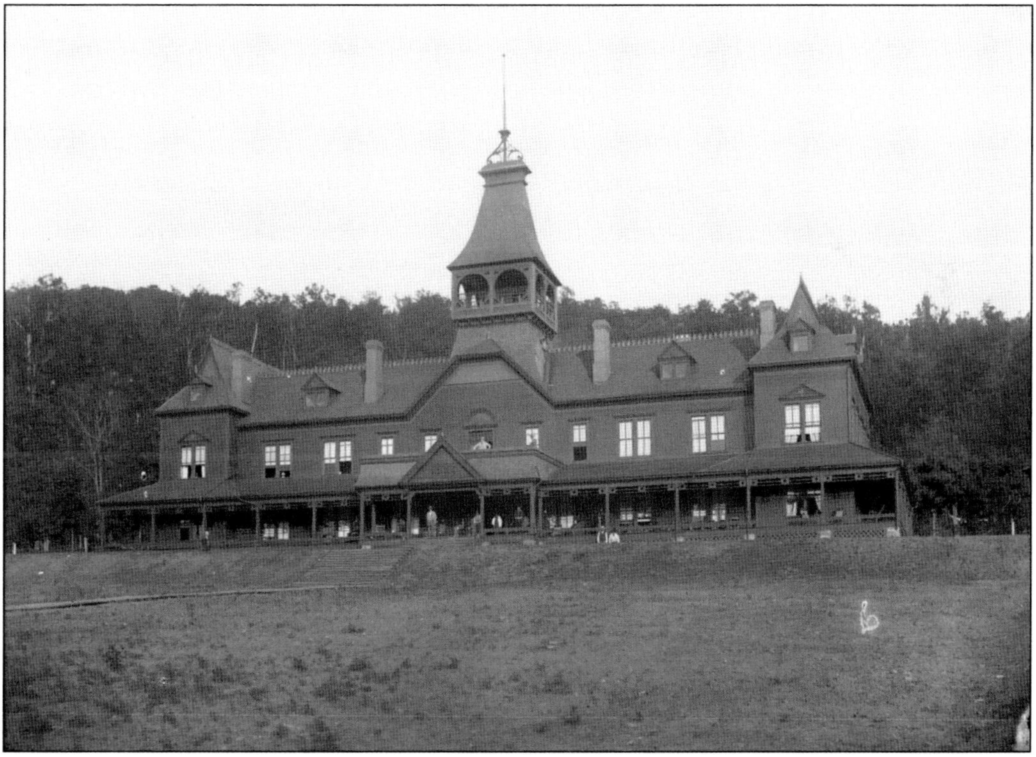

North Alabama College, shown in this early Fort Payne postcard, was destroyed by fire three years prior to the 1906 postmark. Built in 1889 as the Manitou Park Hotel, it reopened as Fort Payne Academy for Young Ladies in 1890, and again as North Alabama College in 1895. (Courtesy of Collins Kirby.)

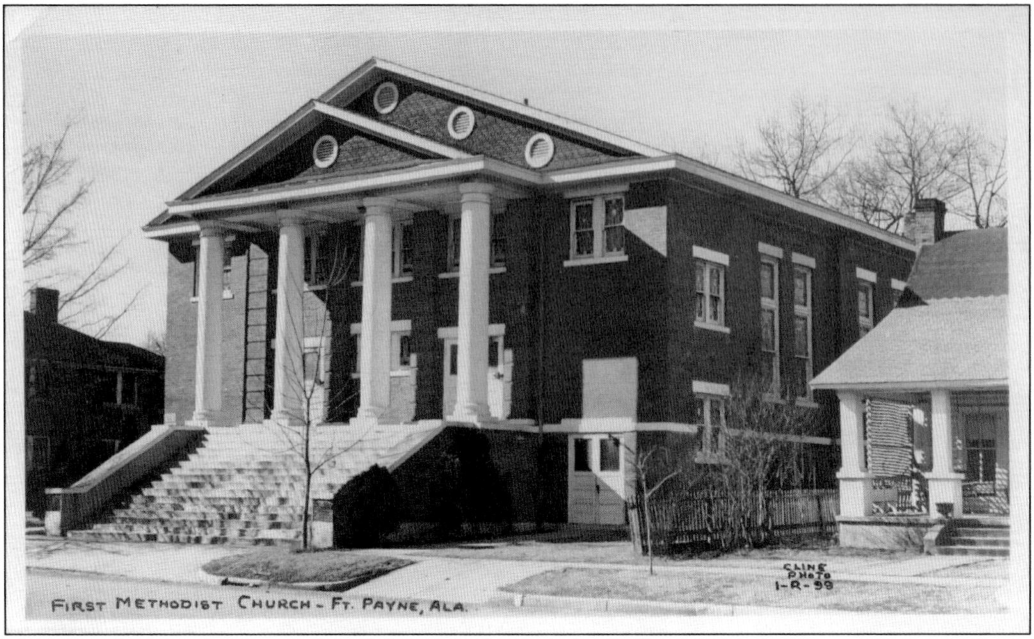

Walter Cline's First Methodist Church photograph, taken on the same day as his First Baptist Church picture, accentuates the broad steps and high portico. A portion of the second parsonage, which is now used as the church's administrative building, is visible at left. (Courtesy of Collins Kirby.)

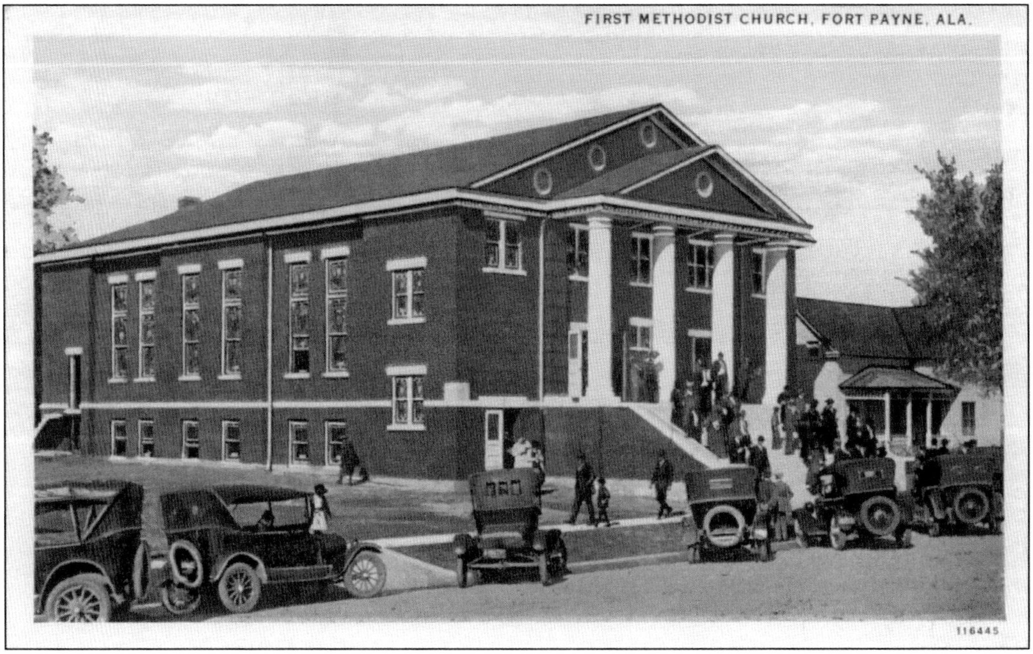

Another of Curt Teich & Company's 1927 Fort Payne series, this view of First Methodist Church demonstrates the building's grand appearance and a casual approach to parking. Built in 1922, the sanctuary remains in use today. (Courtesy of Collins Kirby.)

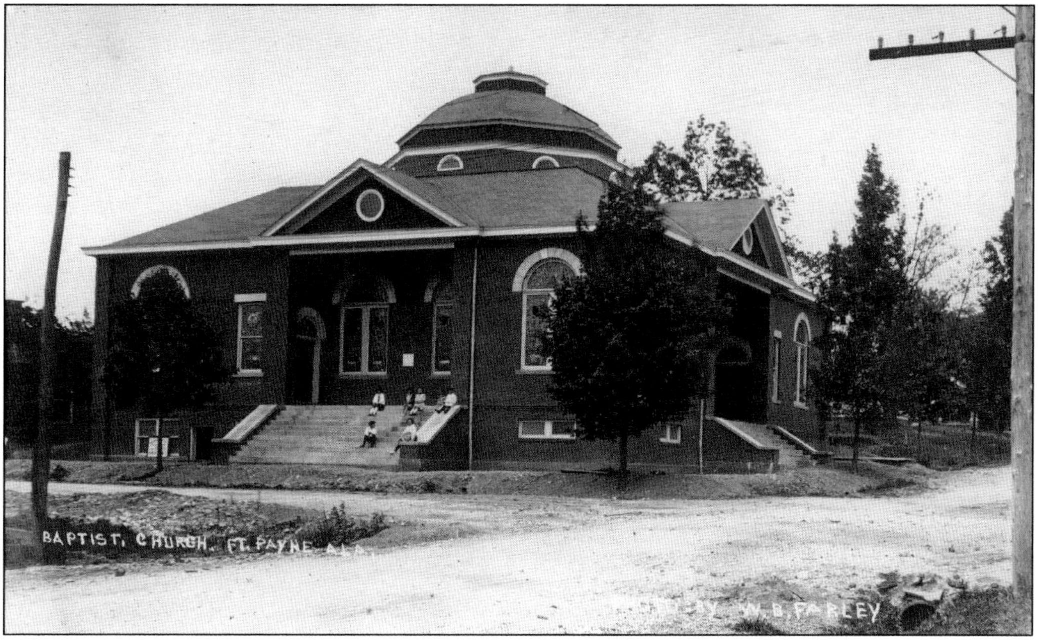

Local photographer W.B. Farley published this real-photo postcard of the First Baptist Church, with its distinctive cupola and entrances on both Grand Avenue North and Second Street Northwest. The picture reveals the dirt streets and open drainage ditches of 1920s Fort Payne. (Courtesy of Collins Kirby.)

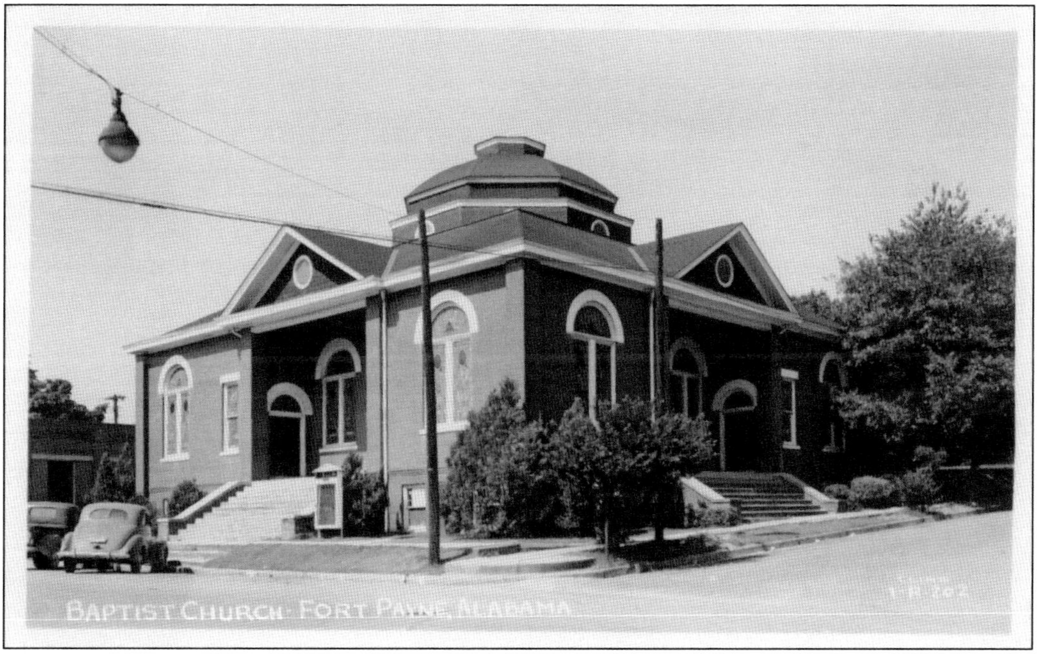

This 1940s view of First Baptist Church was taken by Chattanooga photographer-publisher Walter Cline. It shows a nicely paved Grand Avenue with curbs and gutters and highlights the church's intricate stained-glass windows. The private residence of insurance agent John L. Cross is visible at right. (Courtesy of Collins Kirby.)

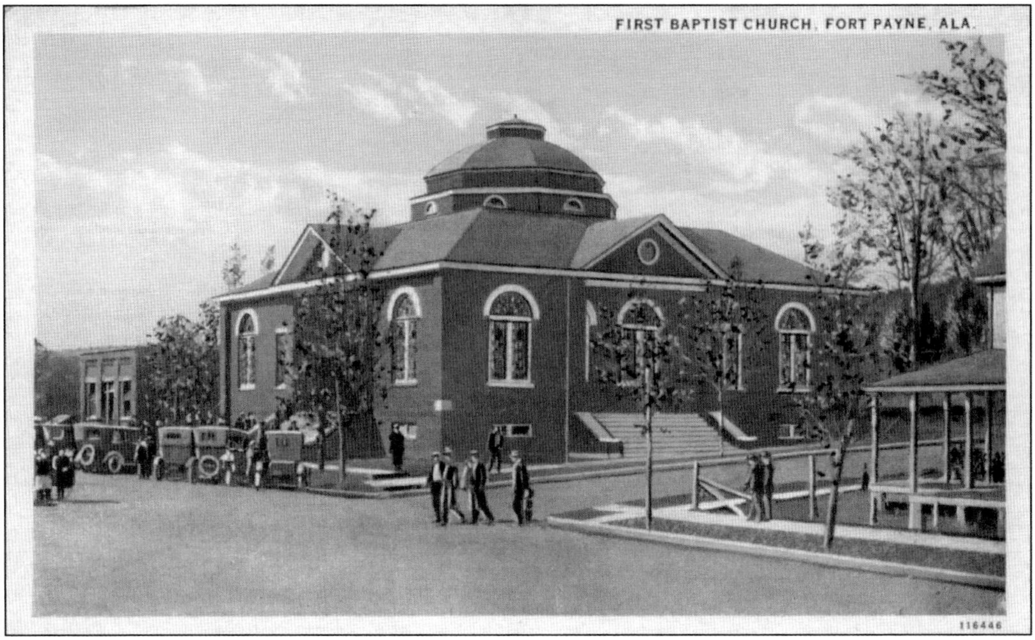

The sanctuary pictured was erected in 1921 and served the Baptist church well until 1958, by which time the congregation had outgrown the building. It was razed during the mid-1960s to accommodate the church's new educational facility. This postcard was published by Curt Teich & Company in 1927. Model T automobiles line the street, and the Isbell law office is visible at left. (Courtesy of Collins Kirby.)

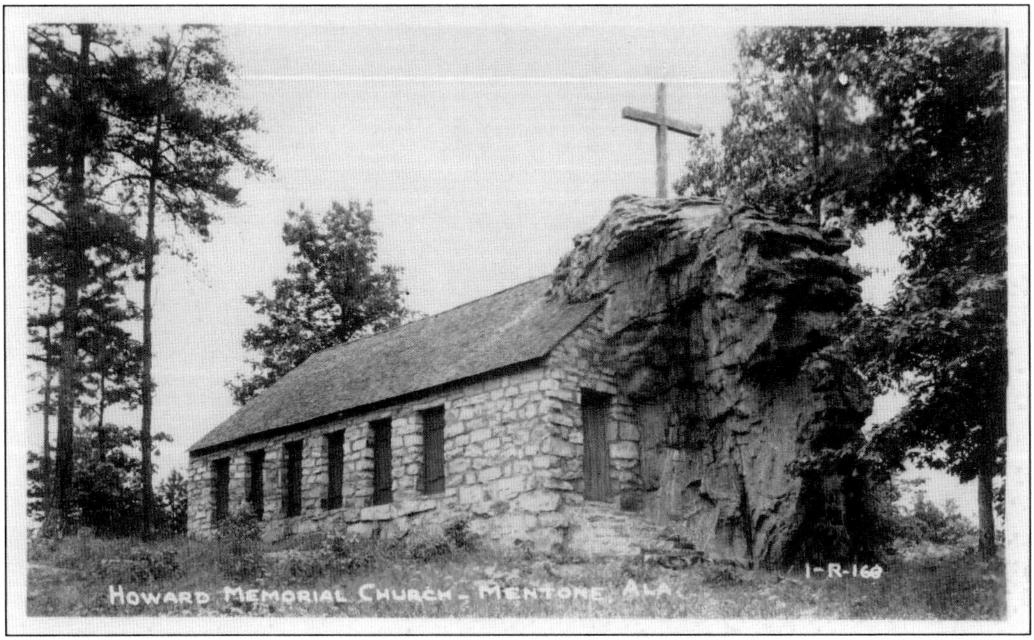

Howard's Chapel (Sallie Howard Memorial Chapel) is one of the most photographed churches in northeast Alabama. Built in the 1930s by author, congressman, actor, and developer Milford W. Howard as a tribute to his deceased wife, the unique structure is literally built upon a rock. Local labor and materials were utilized to create this charming church. (Courtesy of Collins Kirby.)

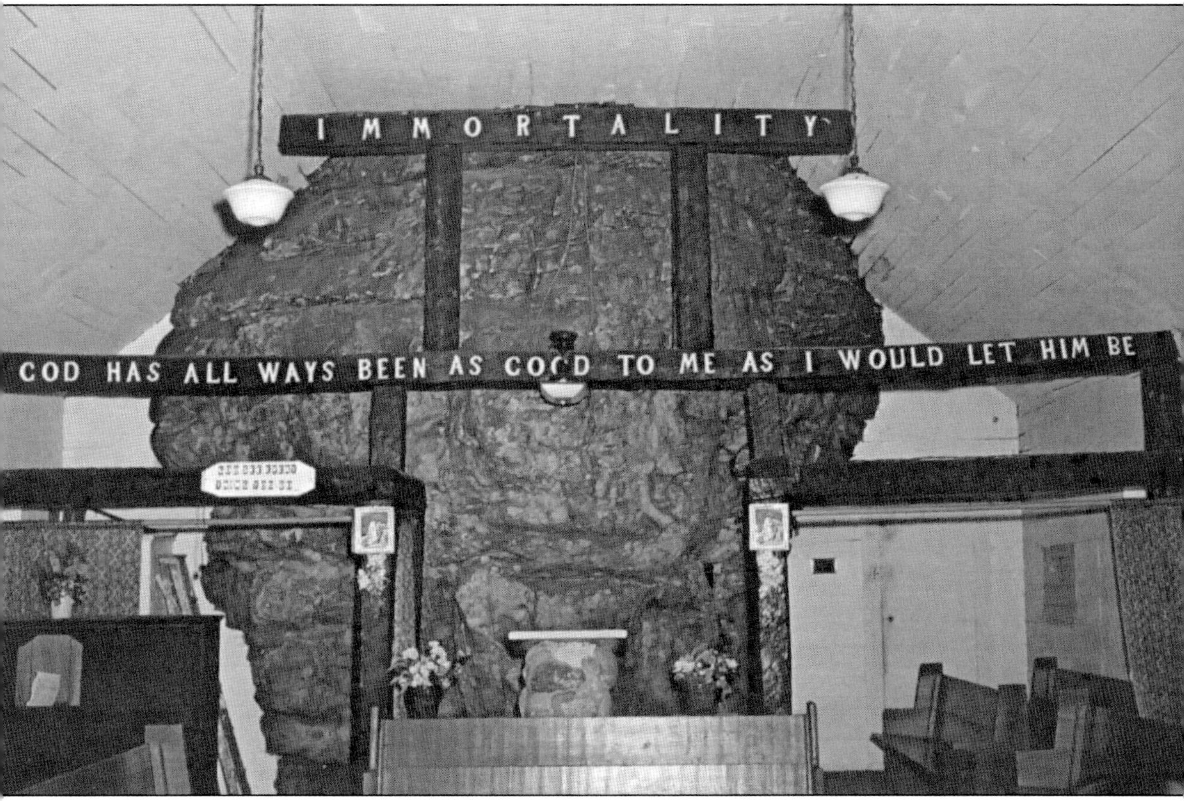

This interior view of Howard's Chapel by Hub Gardner reveals the church's hand-built, folksy style. Milford Howard's ashes are interred in the enclosed portion of the rock. (Courtesy of Collins Kirby.)

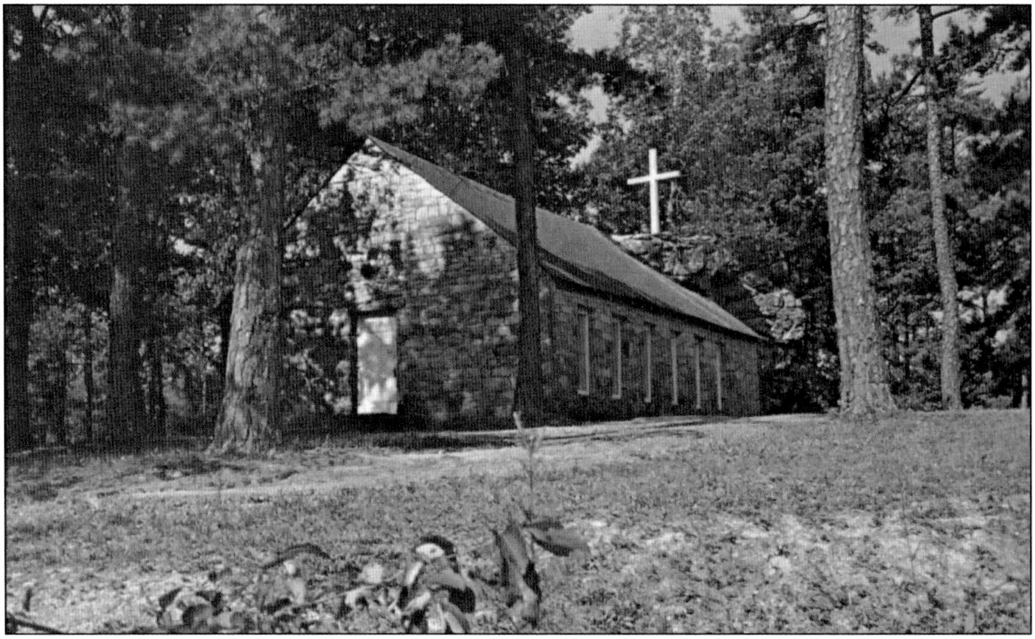

This Hub Gardner postcard from the 1960s captures the peaceful mountain atmosphere of this extraordinary edifice, whose design was inspired by Wee Kirk o' the Heather at Forest Lawn Cemetery in Glendale, California, where Sallie Howard is buried. Perched on this hilltop adjacent to DeSoto State Park on Lookout Mountain, Howard's Chapel receives thousands of visitors annually. (Courtesy of Collins Kirby.)

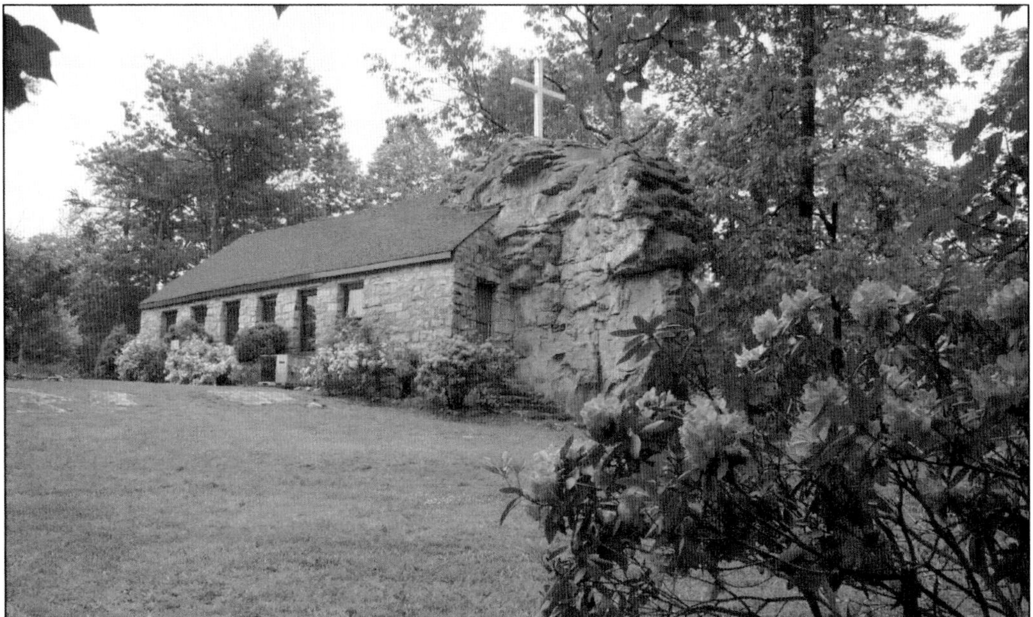

This 2008 view shows Howard's Chapel in spring. This area is near the southernmost point where rhododendron can grow. The chapel, located next to DeSoto State Park, is a beautiful place in the spring and fall as plants normally grown farther north or farther south meet here and all prosper in spring bloom or brightly colored fall foliage. (Author photograph.)

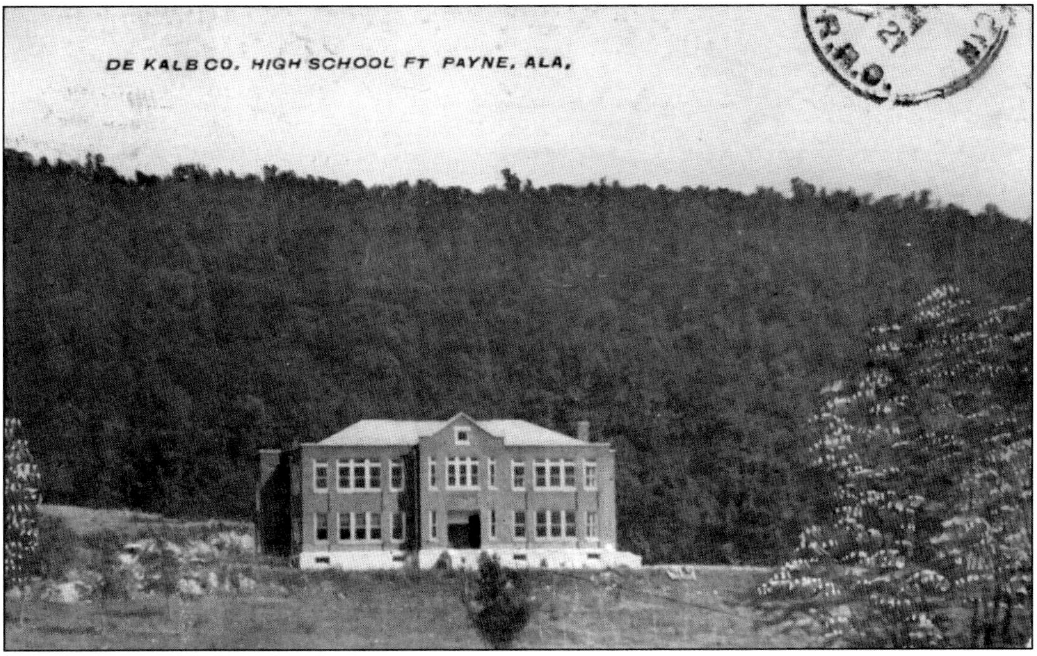

DeKalb County High School was built in 1908 on the site of North Alabama College. It is shown here shortly after its construction but prior to the completion of sidewalks and landscaping. (Courtesy of Collins Kirby.)

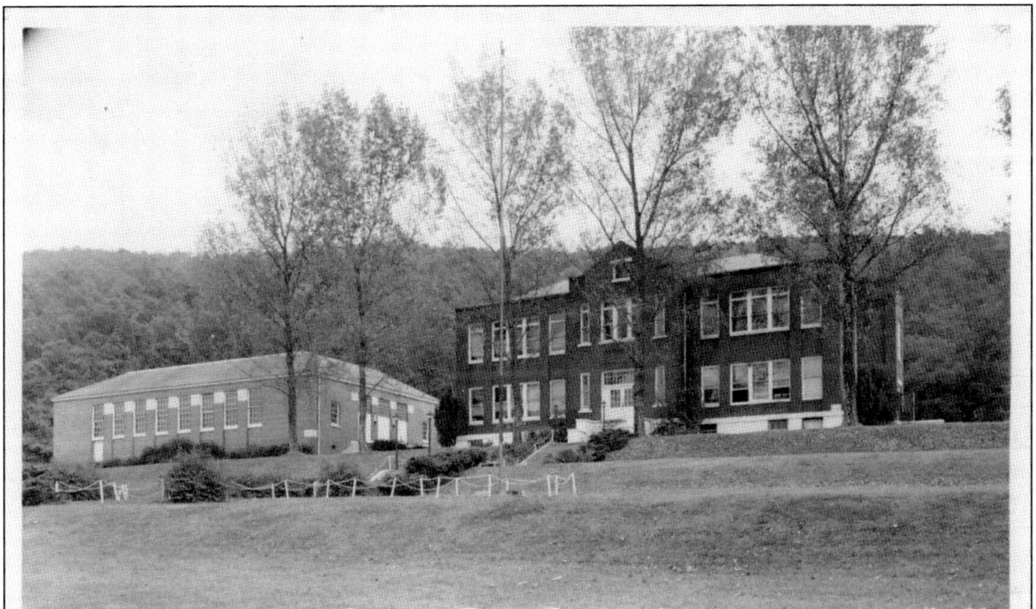

This c. 1950 Cline postcard offers a view of the high school building and auditorium. DeKalb County High School became Fort Payne High School in 1957. The high school was moved to a new facility in north Fort Payne in 1969; in 1972, the original classroom building was demolished. (Courtesy of Collins Kirby.)

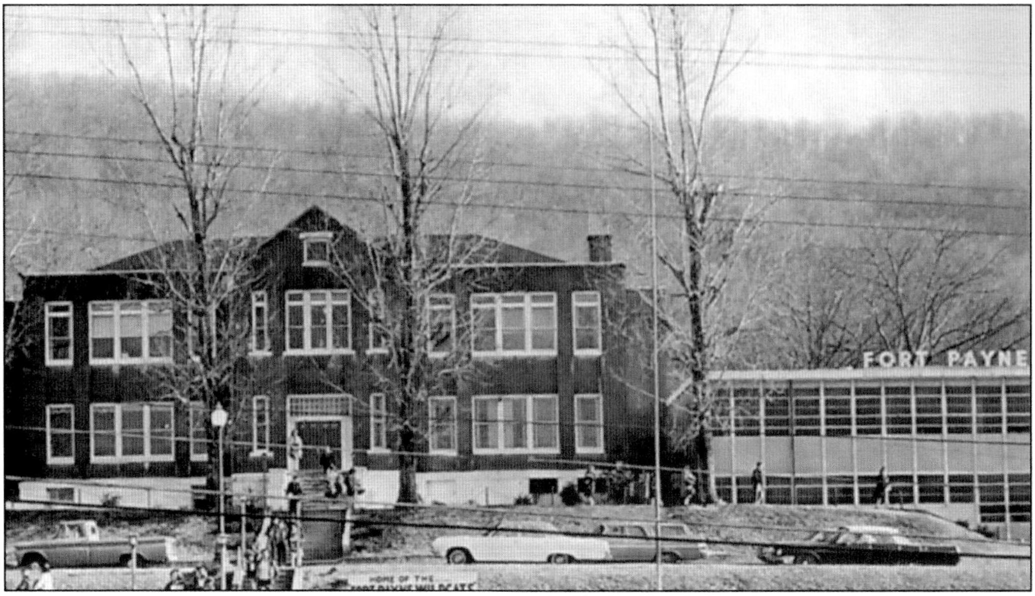

Pictured here is Fort Payne High School in the late 1960s; it shows the newer wing built in the mid-1950s. Prior to this time, it was named DeKalb County High School; however, once other county schools opened, it became Fort Payne High School, home of the Wildcats. A newer high school opened in early 1969. It remains the only high school in Fort Payne. Fort Payne's population has been about 15,000 over the last several censuses, with one school able to serve the high school–age population. (Author's collection.)

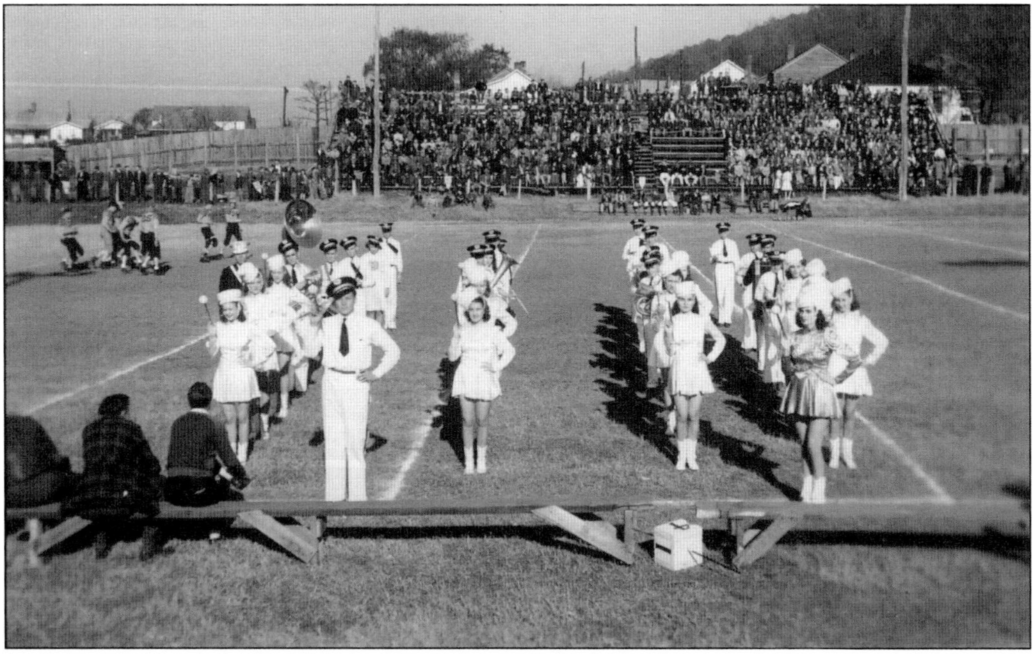

The DeKalb County High School marching band is shown performing at Sawyer Field, which was situated on Rucker Street Northeast; it served as the school's football field prior to the construction of the Fort Payne Sports Complex. Football players are seen warming up at left. (Courtesy of Collins Kirby.)

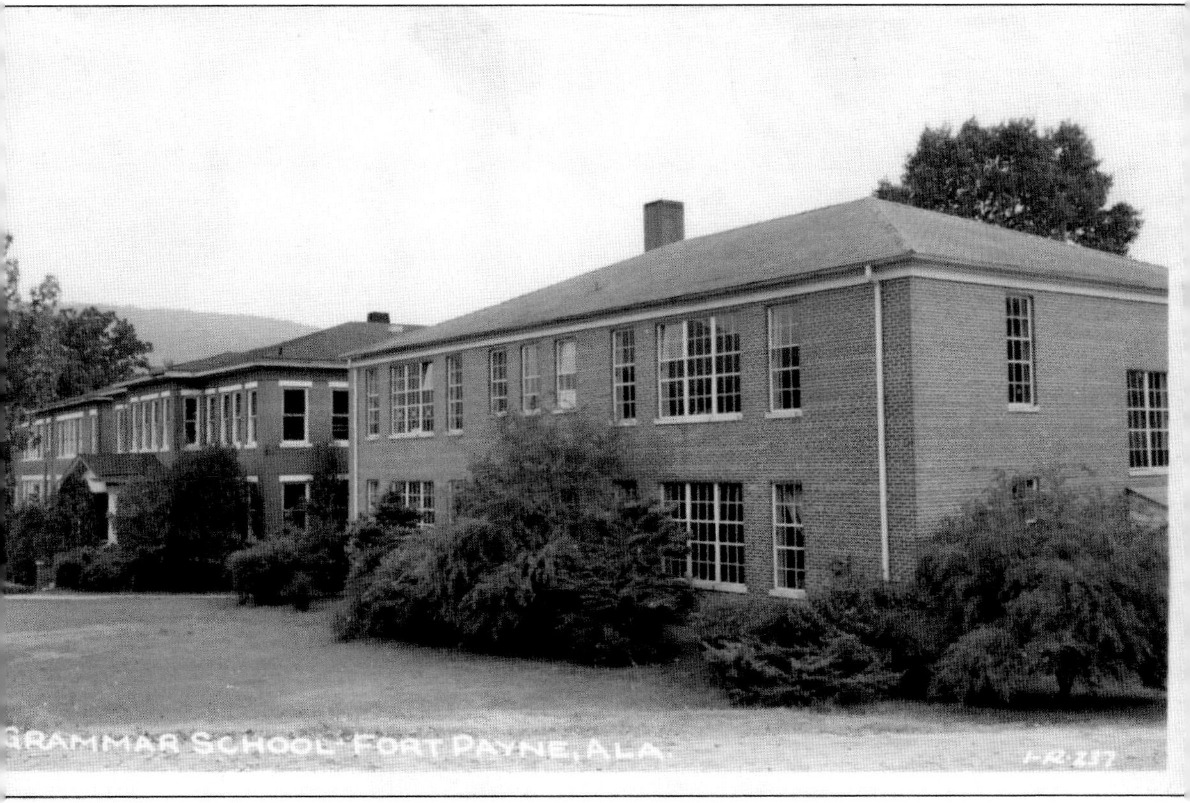

Fort Payne City School (later Forest Avenue School), pictured here around 1950, was the city's only elementary school until 1957, when Williams Avenue School was added. The building at left was erected in 1912 and was condemned and razed in 1962. The building in the center and right foreground was built in 1938 and still stands. The Forest Avenue School complex, with its active elementary school, was closed and vacated in May 1998. This photograph was taken from the corner of Second Street Northwest and Forest Avenue North, looking southeast. The city of Fort Payne restored several buildings in this school complex, and in 2006, it became the new Fort Payne City Hall and Municipal Auditorium. (Courtesy of Collins Kirby.)

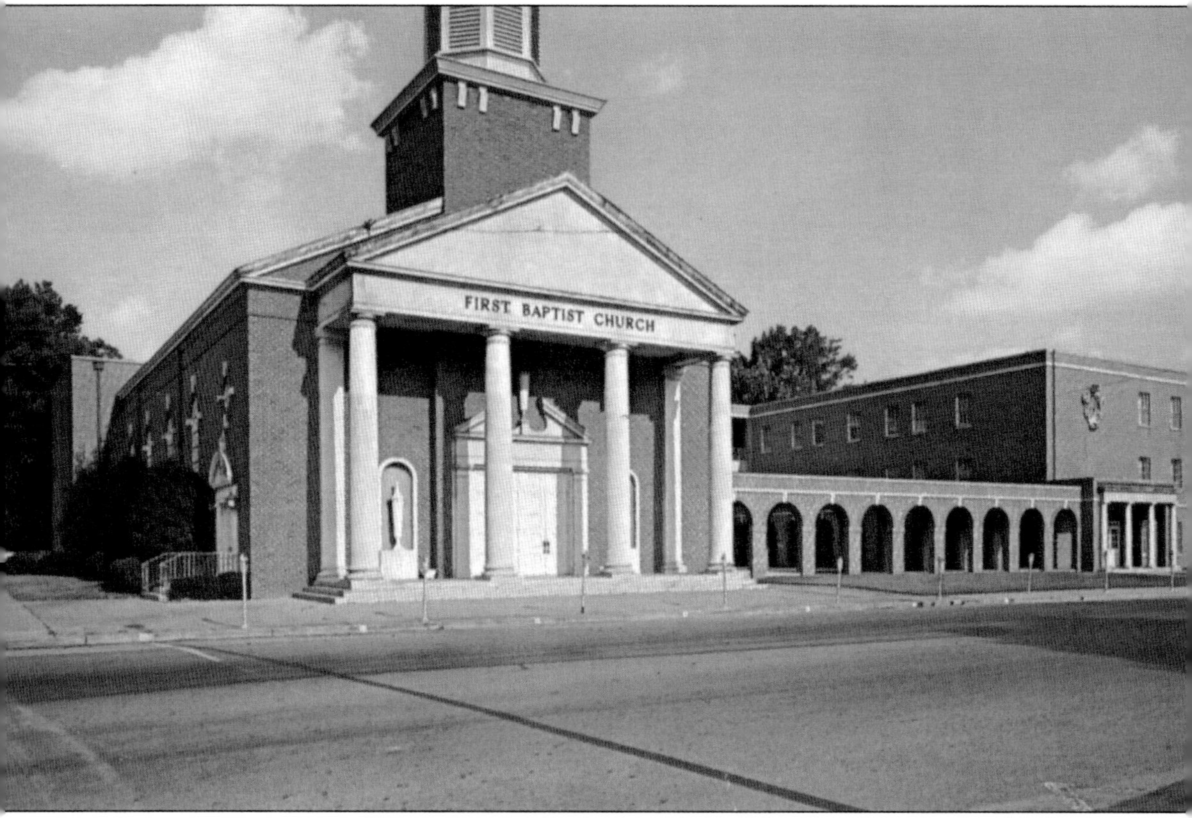

Popular Fort Payne photographer Rogers Culpepper took this photograph, and the postcard was published around 1970. It shows both the 1958 sanctuary and the 1966 educational wing of First Baptist Church in the 100 block of Grand Avenue North. (Courtesy of Collins Kirby.)

Eight

Hotels, Motels, and Businesses

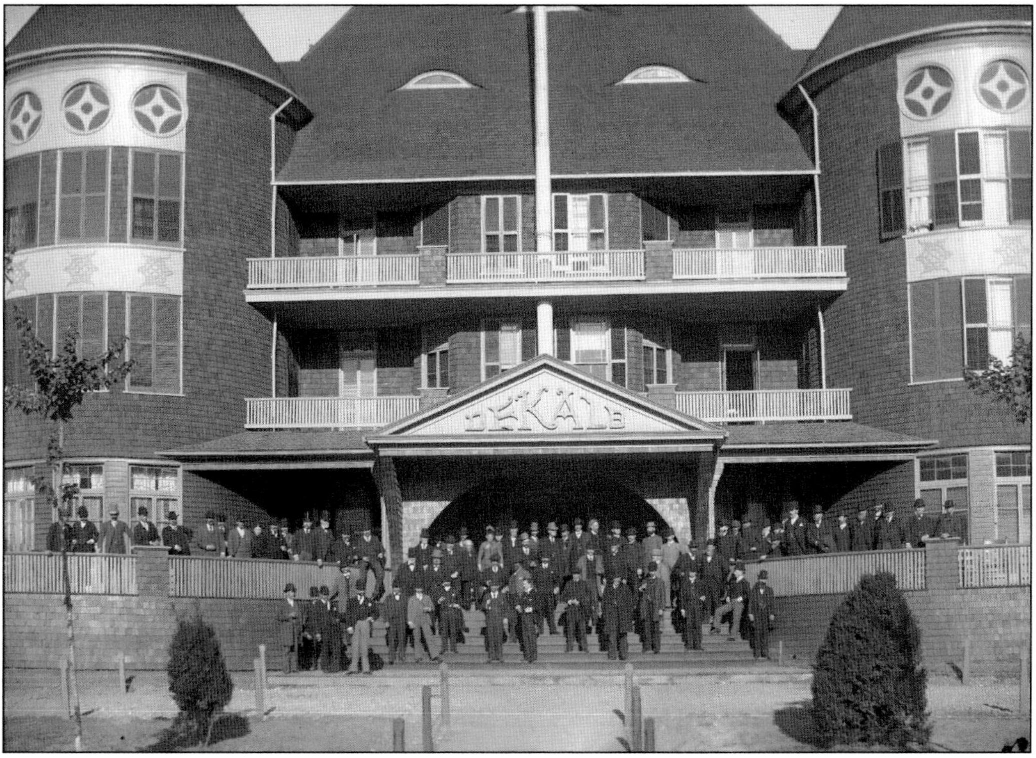

The DeKalb Hotel is seen with local and visiting businessmen. Photographer O.W. Chase came to Fort Payne under contract; Boston businessmen wanted him to photograph the boomtown progress in Fort Payne for the purpose of making a brochure to promote investment in Fort Payne by New Englanders. (Author's collection.)

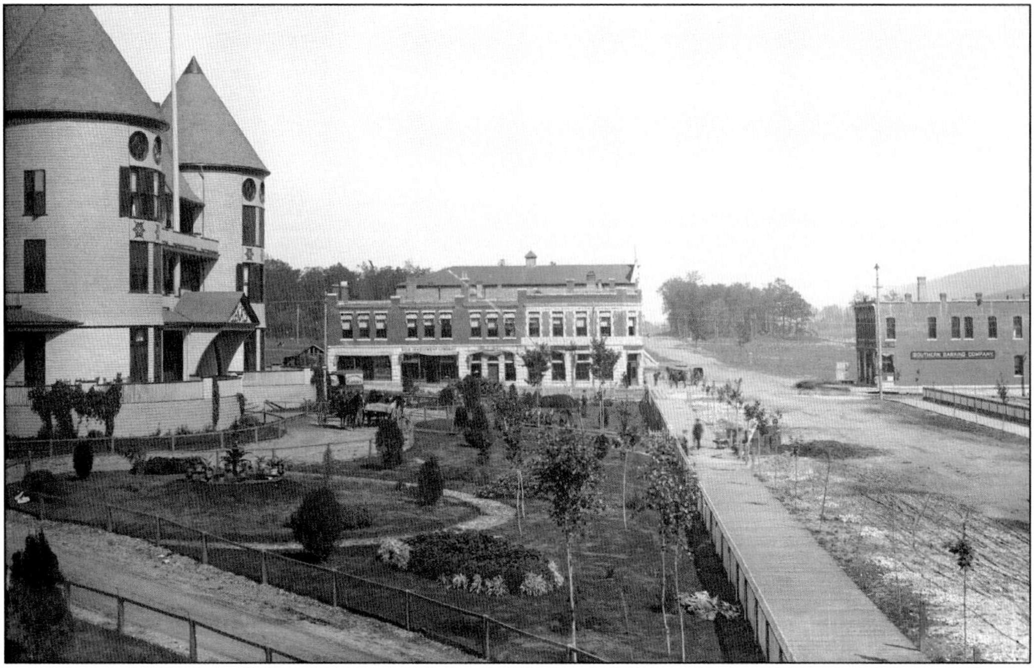

Here is another image by O.W. Chase showing the hotel's new paint job. This picture also showcases the landscaping and the fountain. There were two fountains, one of which was restored recently. The restored fountain is now across the street from this picture in the Fort Payne City Park, which was originally part of the hotel's property. Giant ginkgo trees currently in the park were planted at about the same time as this picture, around 1889–1890. (Author's collection.)

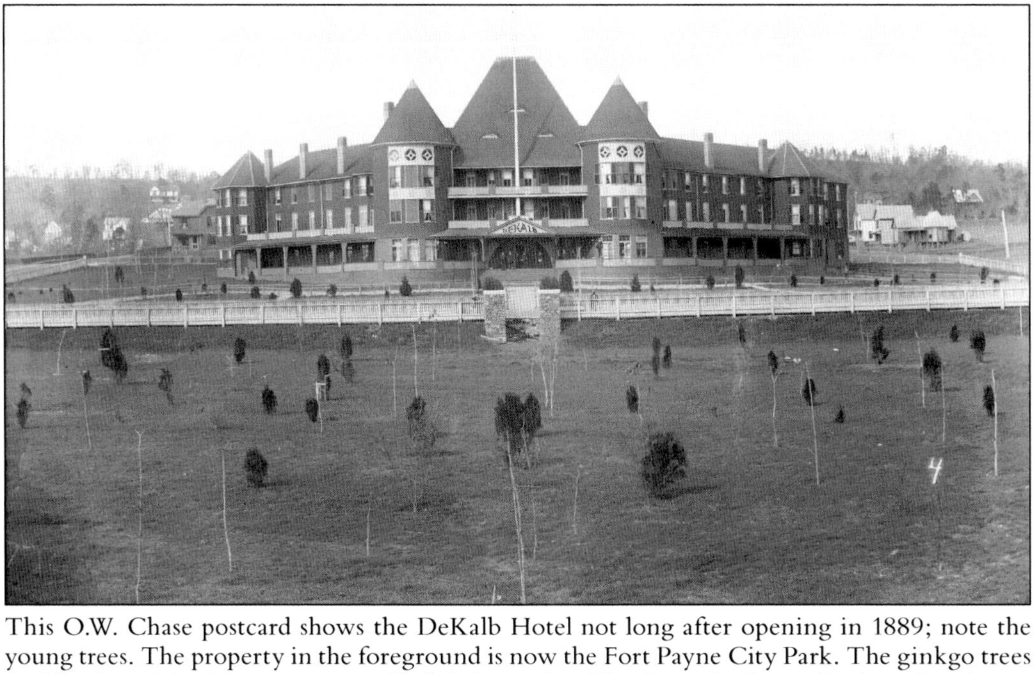

This O.W. Chase postcard shows the DeKalb Hotel not long after opening in 1889; note the young trees. The property in the foreground is now the Fort Payne City Park. The ginkgo trees freshly planted in this picture are still thriving today. The fountain shown in the prior picture sits just to the left of the entry gate at center. (Author's collection.)

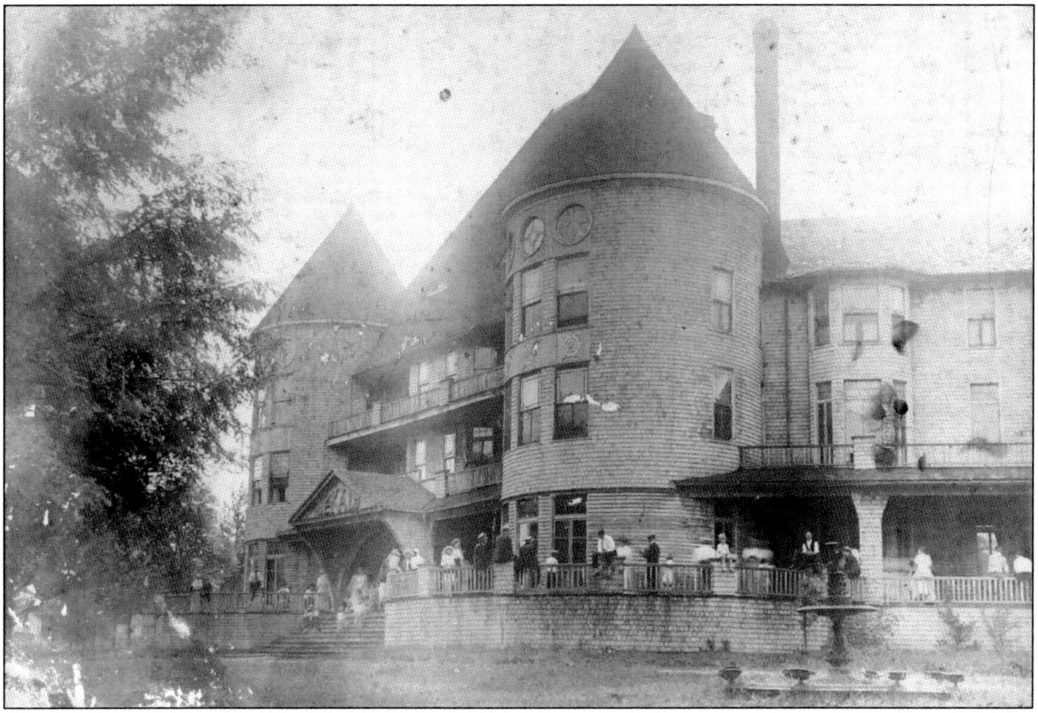

This image of the DeKalb Hotel by O.W. Chase is an original contact print. Chase stayed in Fort Payne and operated a studio where he sold prints. He photographed using a wooden studio camera, which shot 6½-by-8½-inch glass negatives. He made contact prints directly to positive photograph paper. Many of these prints survive to this day and are scattered in private collections. His original negatives survive too, and most of them are part of the Landmarks of DeKalb County Inc. collection. (Courtesy of David Rains.)

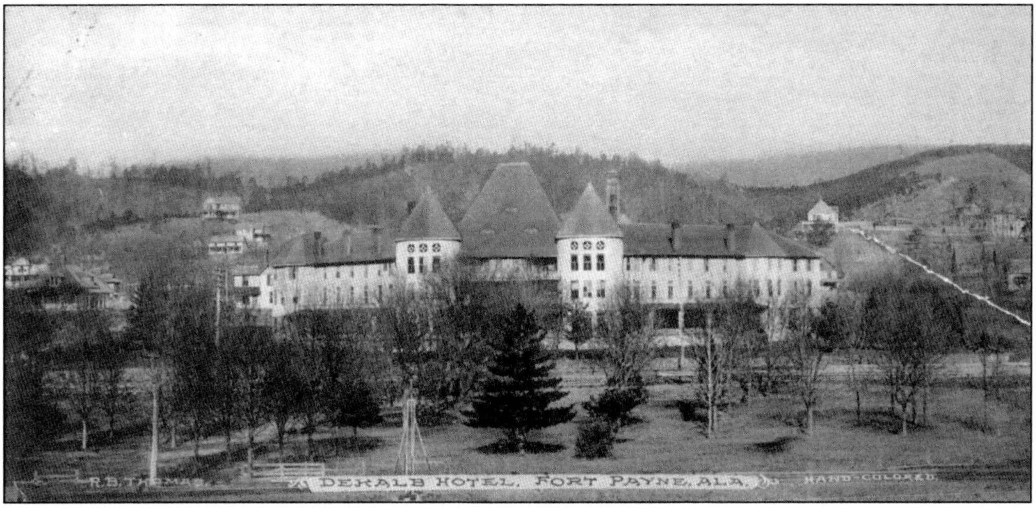

This c. 1910 wonderful hand-colored card by R.B. Thomas shows just how big and beautiful the DeKalb Hotel was. It had 125 rooms. The growth of the trees is evident compared to prior views of the property. Hand-colored cards were very popular in this era, and they remain beautiful to this day. Unfortunately this book cannot show the subtle colors, but cards of this kind can be found at antique stores and postcard shops worldwide. (Courtesy of David Rains.)

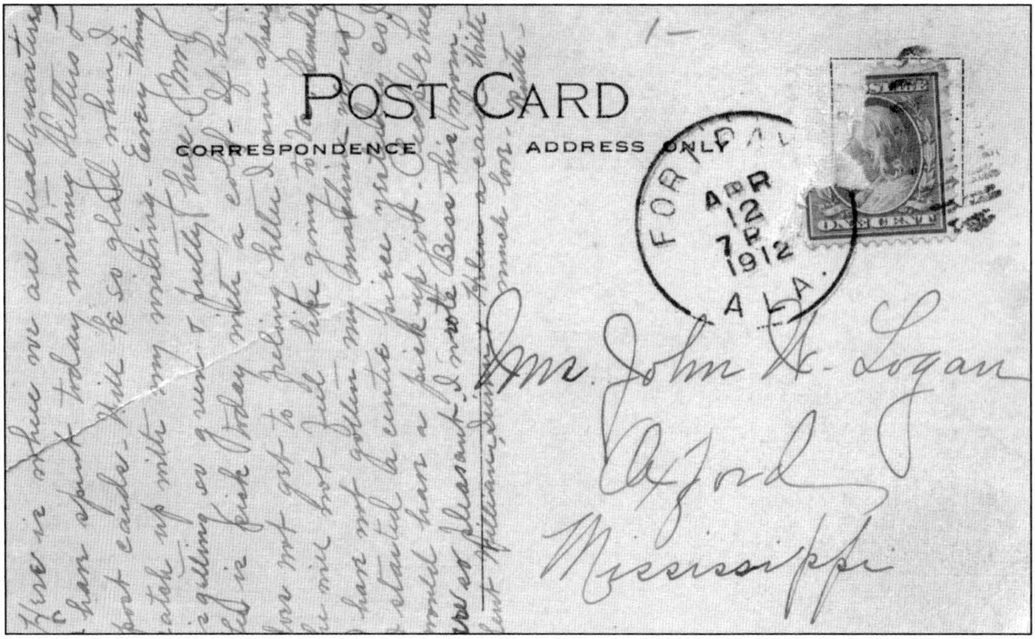

This is the back of the previous card. Postmarked April 12, 1912, it shows the 1¢ stamp and a nice sentiment from the visitor. Prior to 1907, the text had to be written by postal law on the front of the card with only the mailing address on the back. This is why many cards prior to 1907 have writing on the front on the picture. (Courtesy of Collins Kirby.)

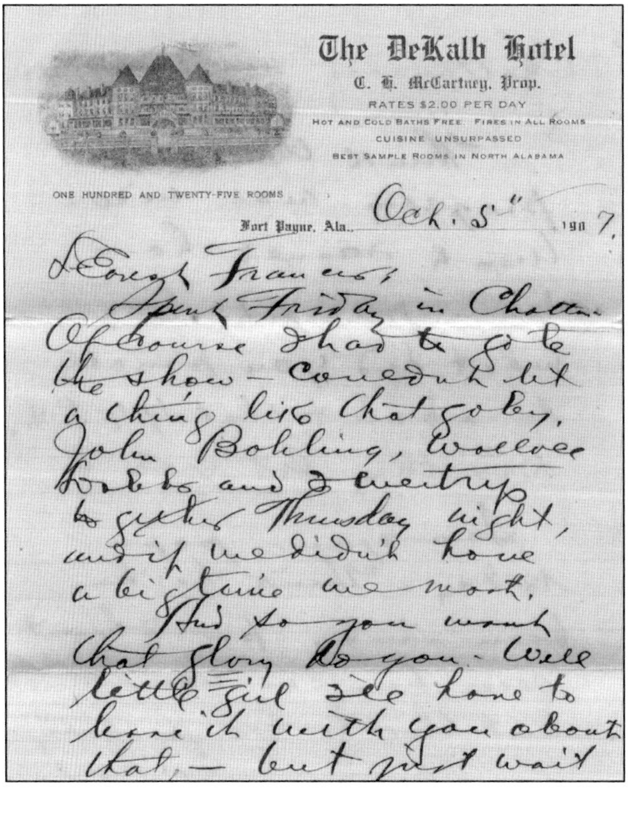

This letter, dated October 5, 1907, was written on the original stationery of the DeKalb Hotel. This shows only part of the letter, but it is a good reminder that all distant communication at that time was done by mail. (Courtesy of David Rains.)

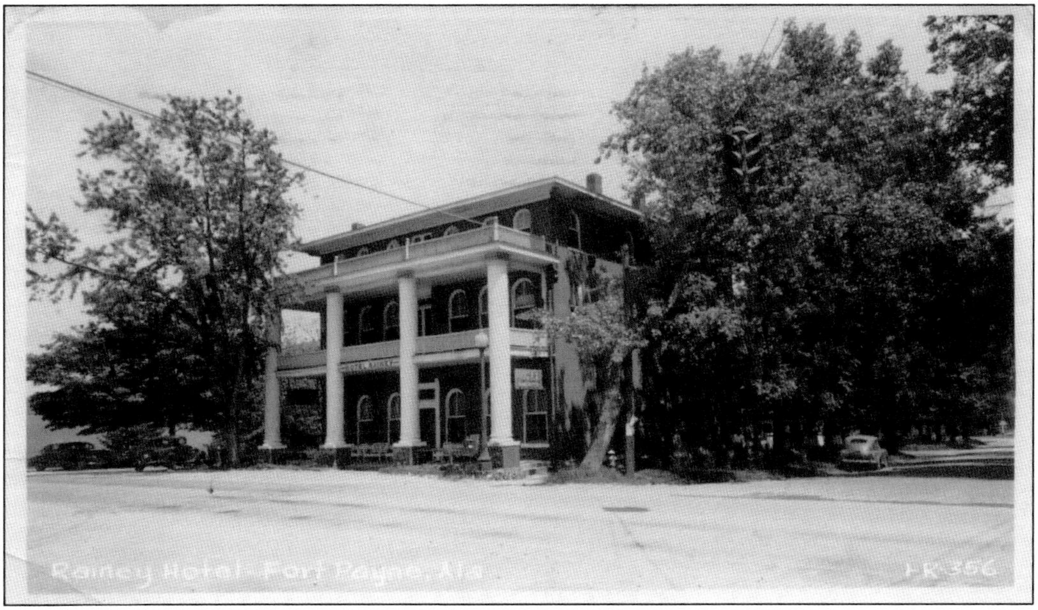

The Hotel Rainey stood kitty-corner to the DeKalb Hotel at the corner of Gault Avenue and Fifth Street. Gault Avenue is the main commercial street running through Fort Payne and is also part of old US Route 11, an original national road that runs in the valleys along the Appalachian Mountains from Louisiana to New York. The hotel was built as a bank during the boom days and converted to a hotel later. Despite the hopes of some local people to buy the hotel, it was torn down in late 1964. (Courtesy of David Rains.)

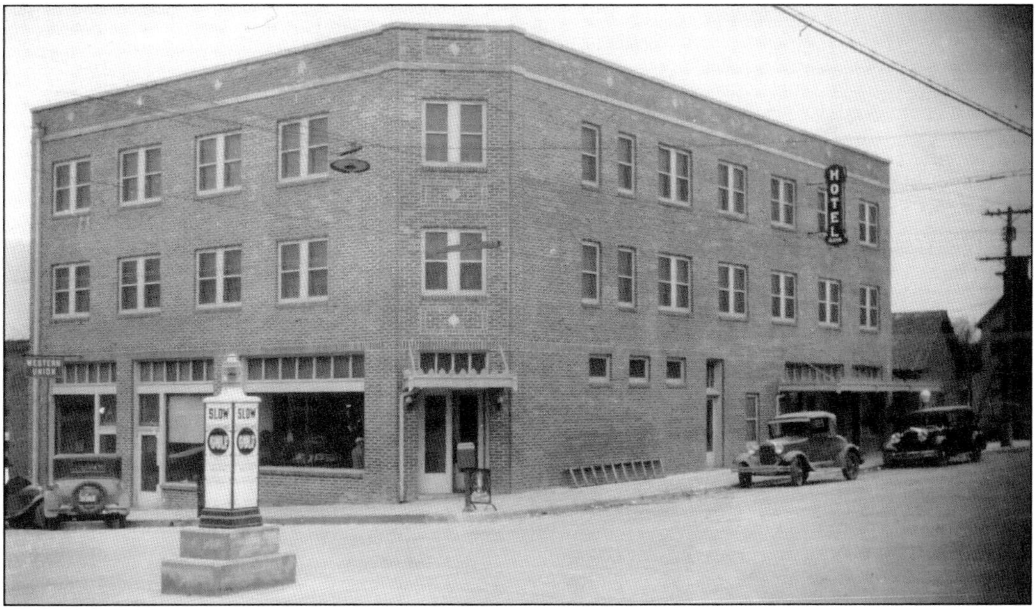

The Quinn Hotel in downtown Fort Payne was on the corner of Gault Avenue and First Street Northeast. The 17,000-square-foot historic building has been sitting empty for a number of years but has recently been acquired by One World Adventure and is to become the W.M. Beck III Discovery Center. The building will serve the organization's hands-on science learning while housing activities to attract tourism and outdoor recreation. (Courtesy of Collins Kirby.)

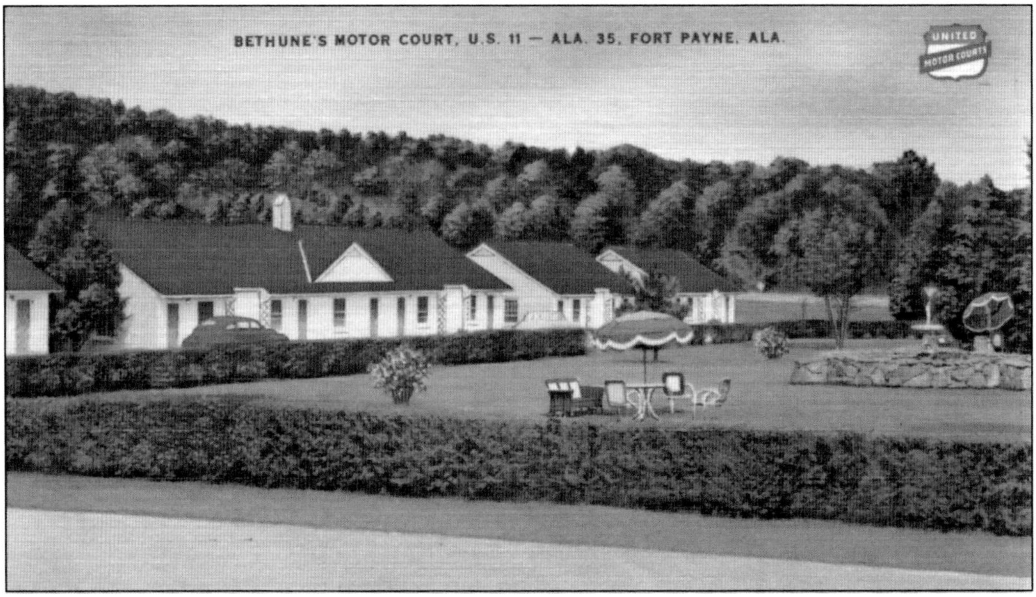

Here is Bethune's Motor Court on US Route 11 in Fort Payne. Until Interstate 59 opened in the 1970s, US Route 11 was one of the main US highways running north-south. In most places in the South, Route 11 runs parallel to Interstate 59. Now, Interstate 59 exits are where travelers find lodging facilities. A majority of those are multi-story with elevators instead of drive-up, ground-floor accommodations. Motels typically mean guests can park right at their room's entrance. Many of these motels have been destroyed or replaced with other buildings, but along Route 11, a good number are still in business. (Courtesy of Collins Kirby.)

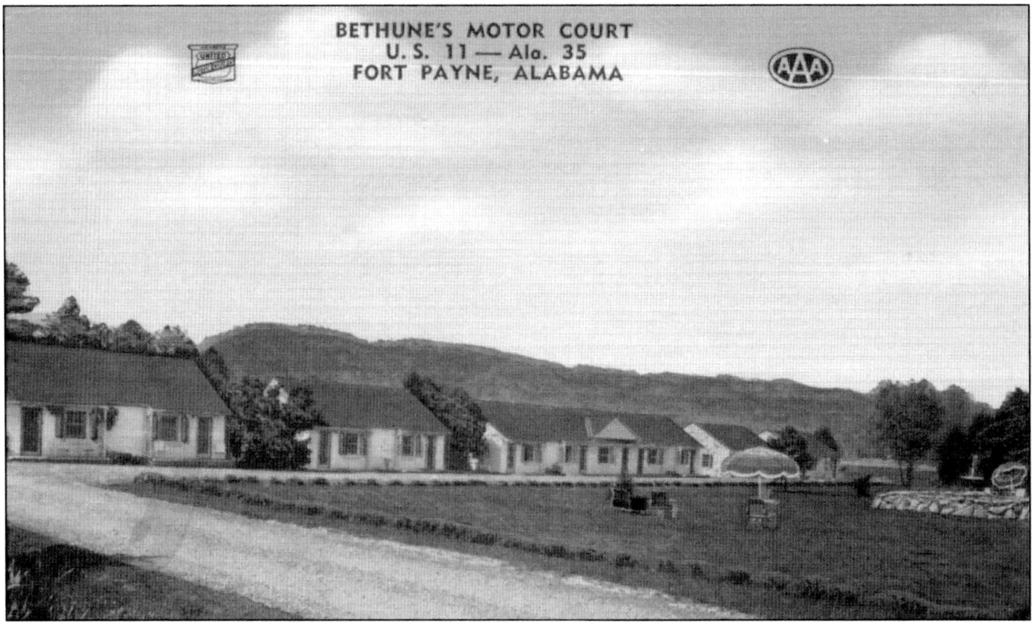

This early 1950s linen card shows Bethune's Motor Court, which was a nice place to spend the night along Route 11. In this day, prior to Interstate 59, the motels were on Route 11, and so were the attractions. Driving Route 11 now, there are both open and vacant motels and attractions. (Courtesy of Collins Kirby.)

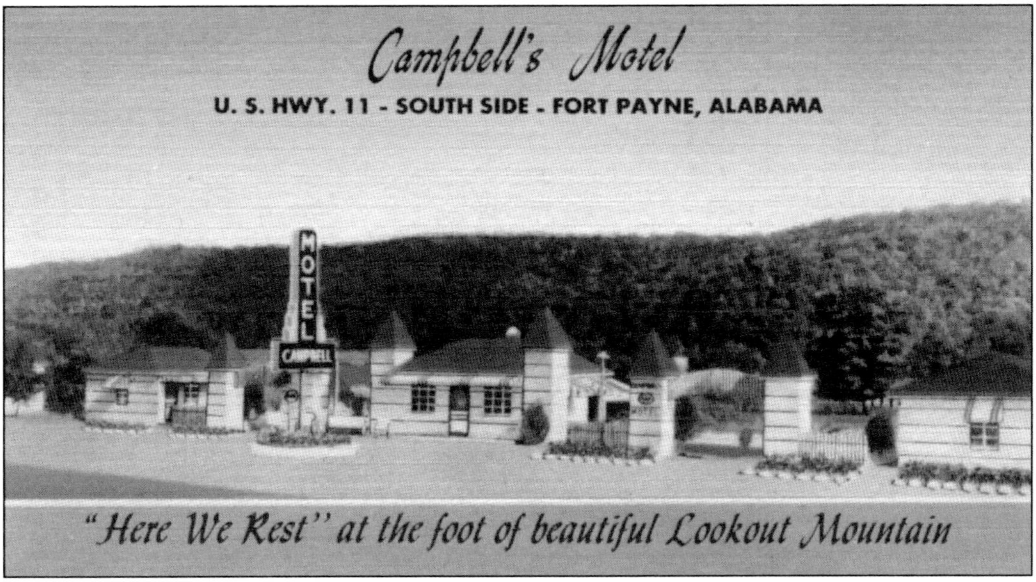

Campbell's Motel is seen here. Much of Route 11 is in the valleys between mountains. In Fort Payne, Route 11 runs at the foot of Lookout Mountain, making for very scenic views for travelers. After checking into a motel, it was common in the 1940s and 1950s for guests to sit outside and enjoy the view and for the kids to play in the yard or swim if there was a pool. In those days, very few motels had air-conditioning, nor did most people's houses. The culture nationwide was to be outside, enjoying the late afternoon and evening. Most motels had lawn chairs outside each room and often a communal outdoor sitting area with a playground for kids. (Courtesy of Collins Kirby.)

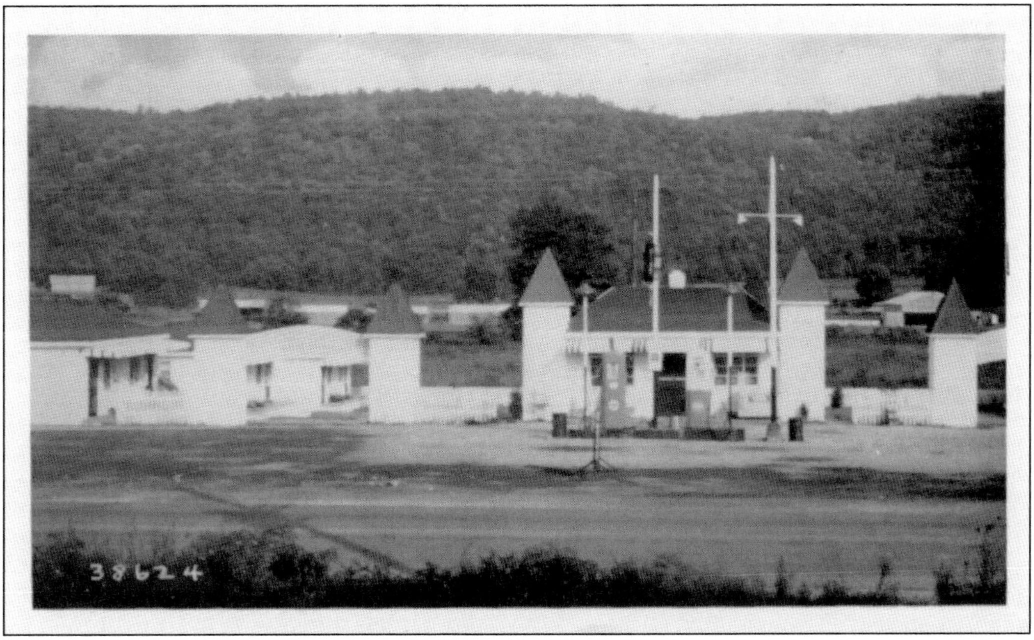

This view of Campbell's Motel shows that it had a gas station and a restaurant. In that era, many motels had restaurants, not just for guests but also for locals. This postcard is most likely from the 1940s or early 1950s. (Courtesy of Collins Kirby.)

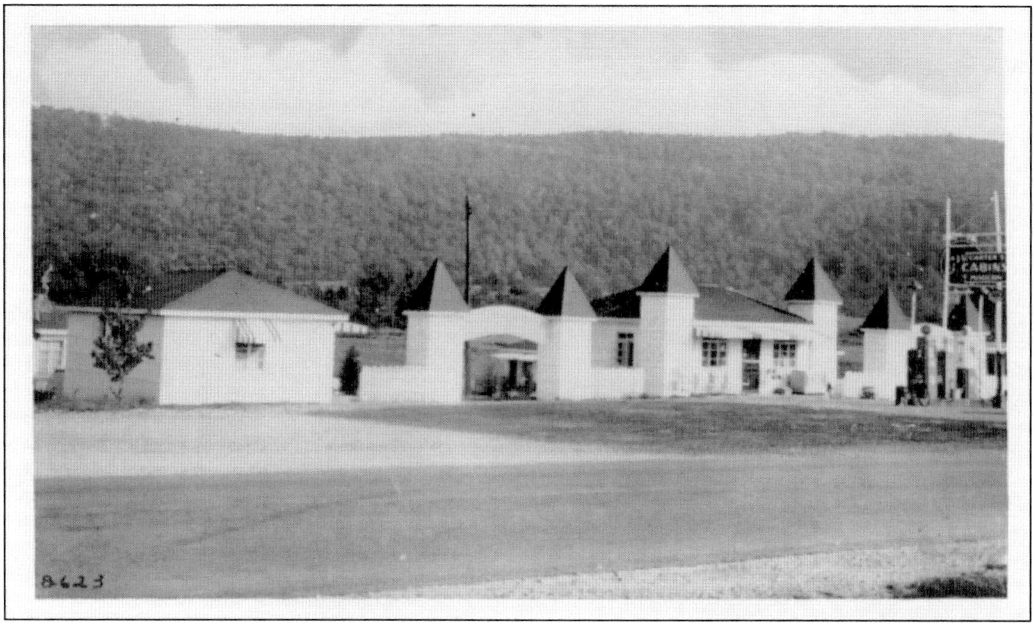

Here is a different view of Campbell's Motel. Many motels had their own postcards made to give out to customers; they were usually in the drawers of the nightstands in all the rooms. The postcard business was big, and there were plenty of people making their living setting up shoots for businesses to have cards made. Marketing postcards was a good job through the 1970s. After that, fewer and fewer cards were being made as technology shifted and more people began communicating electronically. (Courtesy of Collins Kirby.)

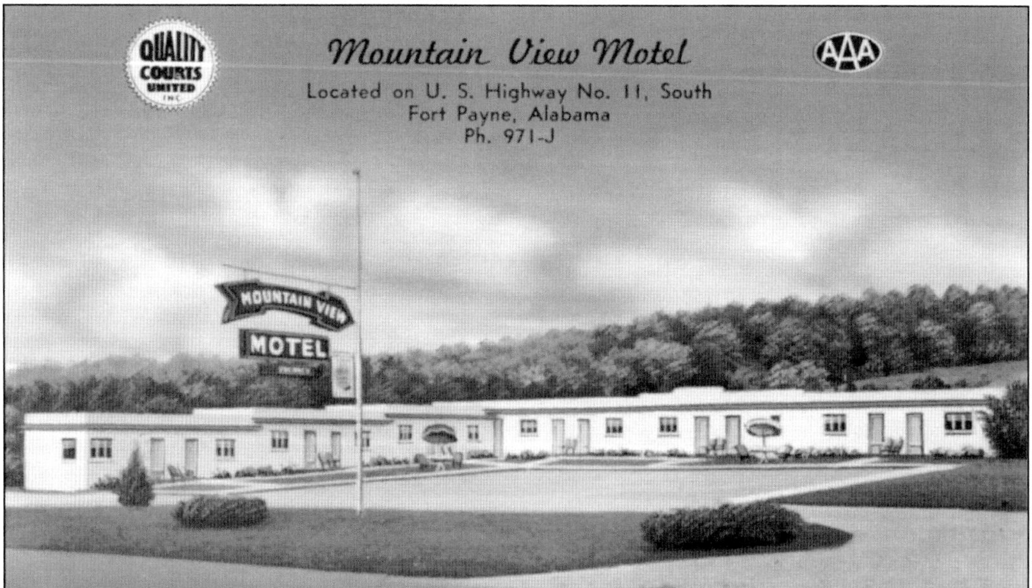

The Mountain View Motel in south Fort Payne on Route 11 is still open under the same name. It was not until 2012 that the sign seen here was replaced by a newer one during a remodel. Do not worry, however: the original sign can still be seen at Vintage 1889 restaurant and bar in Fort Payne, which is located in the 1889 W.B. Davis Hosiery Mill. (Courtesy of Collins Kirby.)

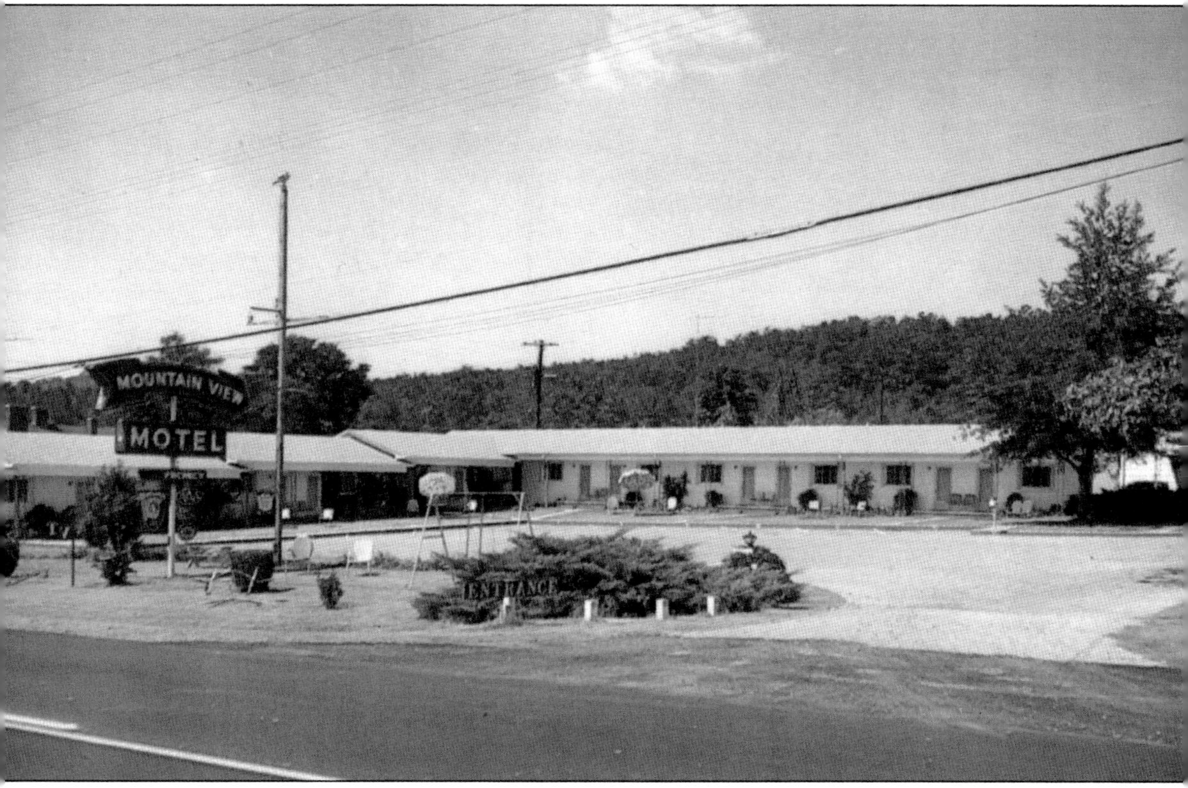

This postcard of the Mountain View Motel is a 1960s commercially printed card. The landscaping has matured from the previous image. Route 11 today looks just like it does here. In most cases, except when passing through metropolitan areas, Route 11 is still two lanes. (Courtesy of Collins Kirby.)

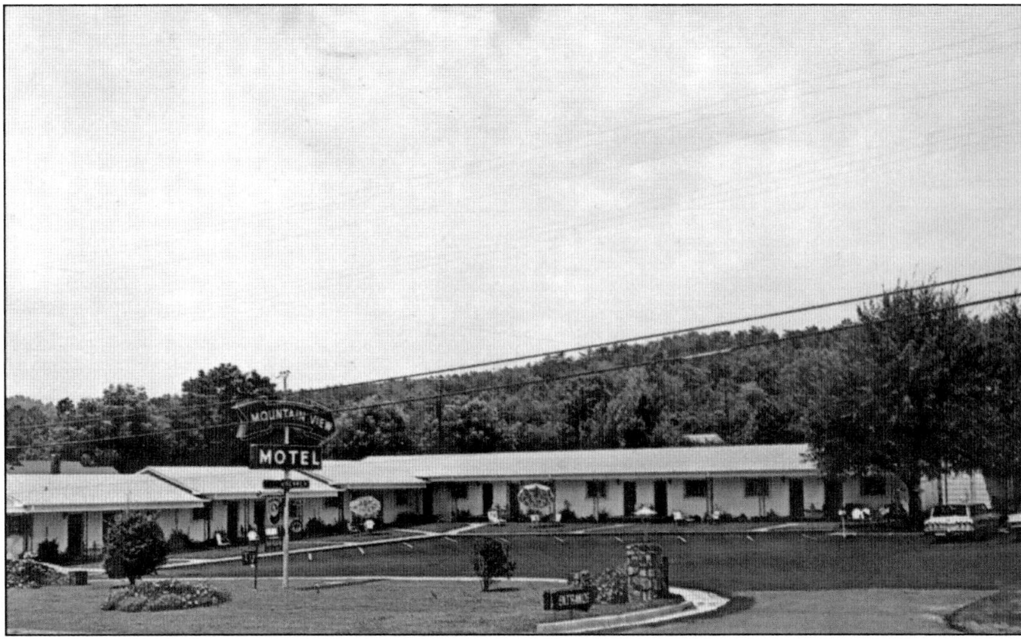

This view is from the mid-1960s. Photographs for motel postcards were almost always taken in the summer when the landscape was green and flowers were blooming. The motel owner knew when the photographer was coming and made sure the lawn was manicured prior to the photographer's arrival. Below is the back of the postcard, postmarked October 28, 1966. The writer drove 800 miles. If that was all in one day, it would have been a lot for that era, especially if it was on Route 11, which passes through towns and cities. (Both, courtesy of Collins Kirby.)

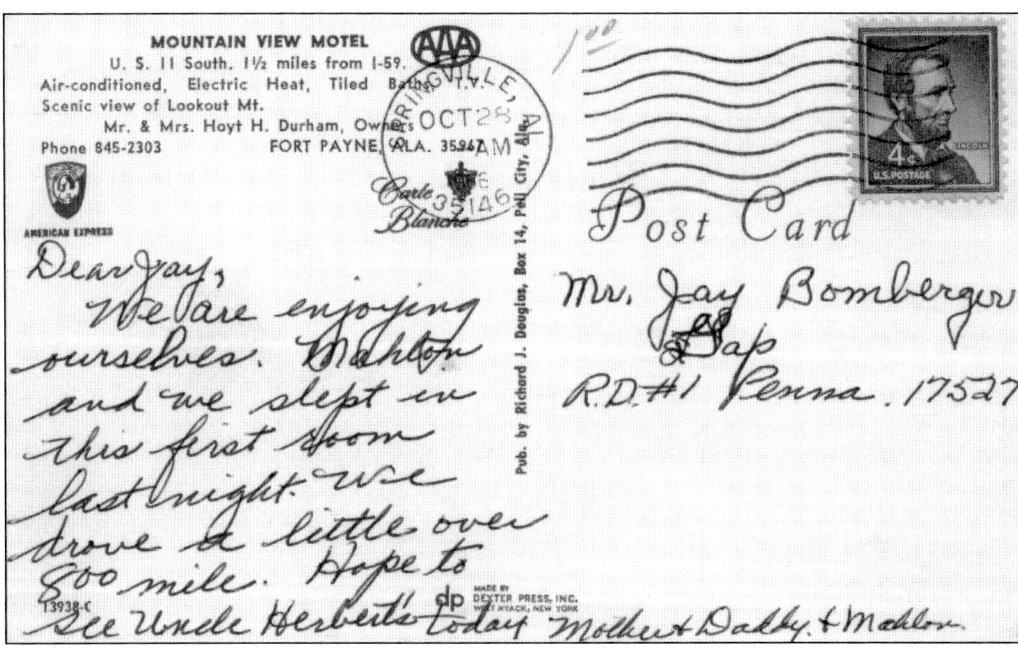

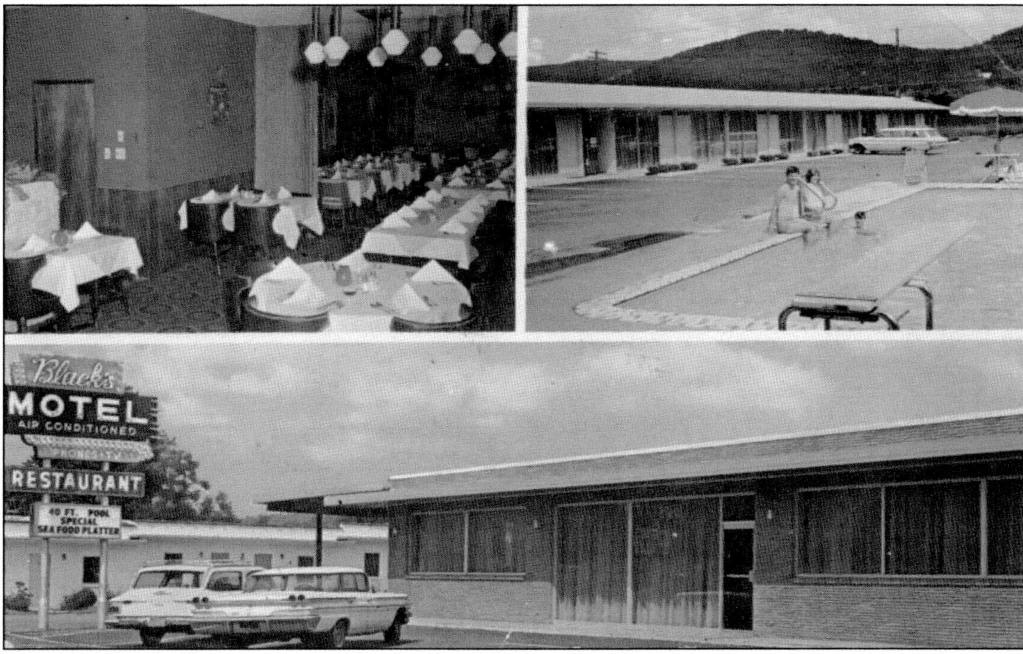

Black's Motel and Restaurant is seen on this commercially printed card from the mid-1960s. It shows all the great things to do while staying at Black's. The motel later expanded and became the Fort Payne Inn. It was located at Nineteenth Street and Gault Avenue. The building was removed in the mid-2000s, and the area has been redeveloped. With the exception of the Mountain View Motel, none of the motels on Route 11 in the Fort Payne area from the 1940s through the 1970s remain open. In some cases, portions of the buildings remain and are used for other businesses, but most have been replaced by other structures. (Courtesy of Collins Kirby.)

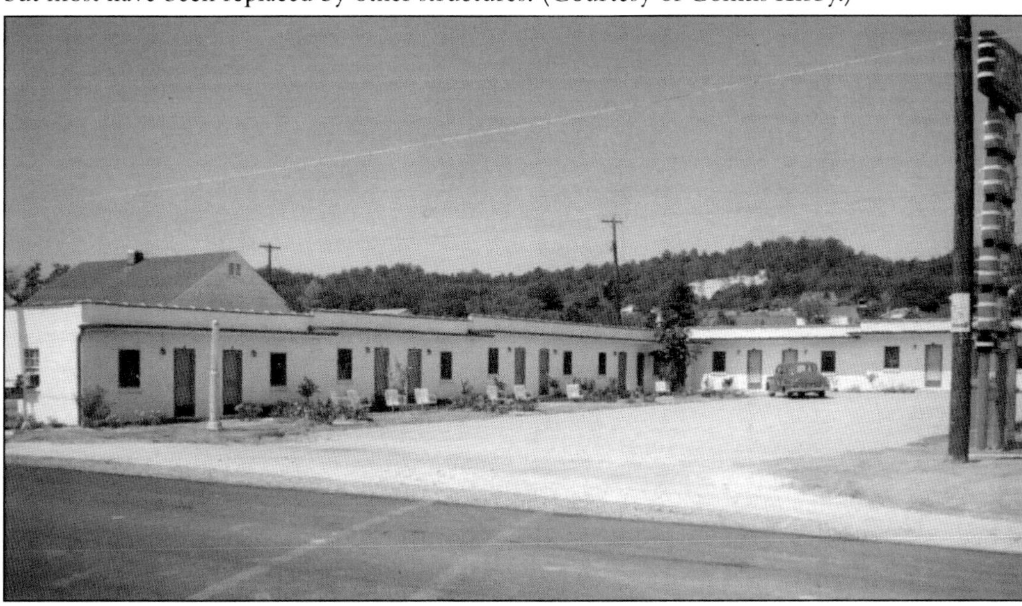

Summertime in Fort Payne is depicted in this early 1950s commercially printed card of Black's Motel. Note the flowers blooming. Also visible are lawn chairs for the visitors, and an air-conditioner hanging out a window at far left, most likely the lobby. (Courtesy of Collins Kirby.)

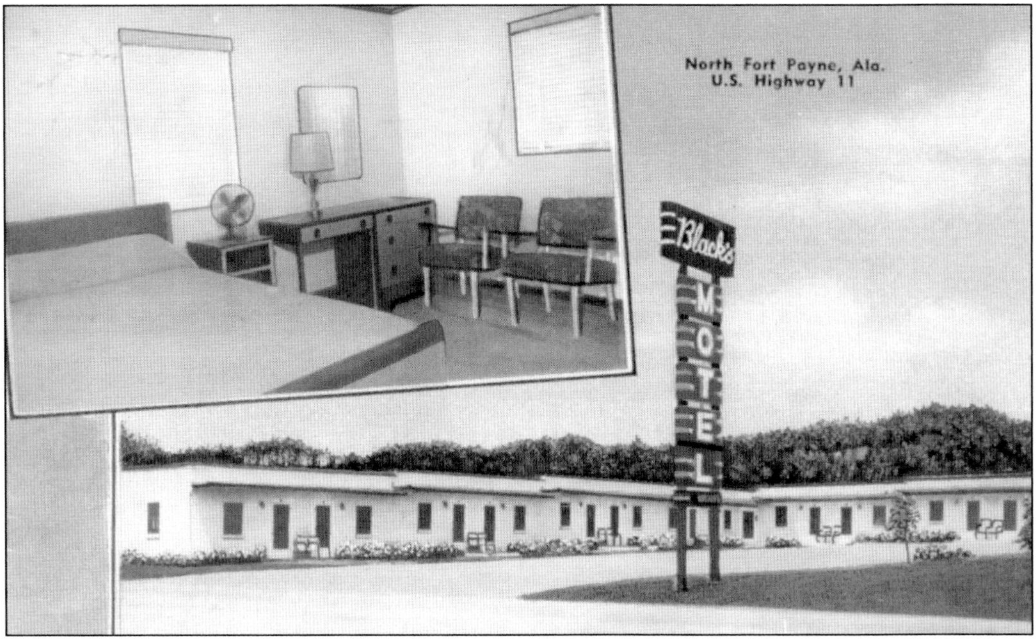

This earlier colorized card shows the inside and outside of Black's Motel. The room furniture is very typical of the late 1940s and early 1950s. Sitting on the bedside table is the room's sole cooling device, other than the open window. (Courtesy of Collins Kirby.)

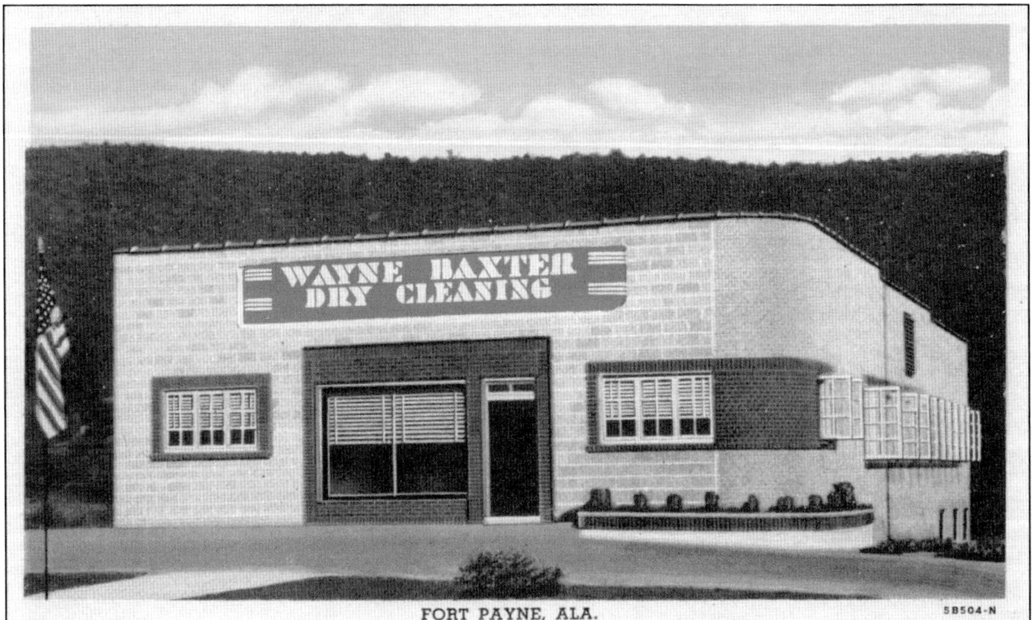

Lod Baxter was the first of several generations of his family, going back to 1933, in the dry cleaning and laundry business. Wayne Baxter built a new building at 601 Gault Avenue in 1945 with unique curved corners. The business was sold to nephew Joe Baxter Brown in 1968. In July 1982, Joe purchased the Fort Payne Laundry & Dry Cleaners from E.T. and Gladola Holleman and maintained both until 1984, when he moved it all to its current location at 817 Gault Avenue North. (Courtesy of Judy Brown.)

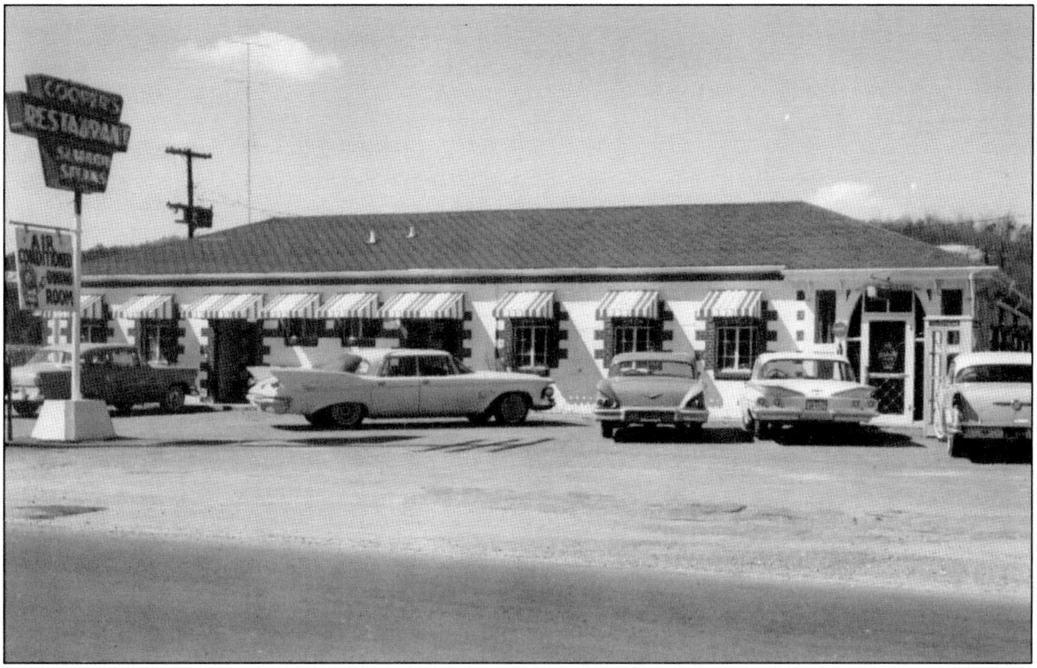

Cooper's Restaurant had an air-conditioned dining room. This c. 1959 linen postcard shows a busy restaurant with some good-looking 1950s cars in the parking lot. Patrons of this restaurant could buy one of these cards. Handing out postcards of one's business was extremely popular among hotels, motels, restaurants, and other attractions. (Courtesy of Collins Kirby.)

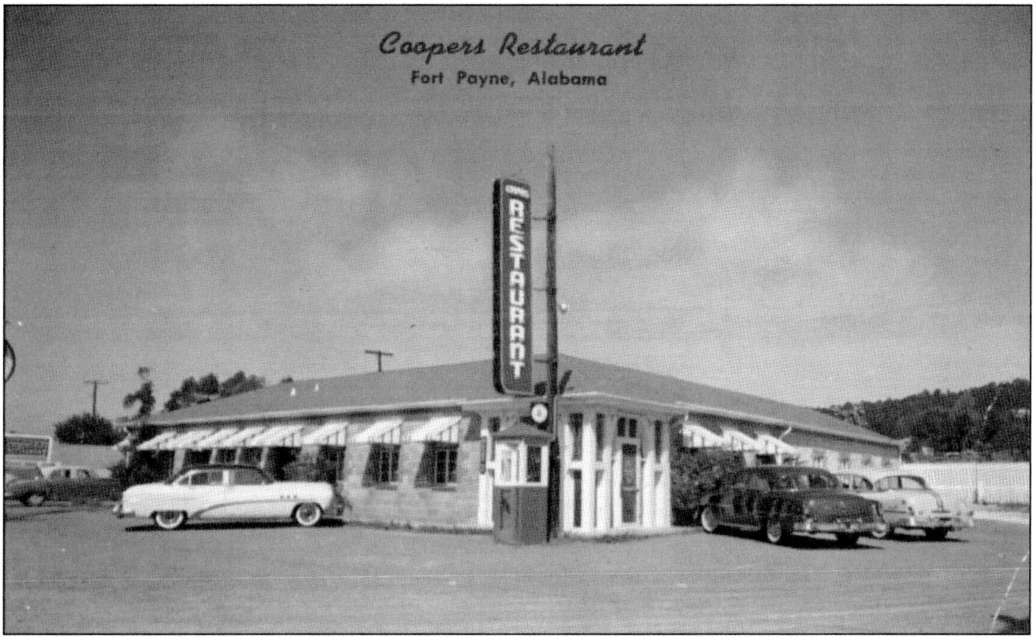

Here is an earlier 1950s view of Cooper's Restaurant. Note the telephone booth by the entrance, which is older than the one pictured at far right above. The postcard itself is of the same linen textured Kodachrome vintage. (Courtesy of Collins Kirby.

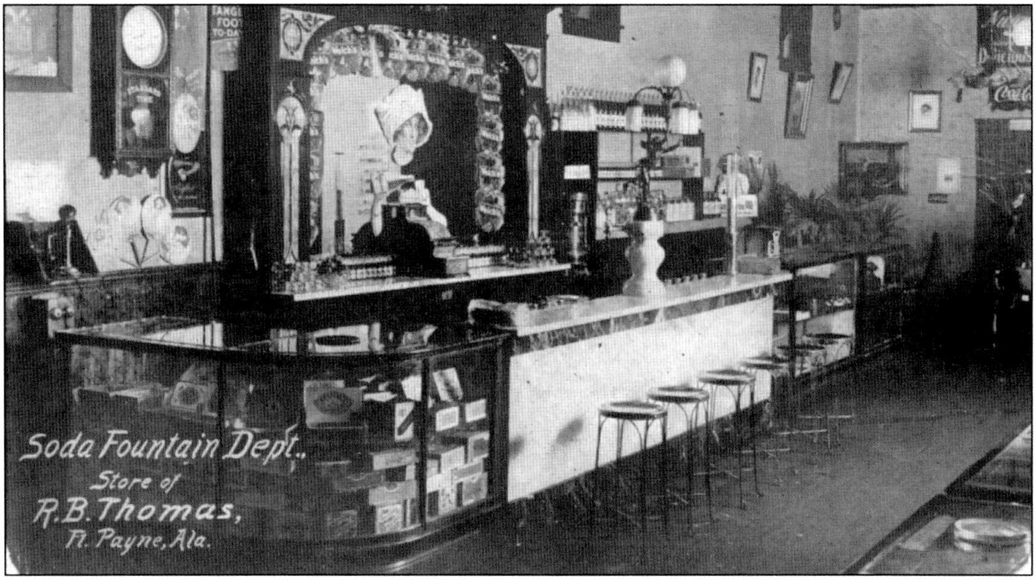

R.B. Thomas Soda Fountain is pictured here. The World War I–era card shows a good interior view of the way most soda fountains looked at that time. It would have been nice to see someone behind the counter and a customer or two, but this photograph was taken for promotional purposes. (Courtesy of Collins Kirby.)

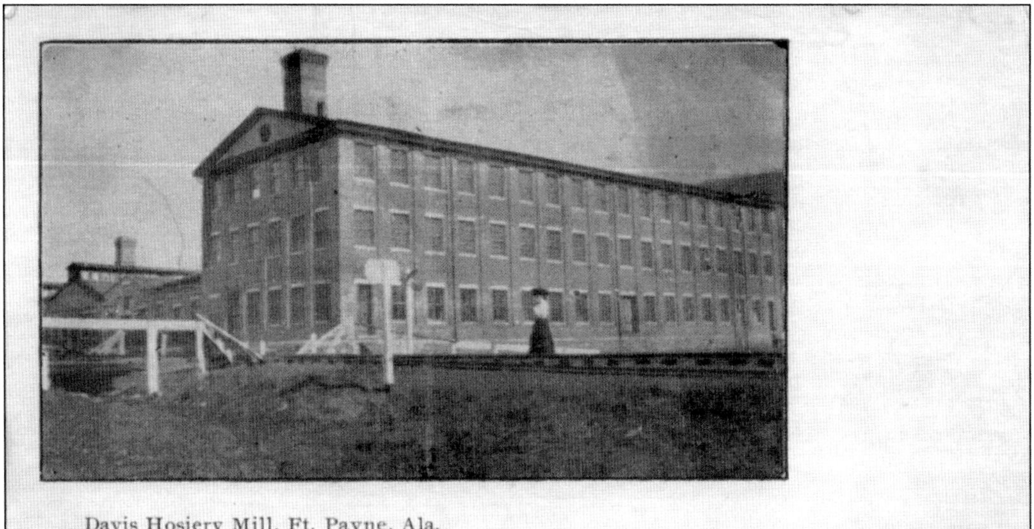

This c. 1910 image shows the W.B. Davis Hosiery Mill prior to its name being painted in big white letters on the brick. Not long after the mill opened, other mills opened in town. It was the hosiery industry that brought back financial well being and the population of the community after the rise and fall of the boom days of the late 1880s and early 1890s. In 2005, there were 350 registered sock mills in the Fort Payne area. For many years, the sock industry ruled the area's economy, giving Fort Payne the distinction of being the "sock capitol of the world." Fair trade agreements in the 1990s slowly but surely killed the industry in Fort Payne. As of this writing, there are less than 20 mills in operation in Fort Payne, but due to recent concerns about offshore quality, some contracts are coming back due to Fort Payne's reputation for top-quality socks. (Courtesy of Collins Kirby.)

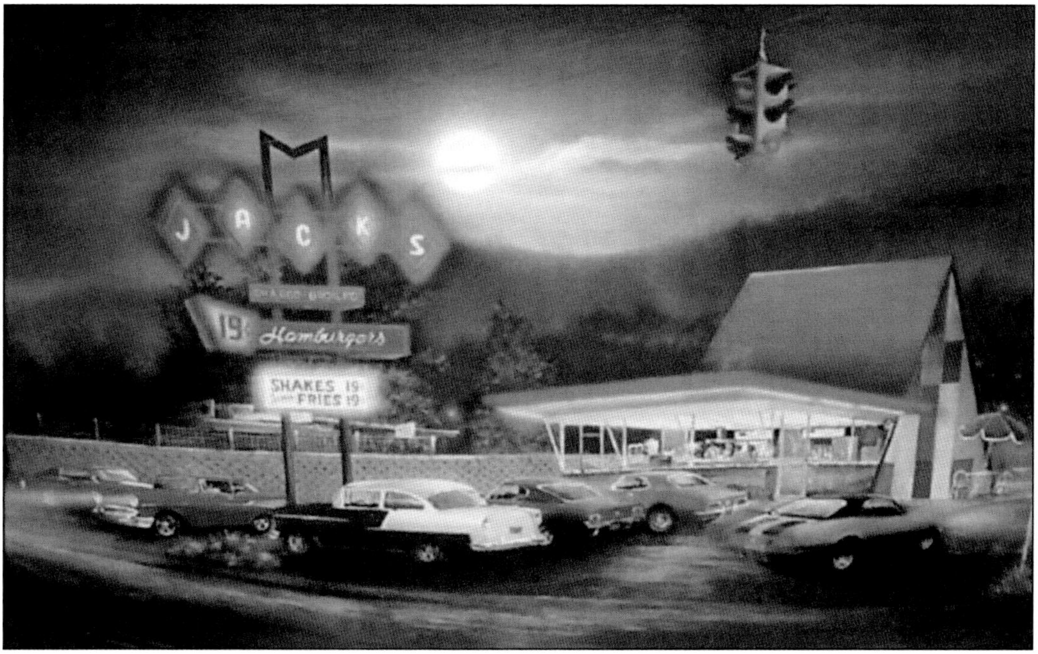

Jimmy Frazier created this artistic rendering of Jacks Hamburgers Drive-In. This was a hot spot for high school students; at one time, it was common for students to drive around town on a Saturday night, stopping at places like this one. Once parked, teenagers would sit on the hoods of cars or on the beds of pickup trucks. All across the country, high gas costs, community regulations, television, computers, and smartphones have pretty much done away with that Saturday night tradition. (Author's collection.)

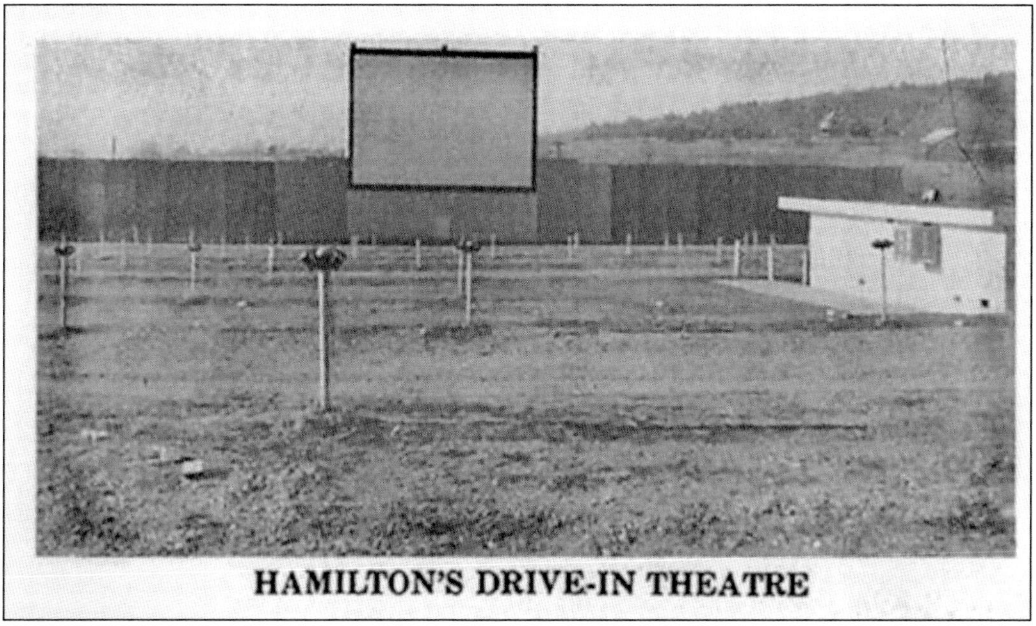

Late in the 1990s, Hamilton's Drive-In Theatre stood empty with the screen still standing. The property was later occupied by a mobile home sales business. Parts of the property remain as bare land today, but much of it has been redeveloped into other businesses. (Author's collection.)

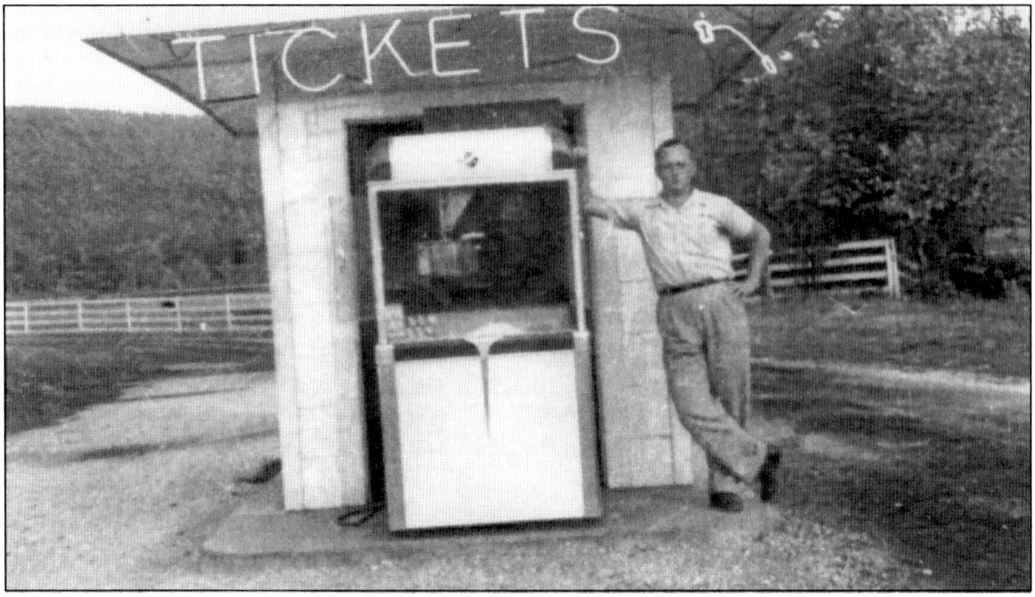

Richard Hawkins is seen working the ticket office at Hamilton's Drive-In Theatre. As tastes changed and new suburban indoor theaters were opened, most drive-ins began to disappear. As of 2012, there were 461 drive-ins still operating in the United States, down from a high of more than 4,000 in 1959. (Courtesy of Judy Brown.)

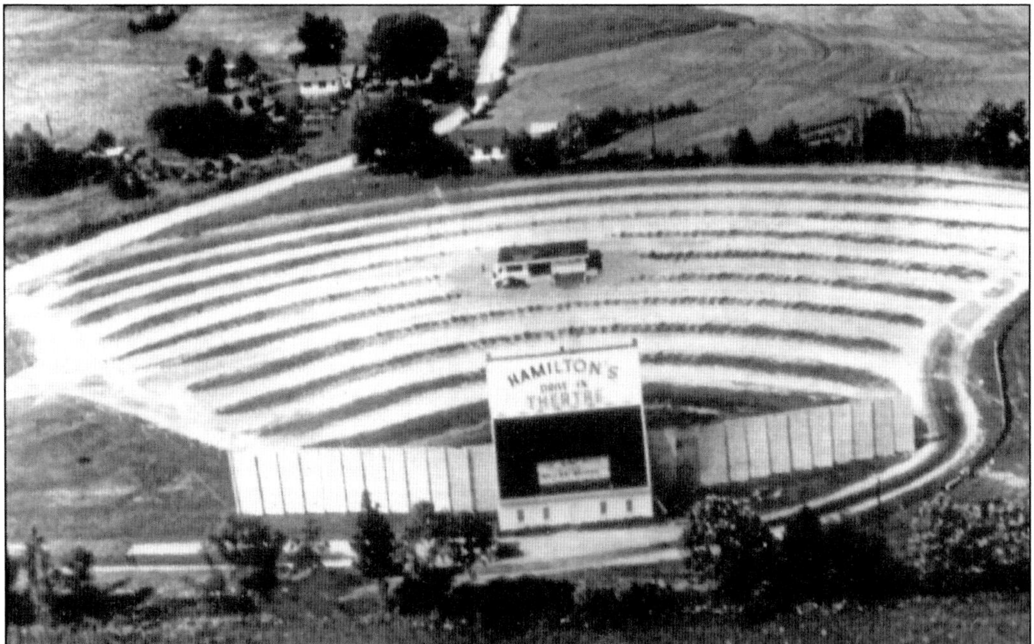

Hamilton's Drive-In Theatre is seen here. This was a very busy and popular location in Fort Payne. Hamilton's Drive-In was built by Dave Hamilton and his son Mack and opened on May 14, 1950. Mack was drafted about that time and was gone for two years during the Korean War. Dave ran it until he returned, and Mack ran the business from about 1952 until it closed in the early 1980s. (Courtesy of Judy Brown.)

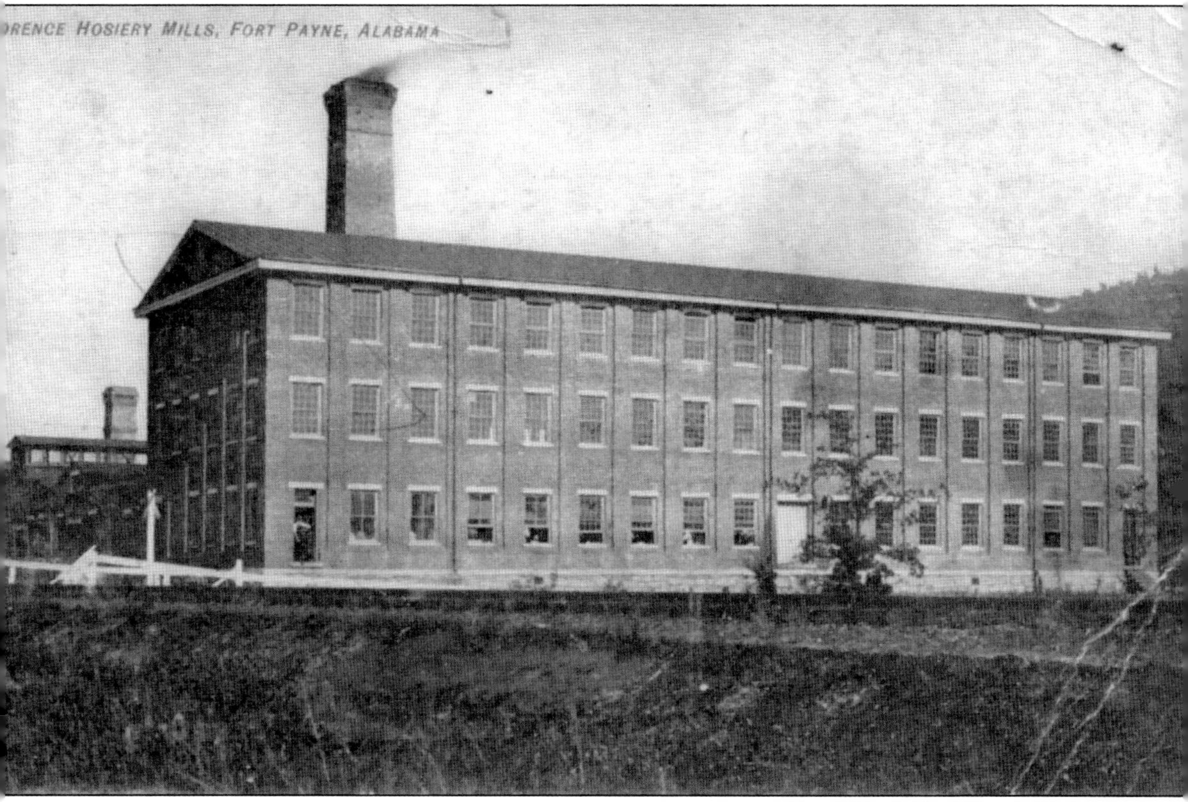

Built in 1889 as the Alabama Builders Hardware and Manufacturing Company, this building at the time of this postcard (pre-1907) was the Florence Hosiery Mill. In 1915, it became the W.B. Davis Hosiery Mill, Fort Payne's largest employer. The name W.B. Davis was painted on the left (west) and front (south) once the company took over. To this day, the name still shows clearly in big white letters on both sides. (Courtesy of Collins Kirby.)

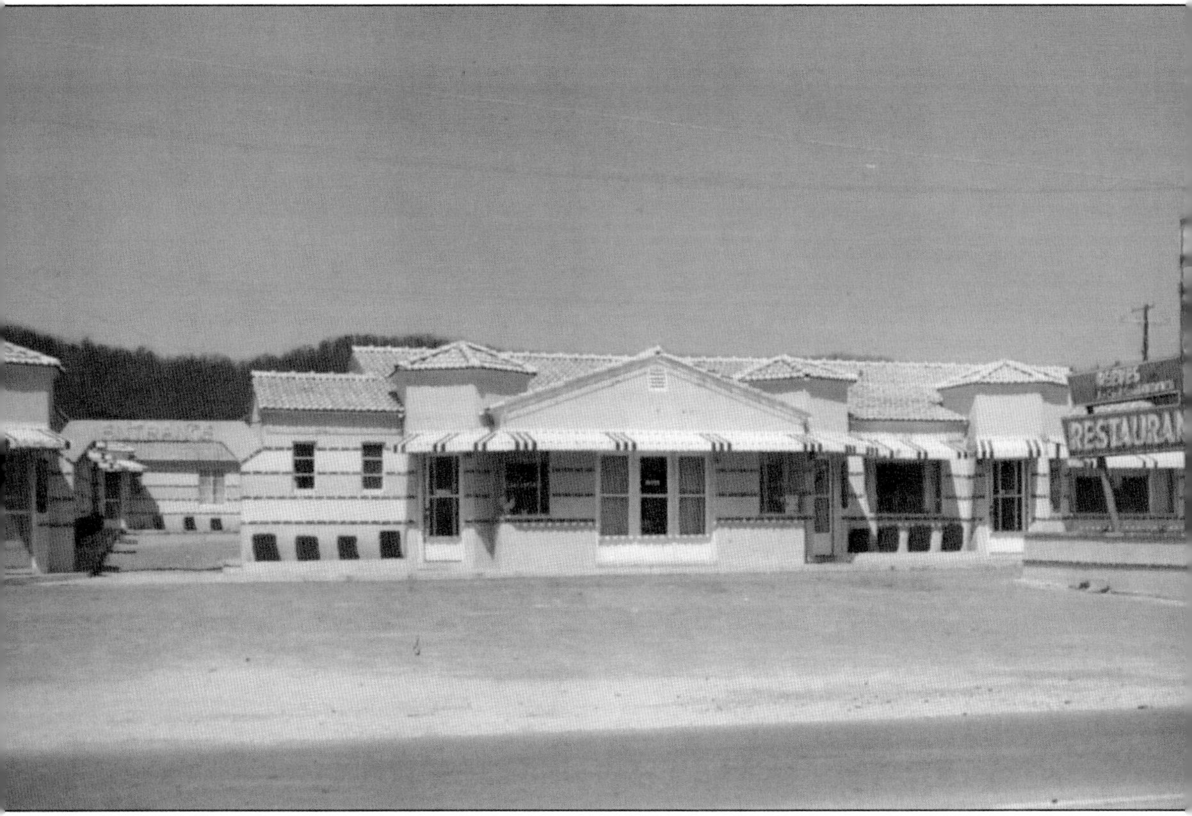

In the days when motels were popular along US highways, many had restaurants. This is Reeves Motel and Restaurant on US Route 11. This linen Kodachrome postcard from the 1950s shows an empty parking lot in front of the motel and restaurant. Motel owners did not want to show people or cars in promotional postcards for fear that they would date the picture and obstruct the view of the property. (Courtesy of Collins Kirby.)

Nine

Lookout Mountain's Parks, Area Caves, and Attractions

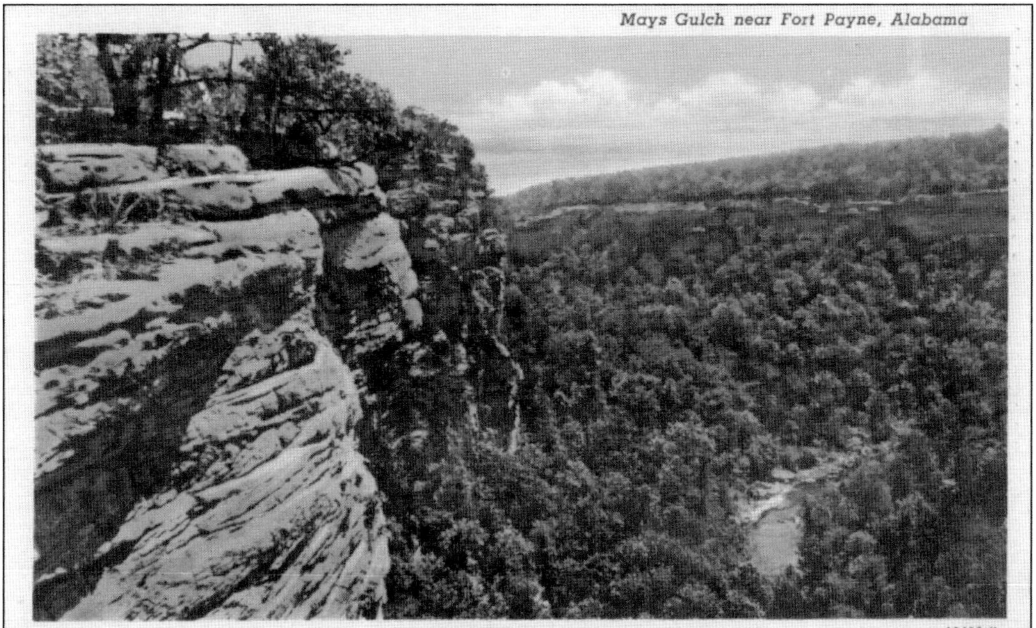

This 1940s linen colorized card by Curt Teich & Company shows a pretty view of Little River Canyon from a bluff on the eastern side of the canyon. This view is almost identical today. (Courtesy of Collins Kirby.)

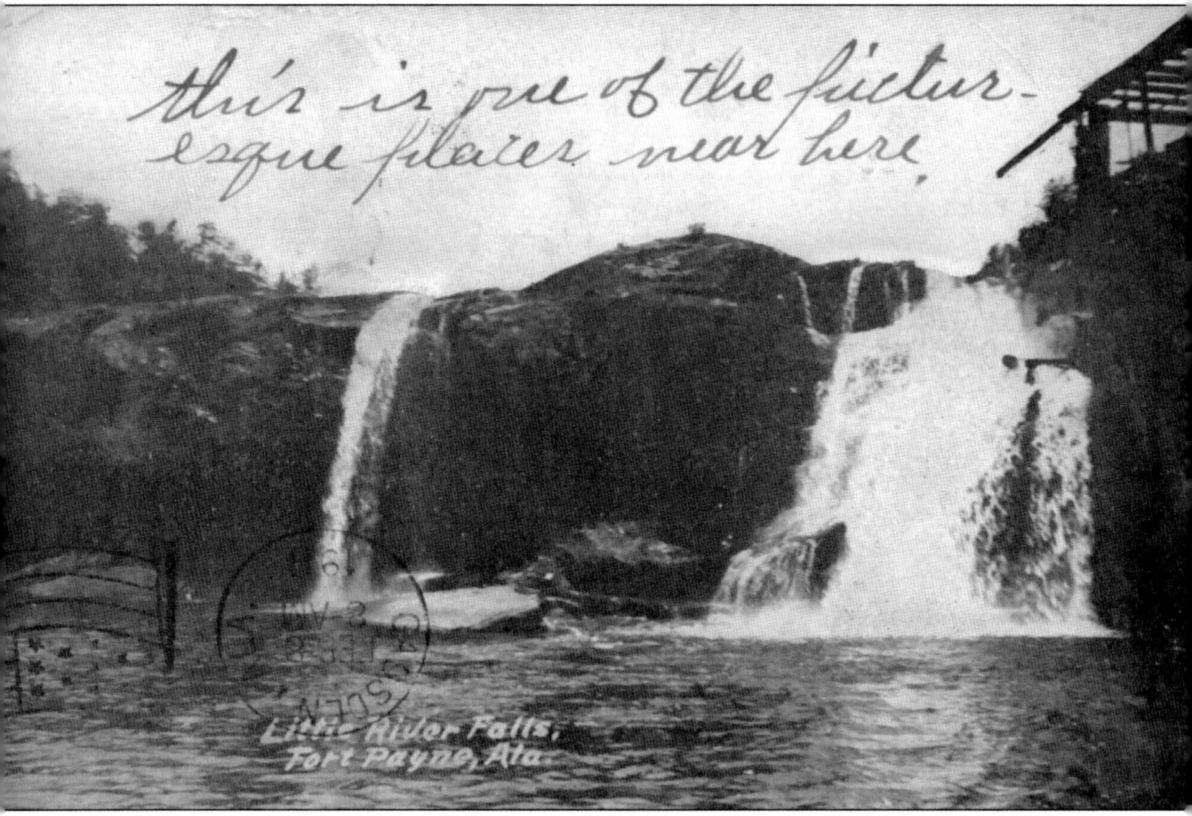

This hand-colored postcard, dated 1911, shows Little River Falls at Little River Canyon with a part of a mill that was in service there during the boomtown years of Fort Payne. A large gear from the mill can be seen in the water pool at the bottom of the falls. The structure in this image is long gone. (Courtesy of Collins Kirby.)

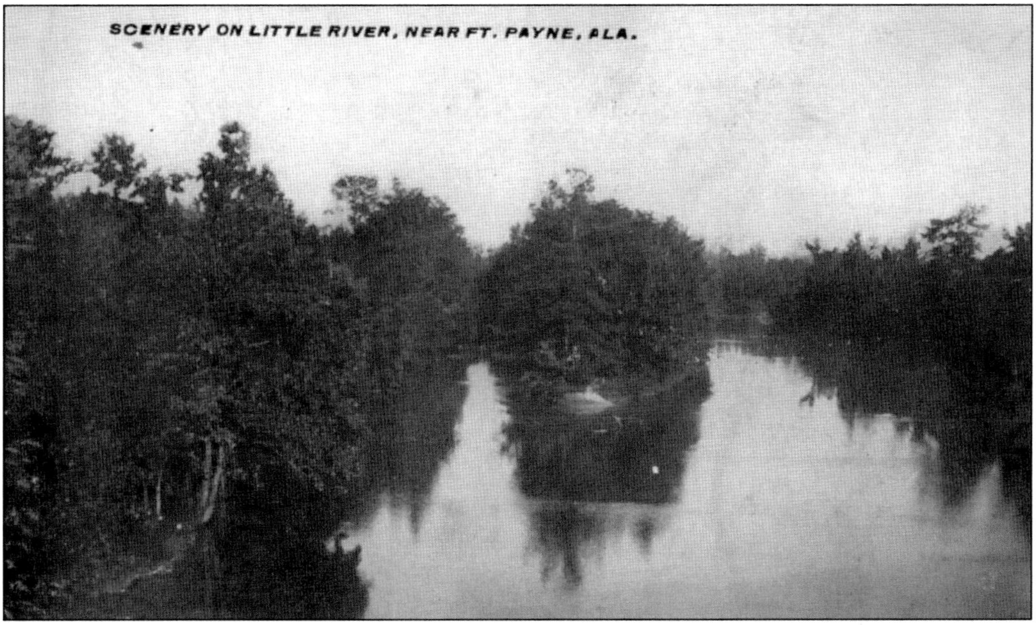

This colorized postcard from 1913 provides a generic and relaxing view of the Little River as it runs across Lookout Mountain. In some areas, the water forms sizable pools that become active swimming holes in the summer. This area is before Little River runs into the canyon; it is easy to access and is good for canoe trips and relaxing by the water. (Courtesy of Collins Kirby.)

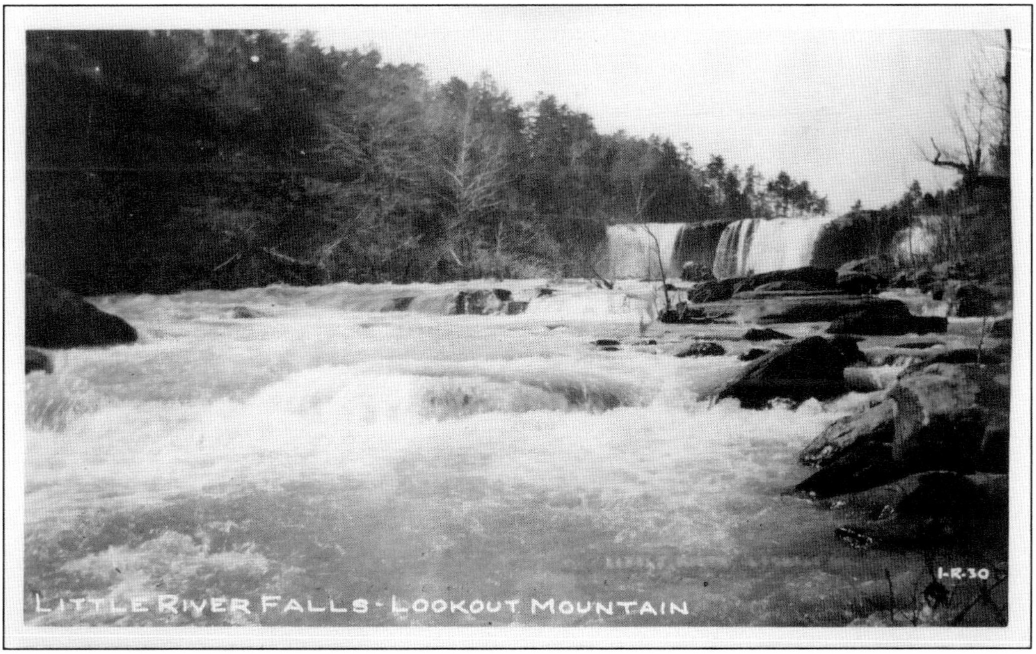

Little River Falls is located on the Middle Fork of the Little River, just as the canyon begins to form from ground level on top of Lookout Mountain. The drop at the falls gradually etches deeper and deeper into the depths of the canyon. This view from 1957 shows the falls after fairly heavy rain. The river is filled by tributaries swollen by ground runoff. The river and the falls fill quickly after a heavy rain. (Courtesy of Collins Kirby.)

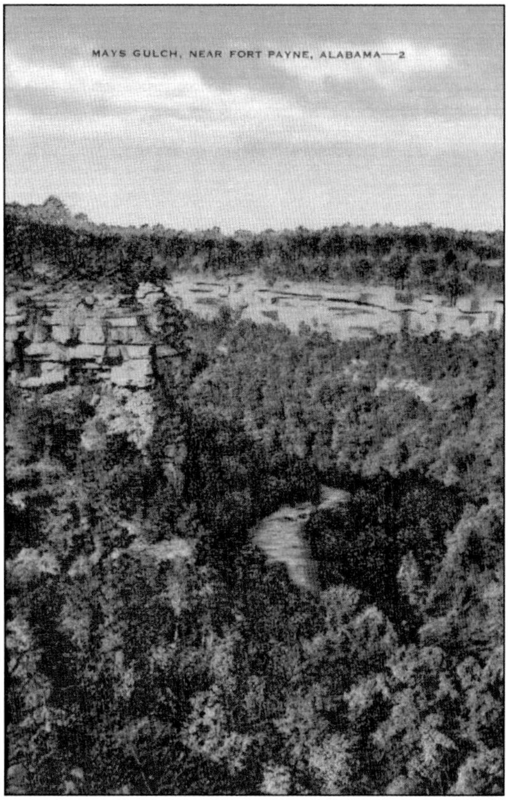

The 1930s linen colorized card by Curt Teich & Company at left shows a similar view from the bluff on the east side of the canyon. Note the name Mays Gulch; Mays was an early pioneer surveyor in the area. It was not until the 1960s that, under ownership of Alabama Power Company and managed by DeSoto State Park, the name Little River Canyon replaced the Mays Gulch name. Some area residents referred to it as Mays Gulf. Below is Little River Falls during an extremely dry summer. (Both, courtesy of Collins Kirby.)

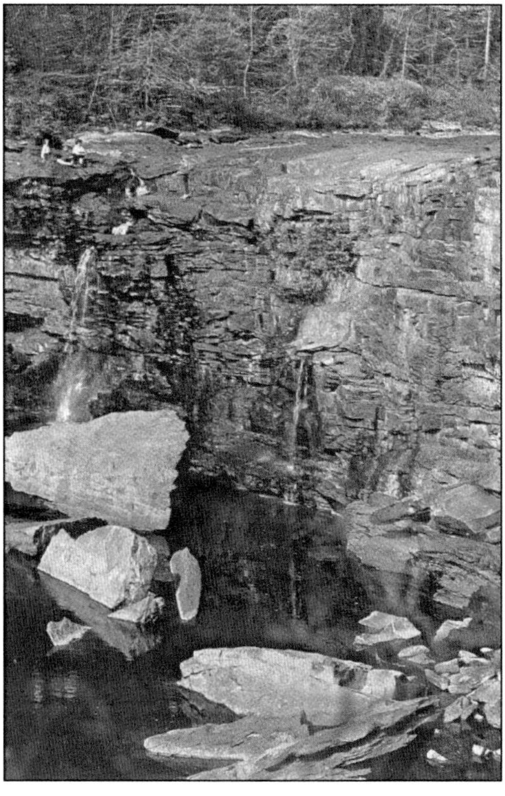

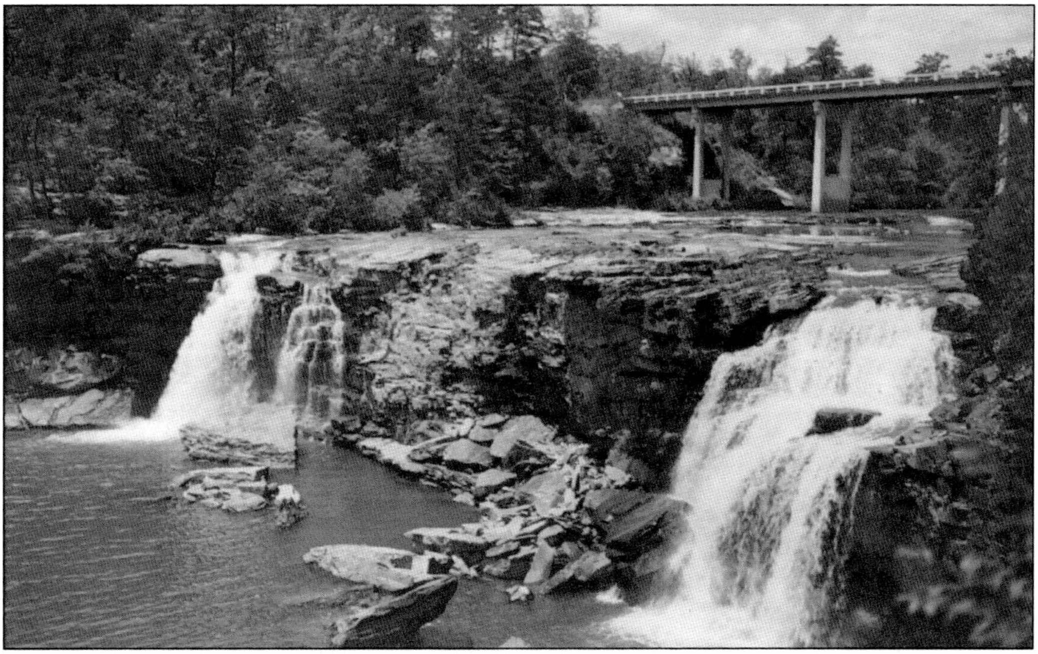

This 1970s postcard shows Little River Falls from its most popular vantage point. Though not yet a park when this picture was taken, this spot was well known for its view, and when the National Park Service took over management, it became a lookout point with its own trail and parking lot. (Courtesy of Collins Kirby.)

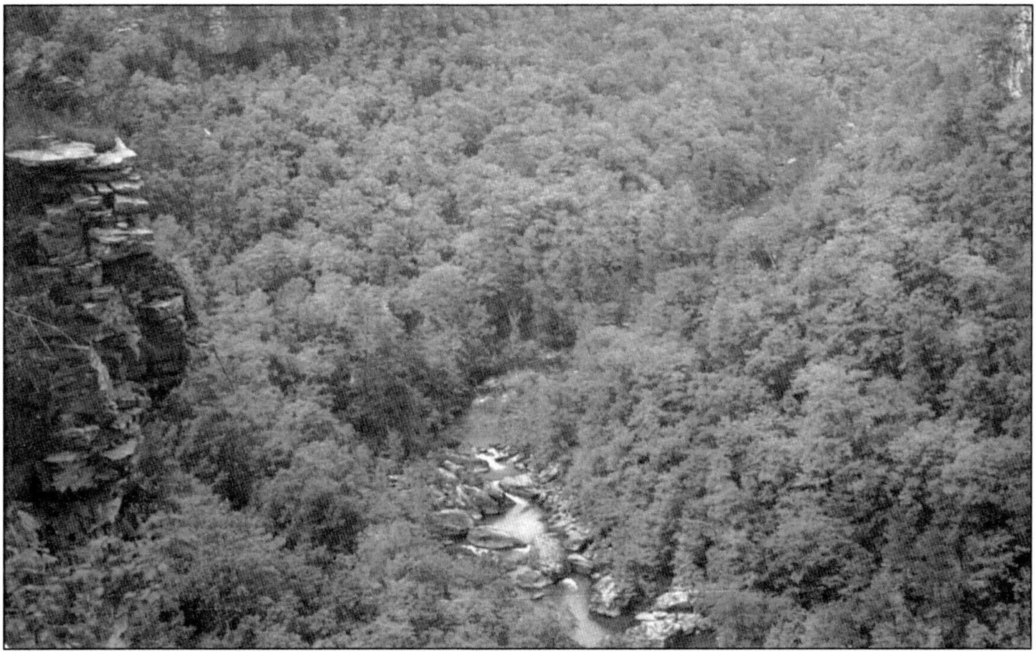

This 1960s postcard shows Little River Canyon from one of the bluffs that follow the staggered, winding trail of the river below. Over millions of years, the river carved out the canyon leaving the bluffs above, which were once on an equal plane with the river. (Courtesy of Collins Kirby.)

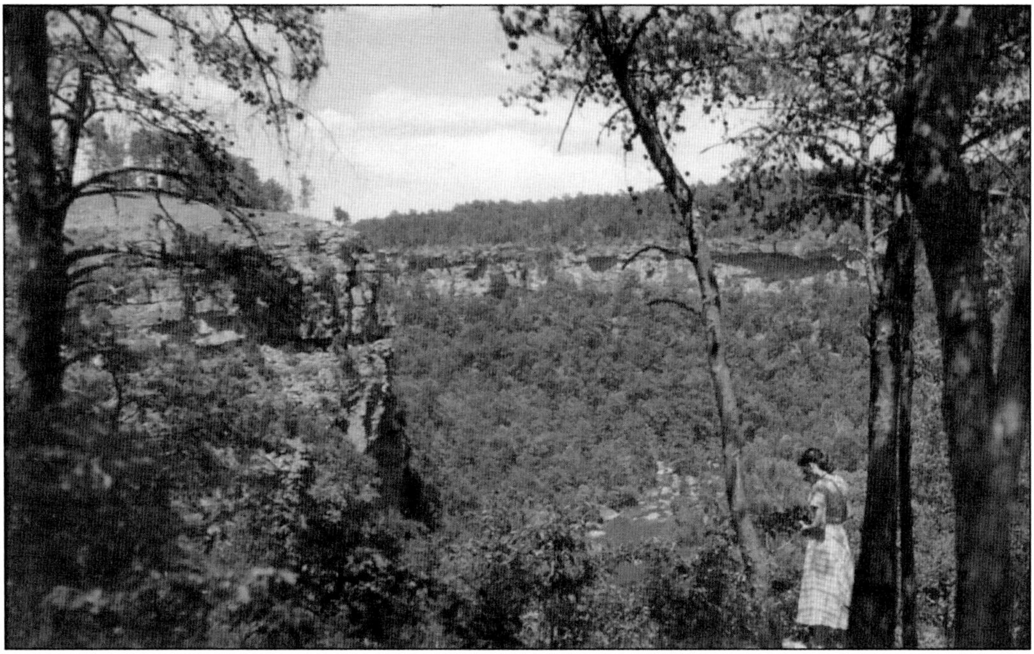

This early 1960s postcard shows a young lady along the bluffs of Little River Canyon National Preserve. It became a National Park Service unit in 1992. Due to its immense size and depth, the canyon has been popular dating back to the Native American cultures that preceded the white settlers. (Courtesy of Collins Kirby.)

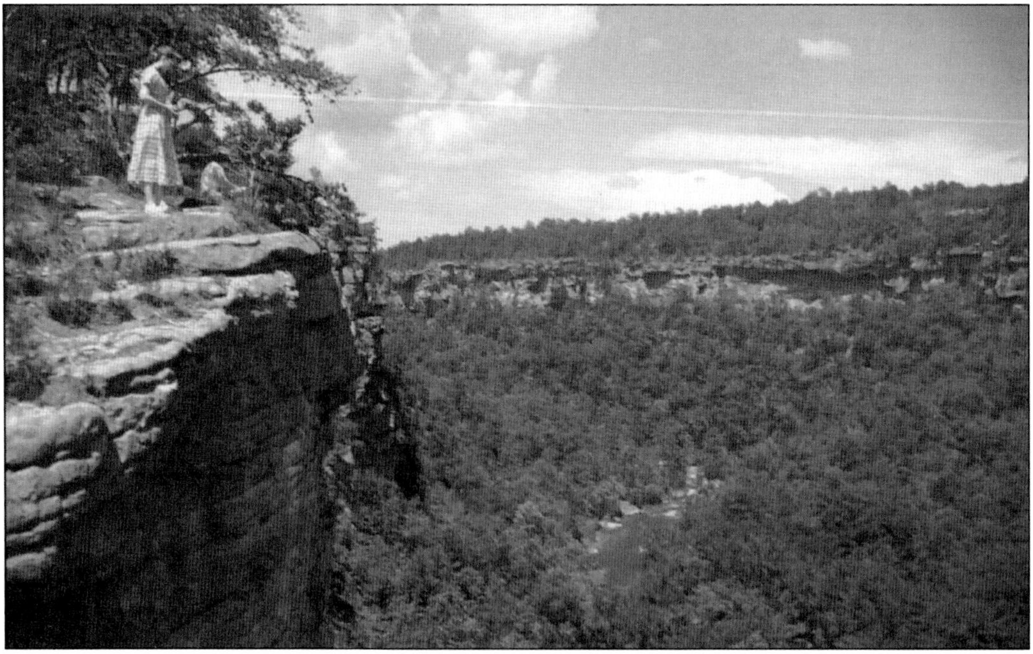

The same woman from the previous picture is seen here with a friend. This photograph was obviously taken on the same day. This magnificent canyon with clear, fresh mountain water and unsurpassed, extremely diverse biocultures attracts scientists from around the world to study the flora, fauna, and the geology of this great natural wonder. (Courtesy of Collins Kirby.)

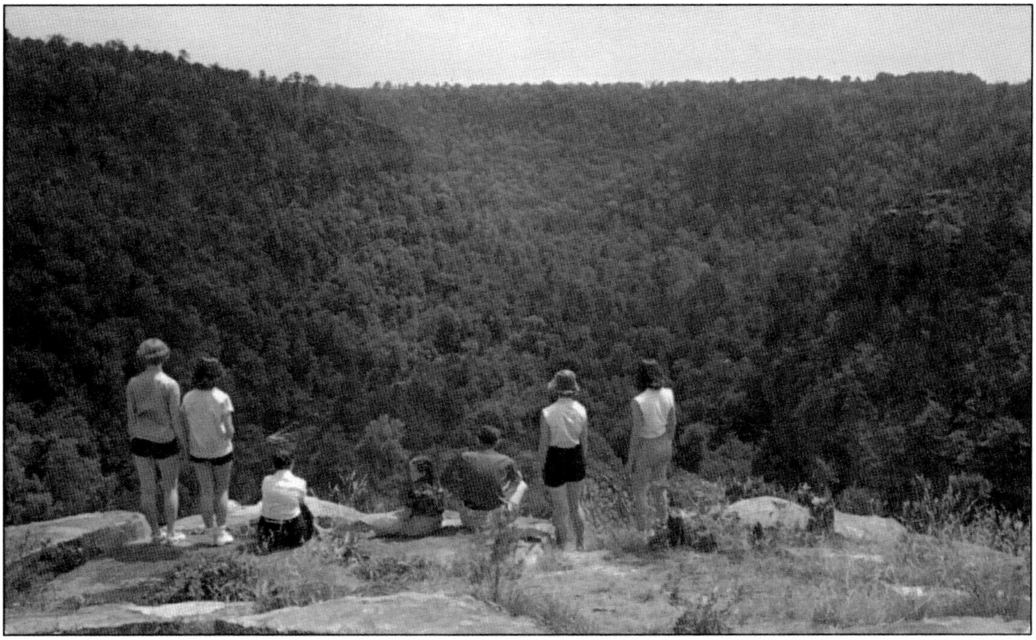

For thousands of years, beginning with the Woodland and Cherokee Indians, people have visited Little River Canyon. At places, the canyon is 650 feet deep. The beautiful river below sparkles in the sunshine as rock outcrops break the flow of the water, producing mini cascades of twinkling beauty. The Middle Fork of the Little River flows below, and its entire length flows from north to south on top of Lookout Mountain. Flowing off the mountain in waterfalls and cascades, the river ends in Weiss Lake. (Courtesy of Collins Kirby.)

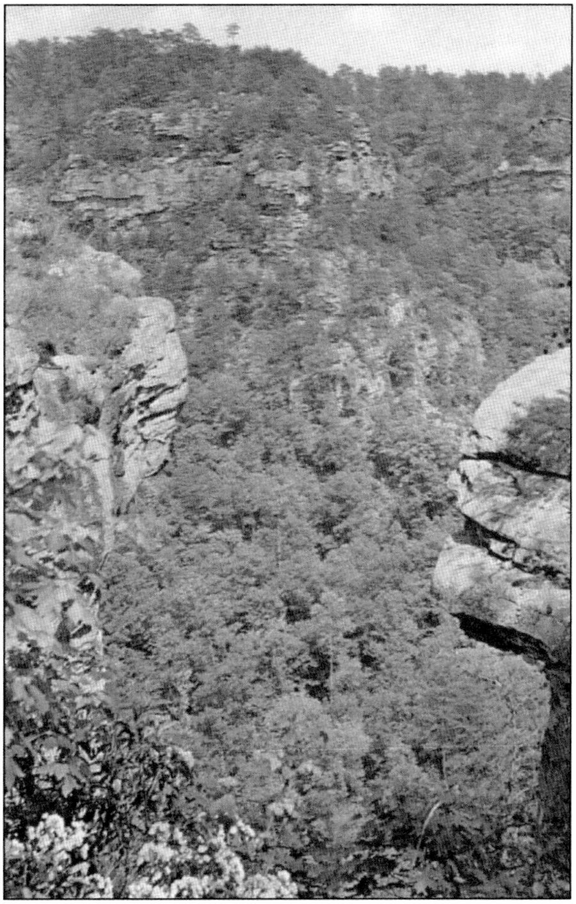

This view shows the bluffs and the quickly inclining landscape on its way to the canyon below. For most of history, these bluffs were unprotected by fences or signs. At the edge, the next step was hundreds of feet below. People climb or walk to the bottom in different locations, but it is a hard hike at almost any point. Prior to the installation of signs or trails, the undergrowth and the difficulty of the climb kept most people out of the canyon along much of its route. (Courtesy of Collins Kirby.)

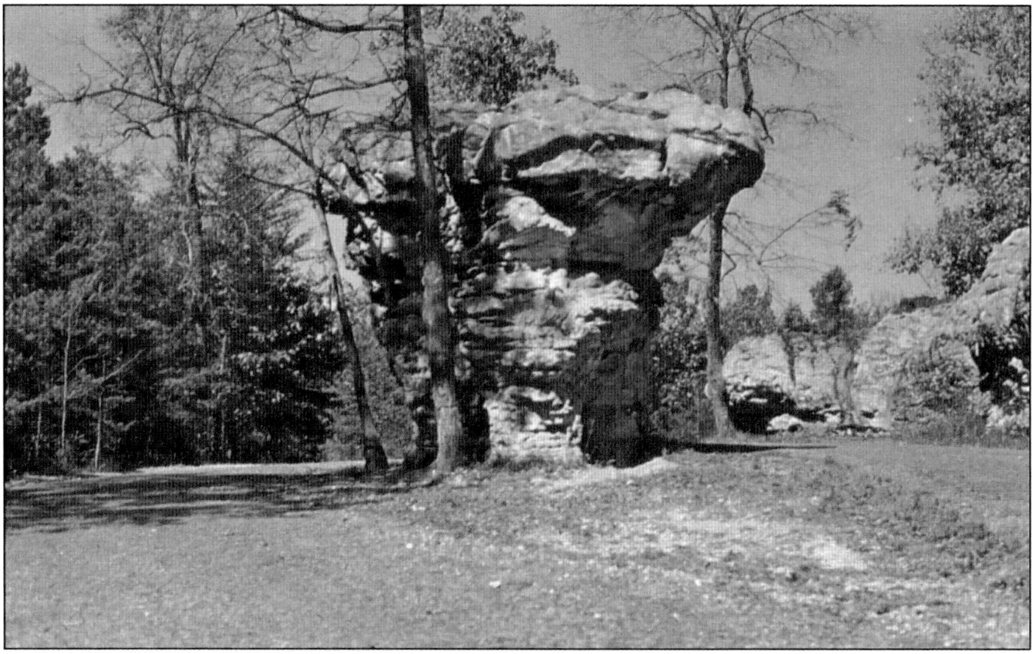

Mushroom Rock at Little River Canyon National Preserve is located on Canyon Rim Drive, Route 176, which runs along the rim of the canyon. Canyon Rim Drive is a secondary route for the Lookout Mountain Scenic Parkway, which is one of 11 state-certified scenic byways in Alabama. Along the way, there are places to picnic, hike, and look down into the beautiful canyon. (Courtesy of Collins Kirby.)

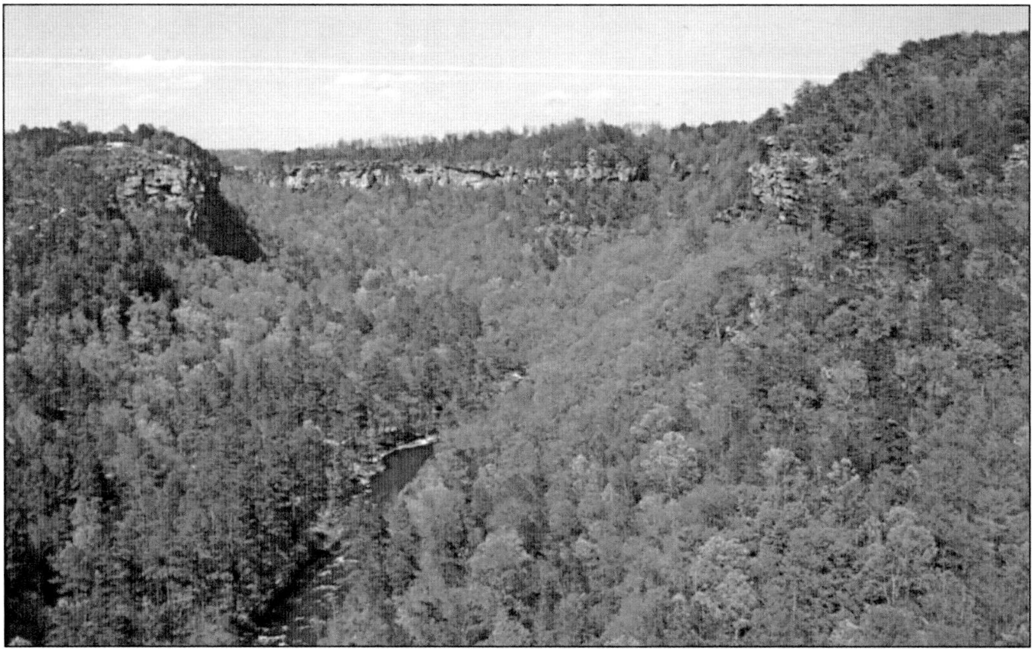

This 1970s commercially printed card shows a deep view of Little River Canyon. On this spring day, the Little River is winding through the canyon, carving deeper and deeper into Lookout Mountain, on which the entire canyon and river are located. (Courtesy of Collins Kirby.)

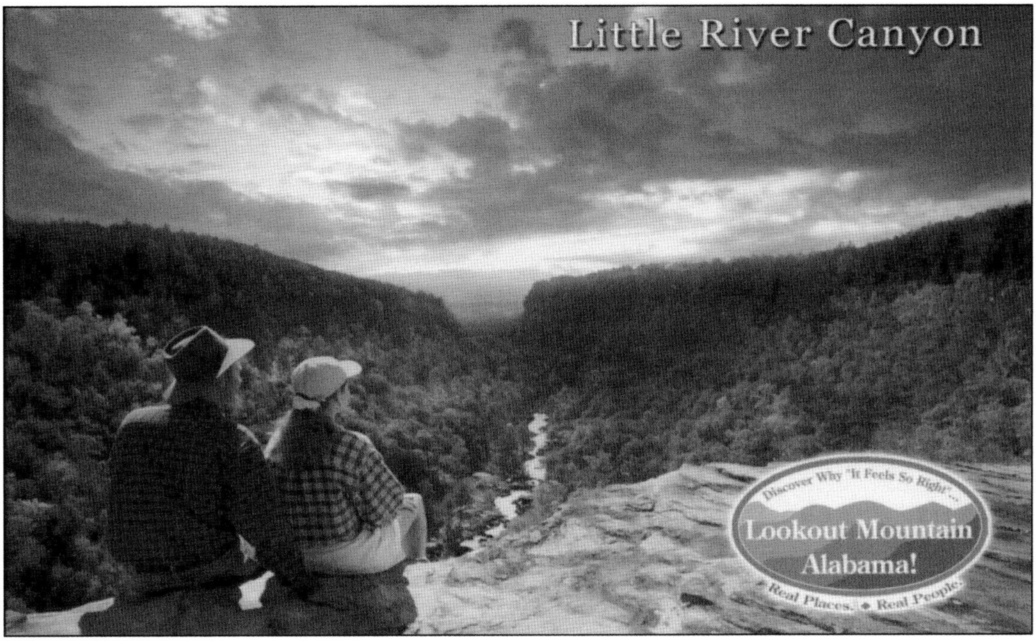

The State of Alabama commissioned this photograph, which was used by DeKalb Tourism to promote tourism to the area. This postcard was made available by DeKalb Tourism in the mid-2000s for use at the Tourist Information Center. Pictured is the Middle Fork of the Little River. (Author's collection.)

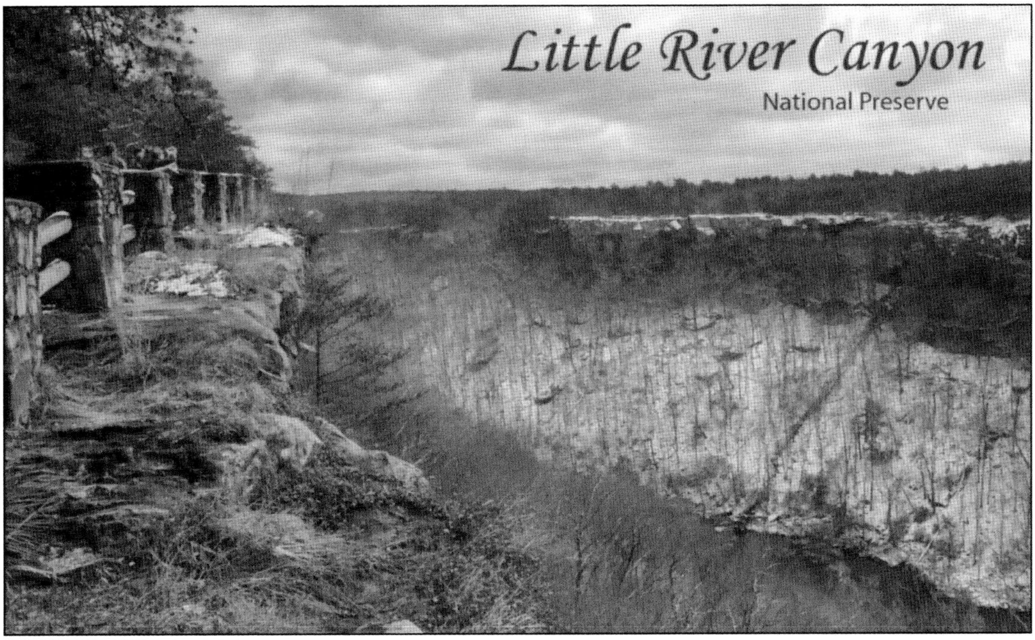

This postcard from 2009 was used to promote the Friends of the Preserve at Little River Canyon. Snow is not uncommon to the area, and during an average winter, it will snow three or more times. Most snows are a dusting from one inch to seven. Snowfalls as deep as 15 to 20 inches have occurred, with the last one being in March 1993 during what was called the "Storm of the Century." (Author's collection.)

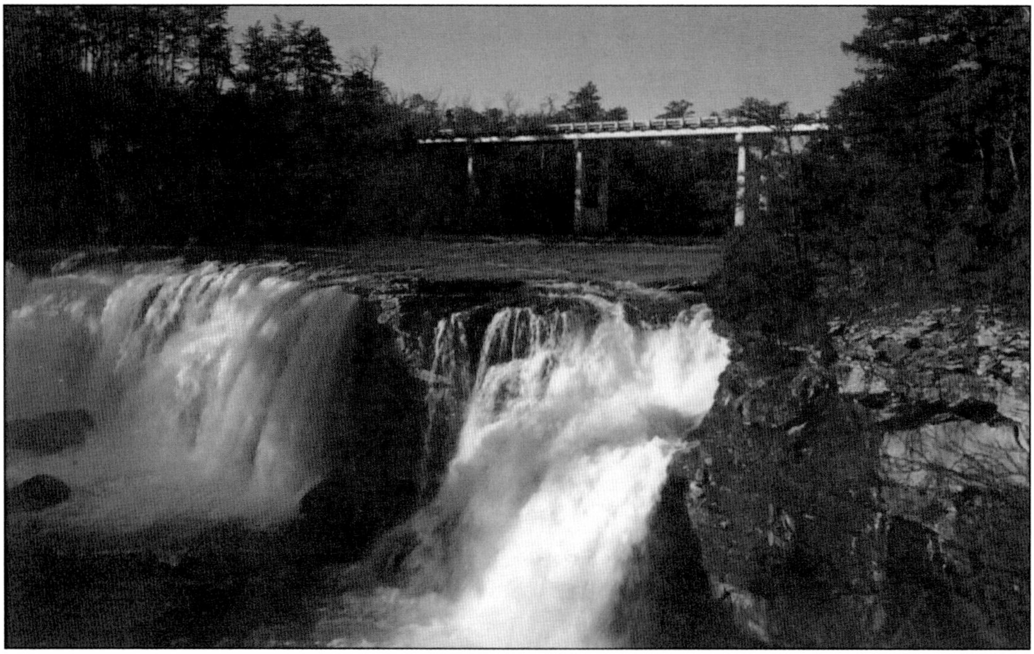

This 1970s postcard shows Little River Falls with significant water coming over the falls. Due to runoff during heavy rains, the river fills quickly. This view of the waterfalls from the east side of the canyon does not require much hiking to get to and is therefore the most common view of the falls, then and now. (Courtesy of Collins Kirby.)

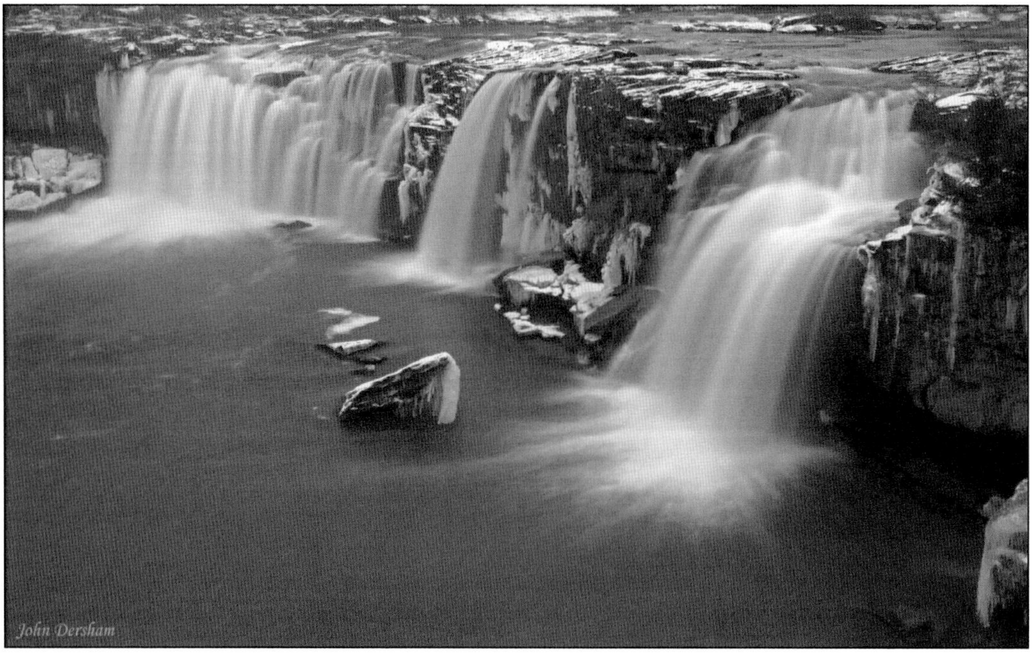

The icy-cold Little River Falls in Little River Canyon National Preserve is pictured in late January 2015. Fort Payne enjoys four distinct seasons, including snow and ice most winters, but is far enough south to enjoy warmer, more temperate seasons each year. (Author photograph.)

This canyon view was captured in the early spring of 2011. The Little River is full, and whitewater is less noticeable than usual. The national preserve encompasses more than 15,000 acres with an alternate route of the Lookout Mountain Scenic Parkway running along the western rim of the canyon. There are overlooks and picnic tables all along the route, and it is beautiful year-round. (Author photograph.)

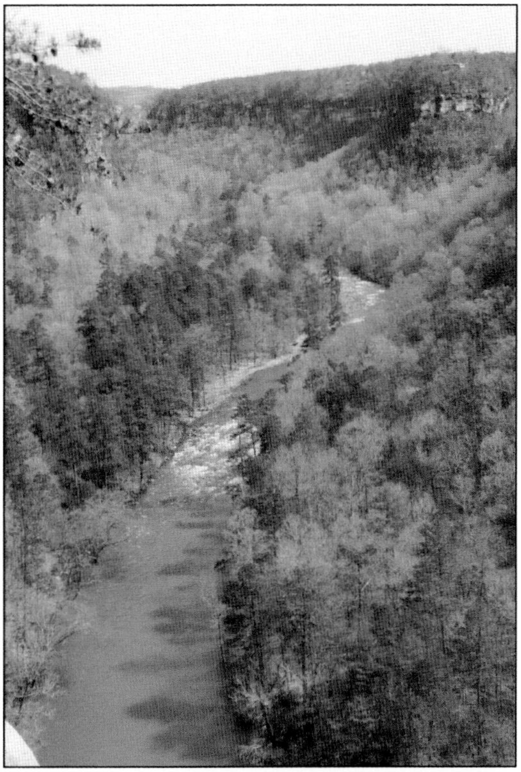

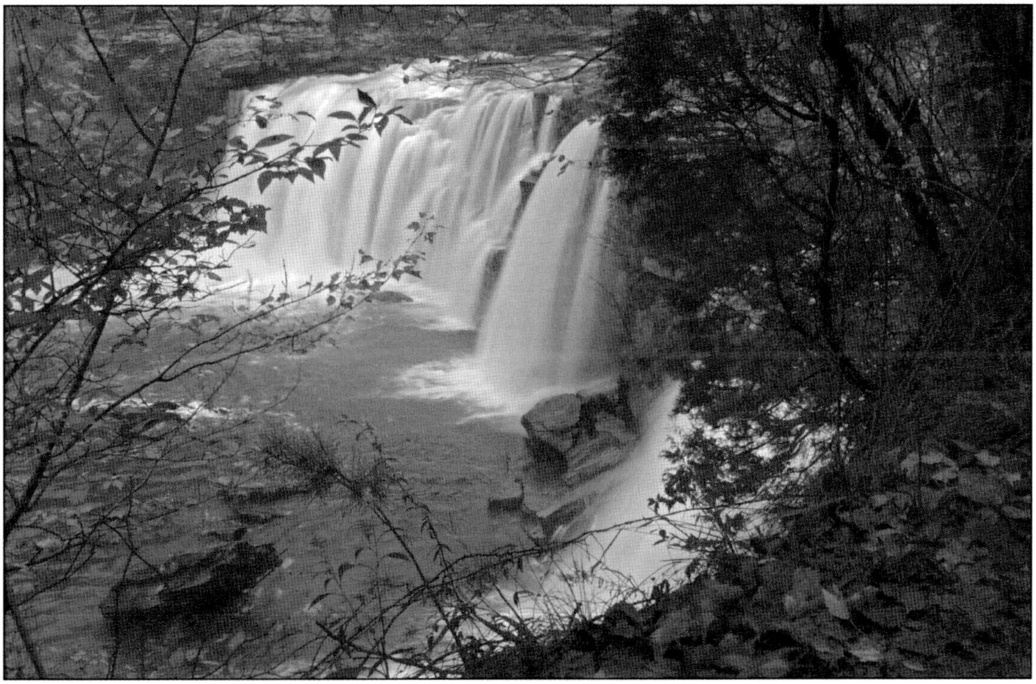

This photograph was taken at the peak of fall color on October 24, 2009. Many fall seasons are dry, and waterfalls are not flowing with this much velocity. In this particular fall, there was some good rainfall that filled the river and made for outstanding views. (Author photograph.)

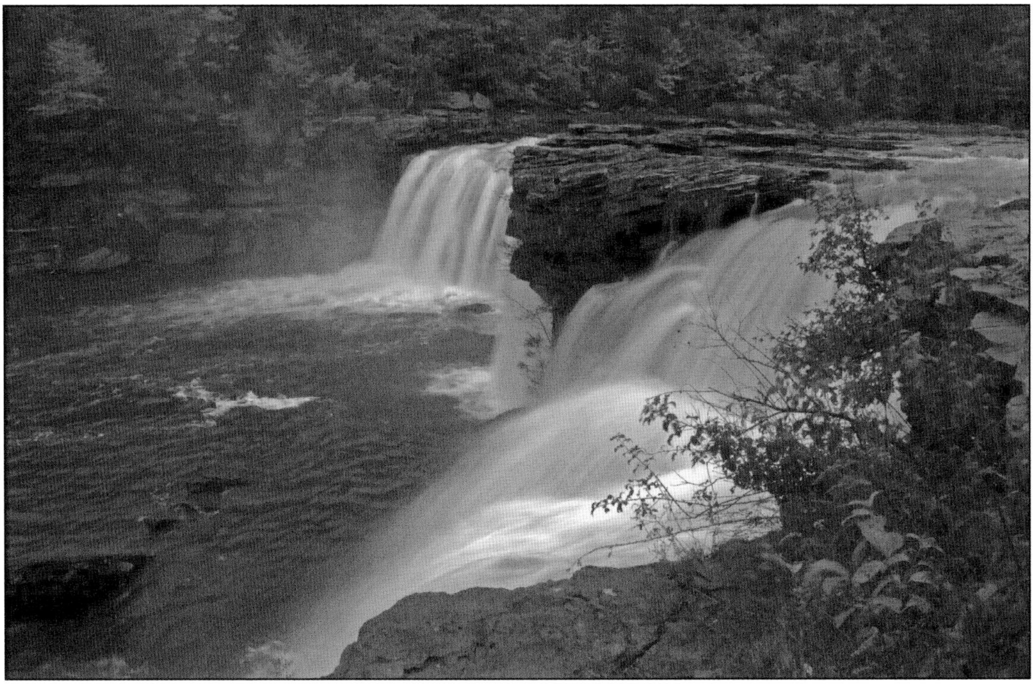

This photograph was taken on the same day as the previous image. It shows a very active Little River Falls. Every day is different in this incredible and diverse ecosystem. (Author photograph.)

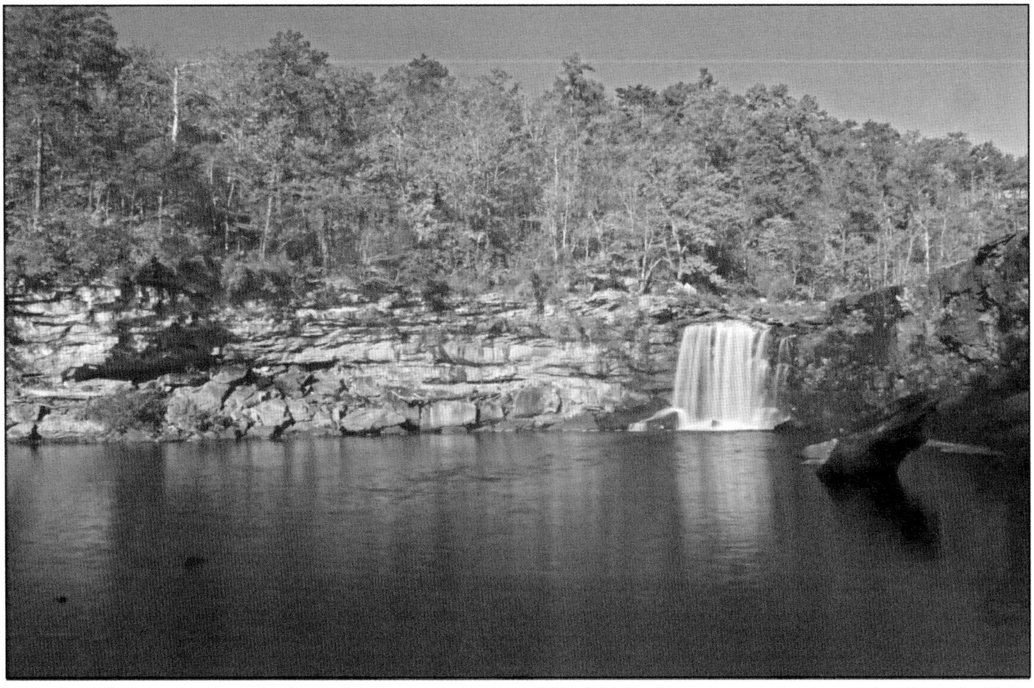

Another photograph depicts much less water in the fall of 2013. This image, captured below the falls at river level, shows the basin. A significant hike is required to get here. (Author photograph.)

This photograph was taken at sunrise in November 2012 during the 20th anniversary of Little River Canyon having become part of the National Park Service. Little River falls varies greatly in how much water is flowing over the falls. The river fills quickly when it rains, and the water roars over the falls. In the fall, when it is typically dryer, it usually looks as it does here. The falls never go dry and are a beautiful sight year-round. (Author photograph.)

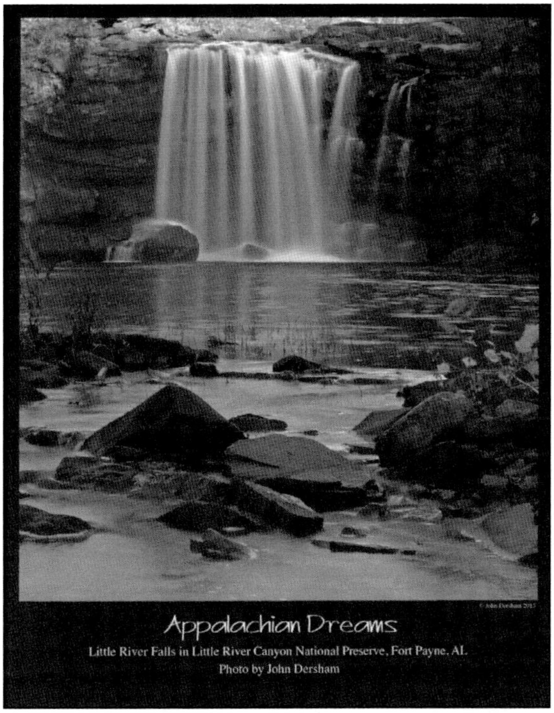

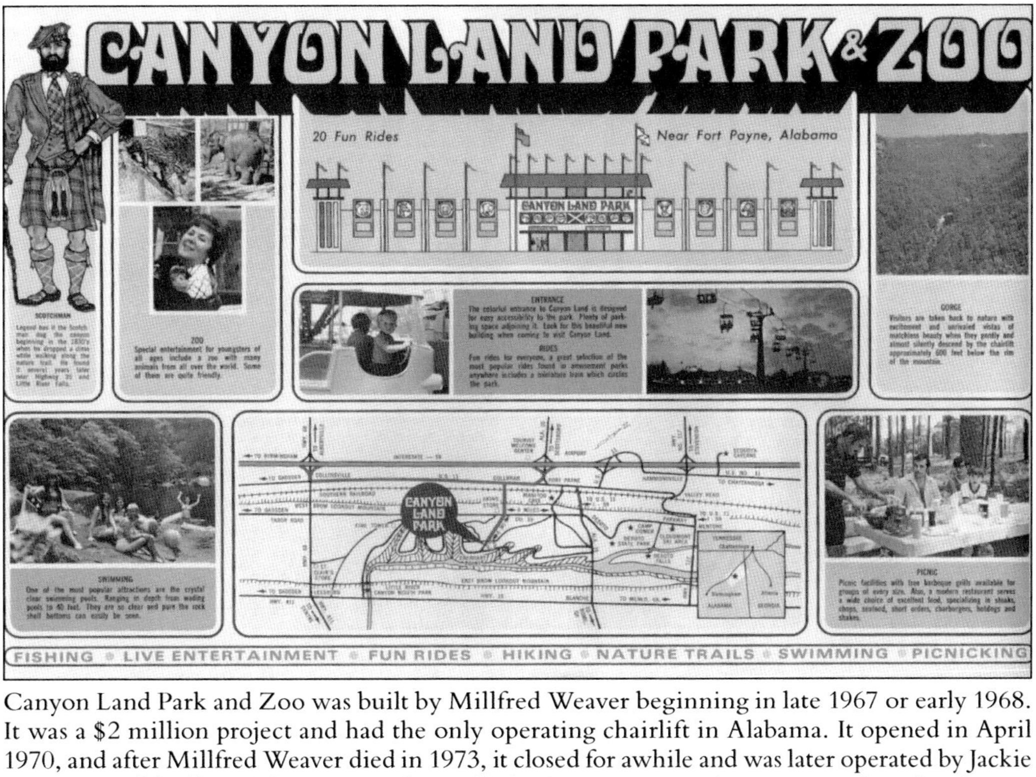

Canyon Land Park and Zoo was built by Millfred Weaver beginning in late 1967 or early 1968. It was a $2 million project and had the only operating chairlift in Alabama. It opened in April 1970, and after Millfred Weaver died in 1973, it closed for awhile and was later operated by Jackie Weaver (Millfred's son) for a time. After Jackie's stint as owner, other operators kept it going on and off through 1985. It never reopened after that year. (Author's collection.)

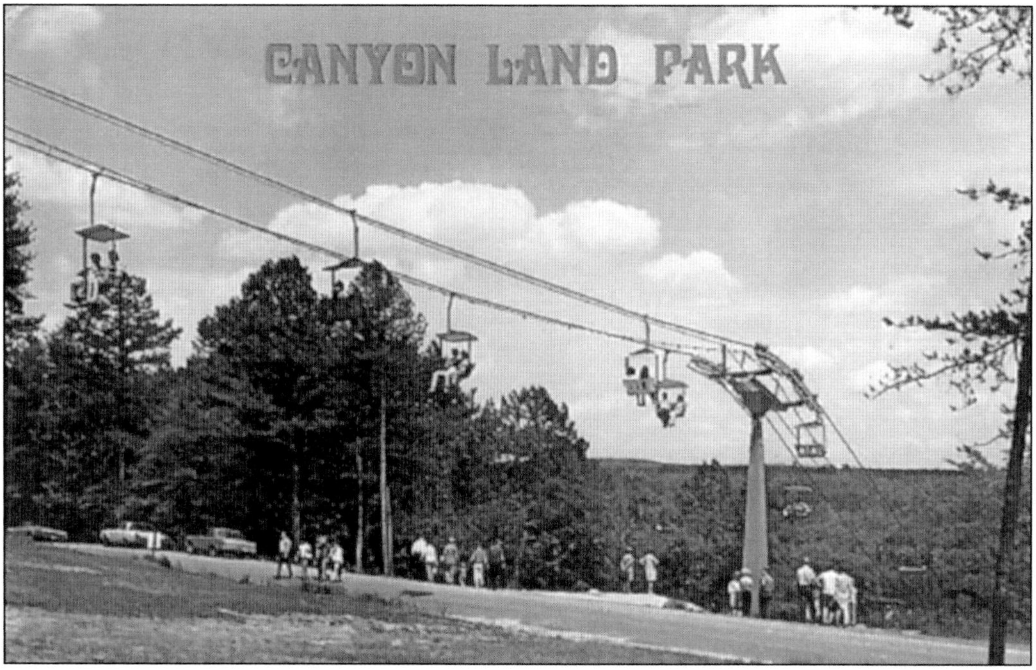

During the time Canyon Land was open, DeKalb County had the only chairlift in Alabama and also the only ski resort, Cloudmont Golf and Ski Resort in Mentone, Alabama. Cloudmont still operates today. (Courtesy of Collins Kirby.)

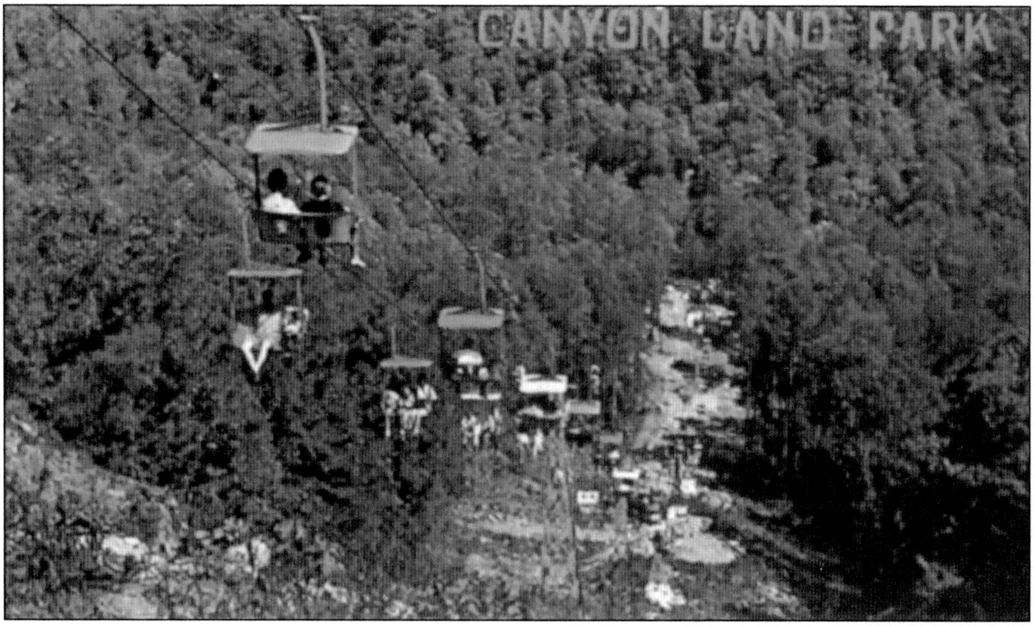

Writing about Alabama's newest attraction, Canyon Land Park, the June 17, 1970, *Cherokee County Herald* reported, "one of the most outstanding of the park's attractions is the chair lift which extends 600 feet into the deepest gorge east of the Mississippi River. The lift, which is equipped with 82 chairs, extends a distance of 1,480 feet, and is the only chair lift or sky lift in Alabama." (Courtesy of Collins Kirby.)

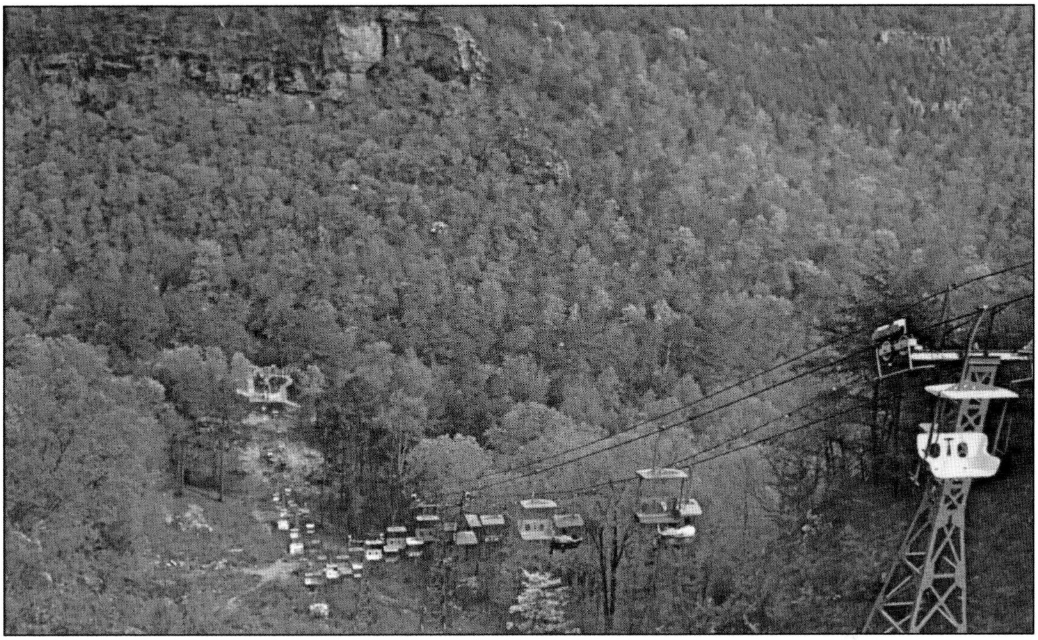

A couple of the buildings and the hardware from the chairlift are still visible today on the former property of Canyon Land. Over the years, the property has changed ownership, and some of the elements of the attraction, like the campground and the restaurant, were reopened and closed. (Courtesy of Collins Kirby.)

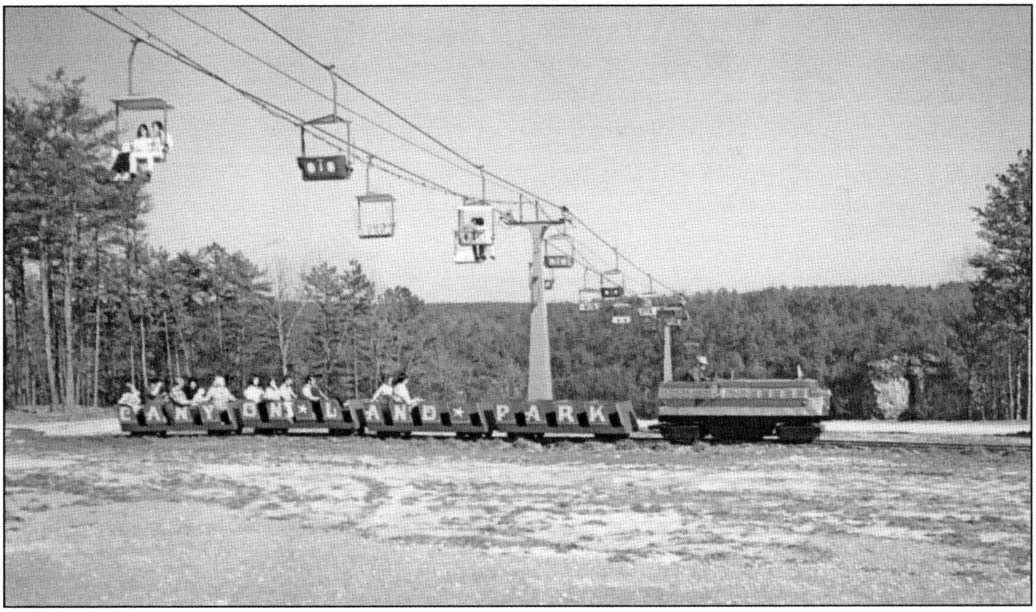

Canyon Land provided a perfect vacation spot at beautiful Little River Canyon; it had everything from a train, zoo, and campground to live concerts in the canyon and a restaurant. In a newsletter released by the Alabama Tourism Bureau in 1971, Canyon Land was said to be a booming tourist facility, having given 35,000 chairlift rides in its first year of operation. The newsletter also stated that Canyon Land was the state's tourist attraction of the month. (Which month is not specified.) (Courtesy of Collin Kirby.)

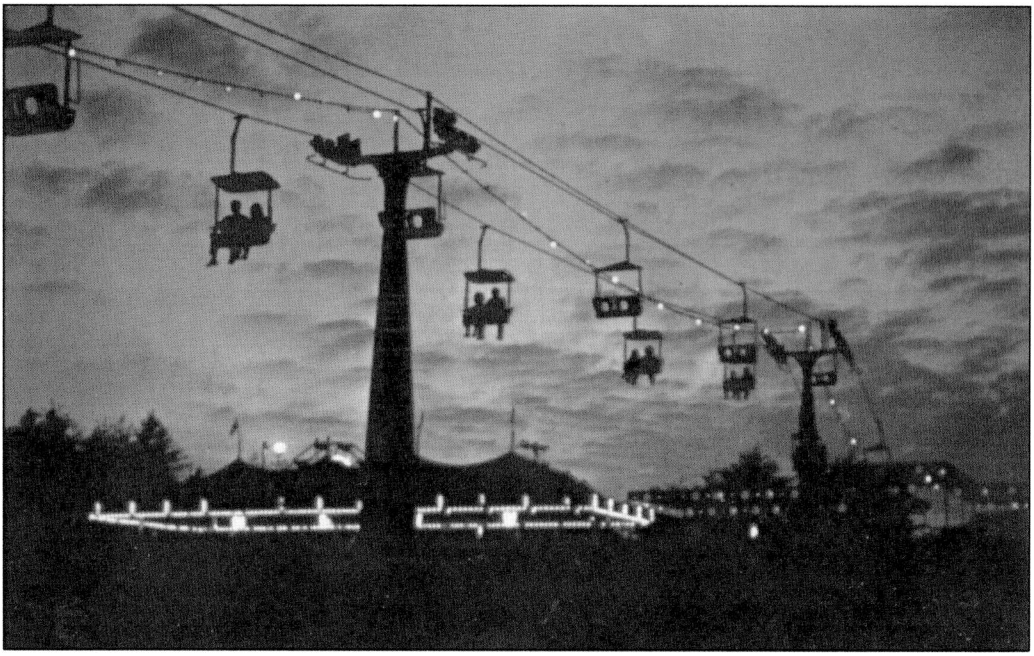

This great photograph taken at twilight shows riders on the chairlift as well as the amusement area of the park. This park was a really special attraction during its tenure. Many who make their living in tourism in this area wish it were still operating. (Courtesy of Collins Kirby.)

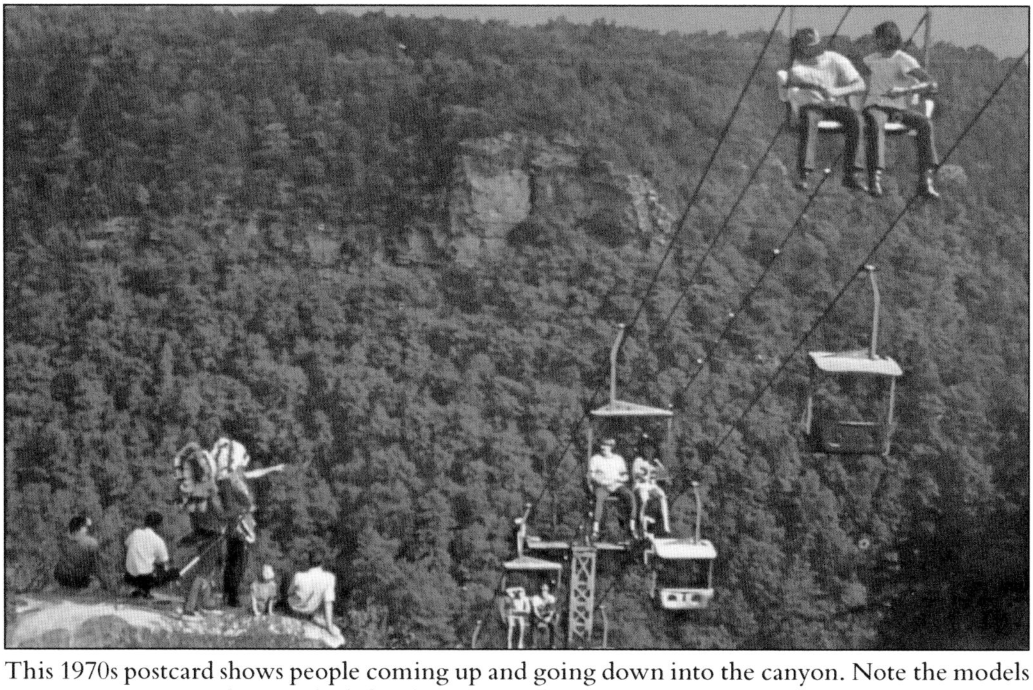

This 1970s postcard shows people coming up and going down into the canyon. Note the models in Native American dress to the left. This was another part of the entertainment at Canyon Land Park and Zoo. (Courtesy of Collins Kirby.)

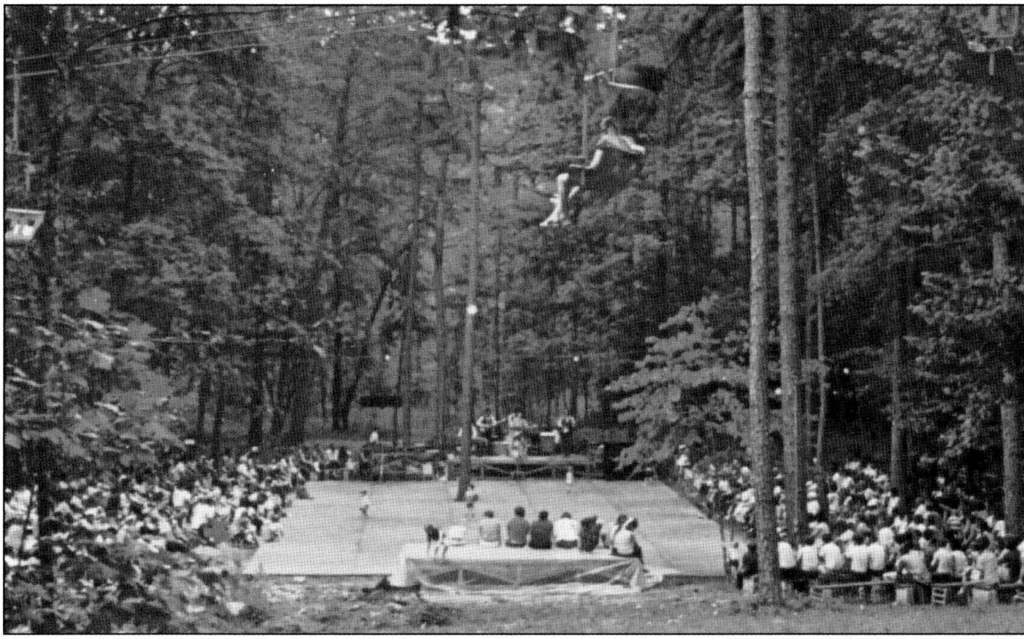

Live concerts were held at the bottom of the Little River Canyon. The chairlift would deliver guests down to this outdoor concert facility, as seen in this postcard. A young group called Wild Country played there on a regular basis. Later the group was renamed Alabama. (Courtesy of Collinsville Alabama Historical Association.)

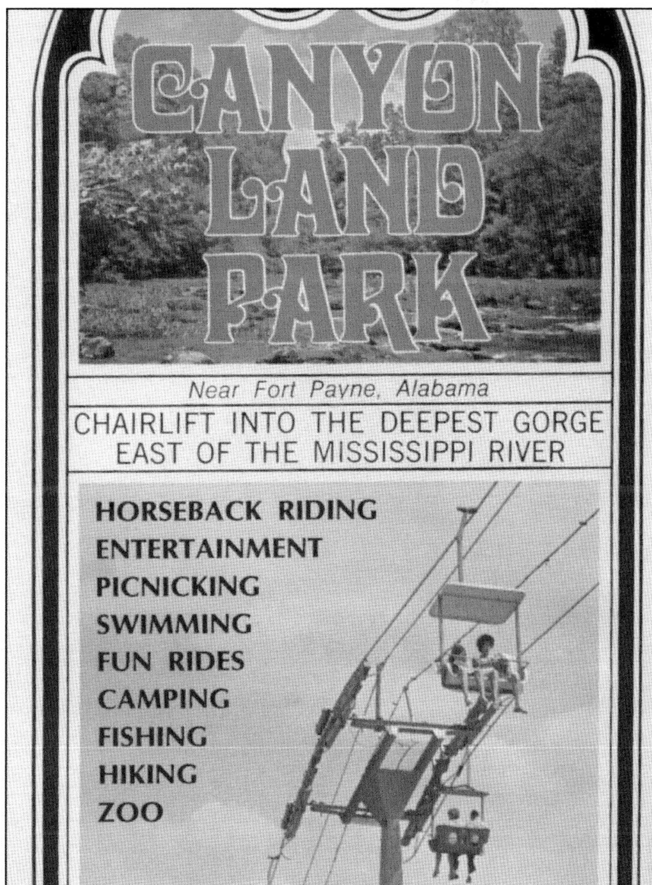

There were so many things to see and do at Canyon Land Park and Zoo. It was an incredible attraction that is missed in the area. Little River Canyon did not become a national preserve until 1992, which was well after Canyon Land closed. To this day, there is no access down into the canyon, except by foot or repelling. (Author's collection.)

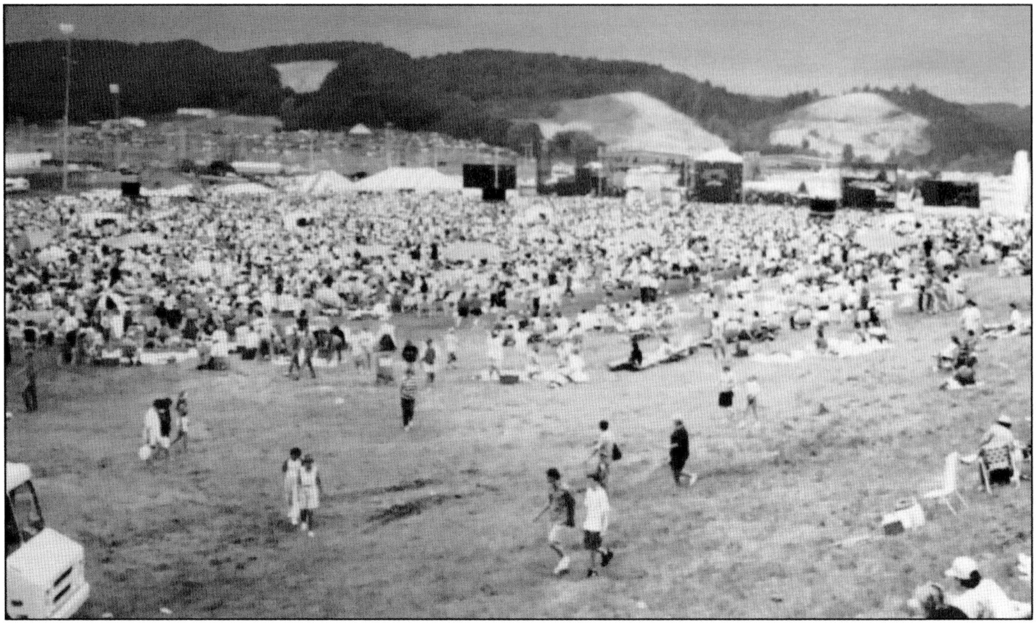

Members of the band Alabama were born here and live here to this day. They have been a major tourist attraction since the early 1980s, when they first became internationally famous. In the 1980s and 1990s, Alabama hosted June Jam in Fort Payne. It was a major outdoor music concert that lasted for days and featured top artists, including Alabama. (Author's collection.)

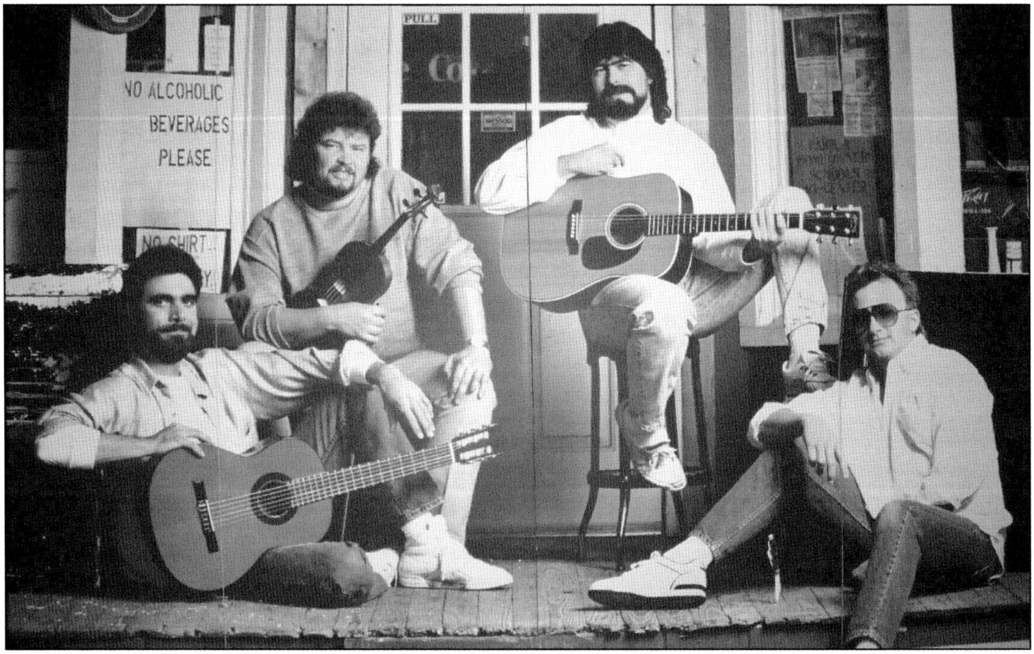

Pictured are the members of Alabama. This image is on the wall of the Alabama Fan Club and Museum in Fort Payne. The band's contribution to the notoriety of Fort Payne and their personal commitments to Fort Payne have been sizable over the years. The group's annual fan appreciation weekend each June and their fan club and museum, open year-round, provides Fort Payne and surrounding areas millions of dollars in revenue each year. (Author's collection.)

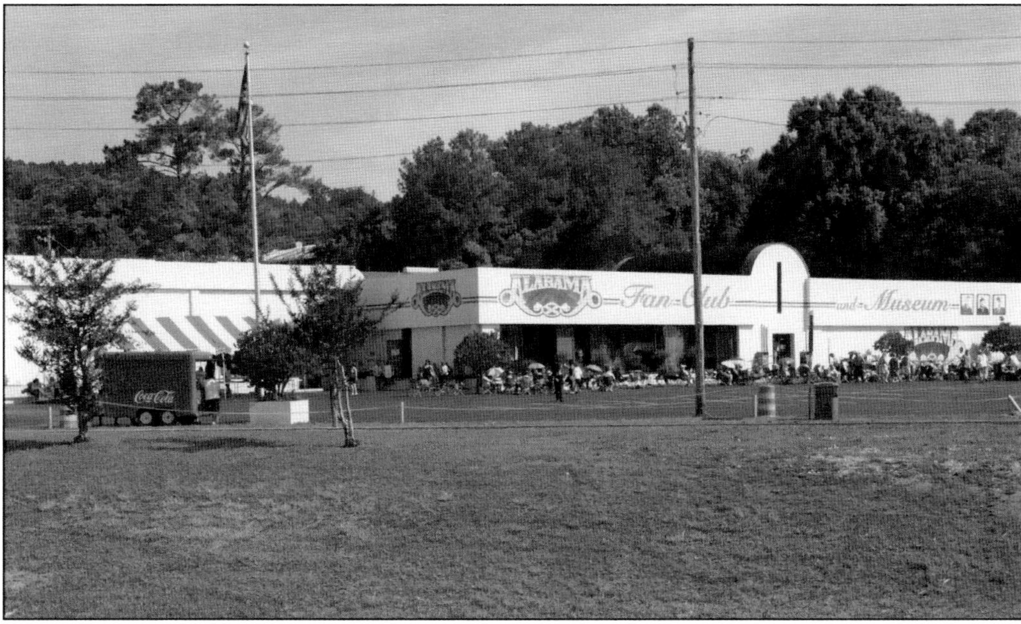

The Alabama Fan Club and Museum is seen here. This photograph was taken prior to a free Alabama performance in June 2014. Beginning early in the morning, crowds line up for the evening concert. (Author photograph.)

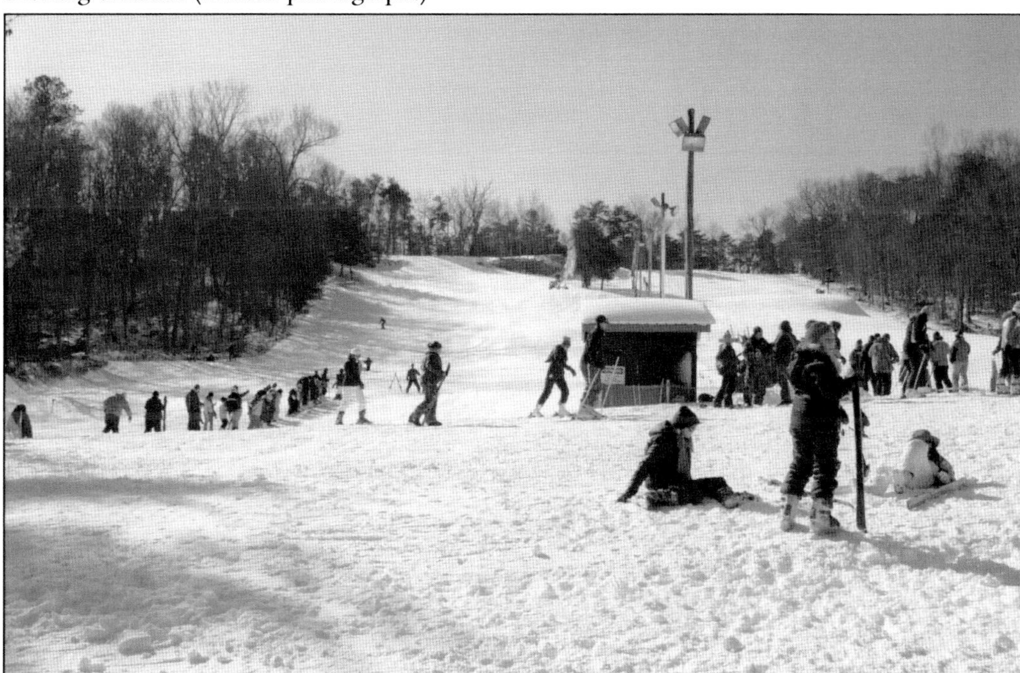

Cloudmont Golf and Ski Resort on Lookout Mountain is located in Mentone. Since opening in the 1970s, Cloudmont is the only ski resort in Alabama. This photograph shows crowds enjoying a bright snow cover on a Saturday morning in January 2013. The resort makes its own snow when temperatures stay below freezing. The area typically will get three to five annual snows. (Author photograph.)

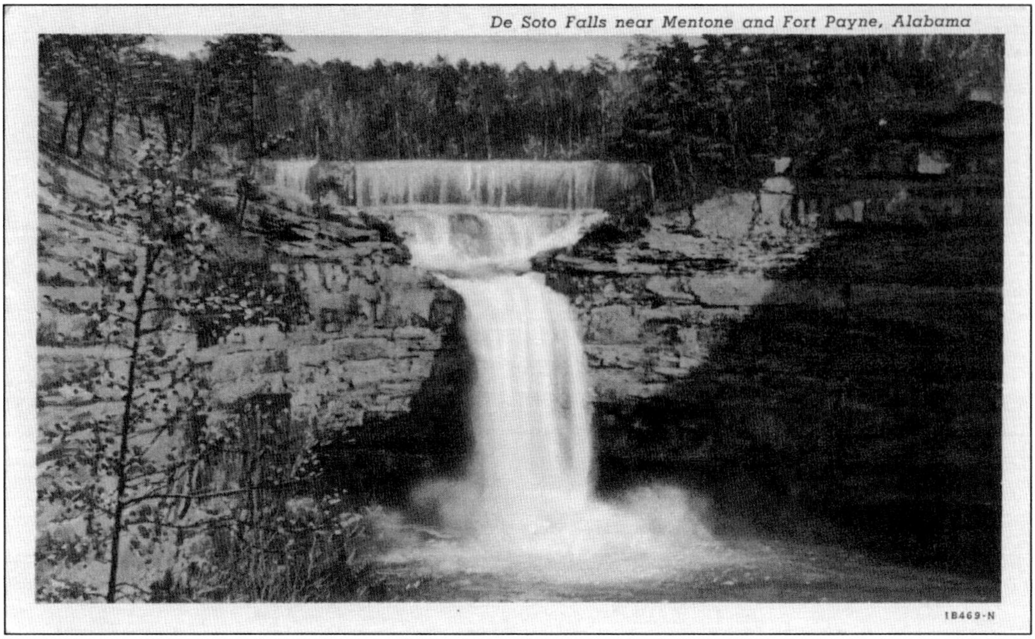

This beautiful hand-colored card with linen texture was common in the 1930s and 1940s. DeSoto Falls had a heavy flow in this springtime picture. The falls makes approximately a 104-foot fall to the basin, depending on the volume of water below. (Courtesy of Collin Kirby.)

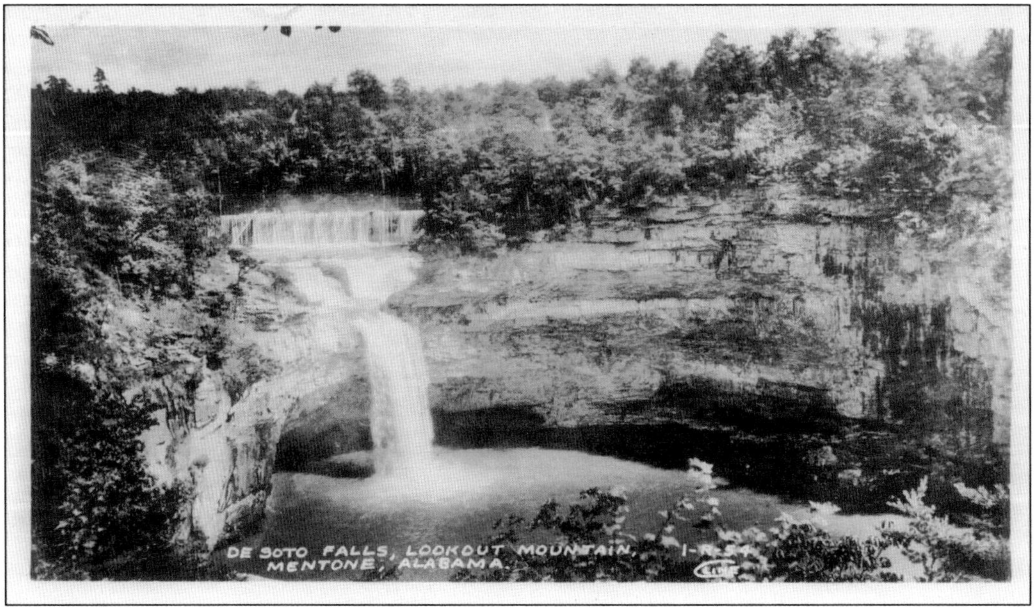

This is a 1940s real-photo postcard by Walter Cline of Cline's photo cards and consumer photofinishing out of Chattanooga. Cline held on to the real-photo postcard process well after most companies went to commercially printed copies. Later, when Cline moved to the commercial printing process, his cards were still known to be of the best quality. In the 1950s, the Kodachrome postcard became popular because it carried the look of the film that was used, which was Kodak Kodachrome. Kodachrome film was the dominant color film for decades; only in 2009 was it dropped from Kodak's production after nearly 75 years. (Courtesy of Collins Kirby.)

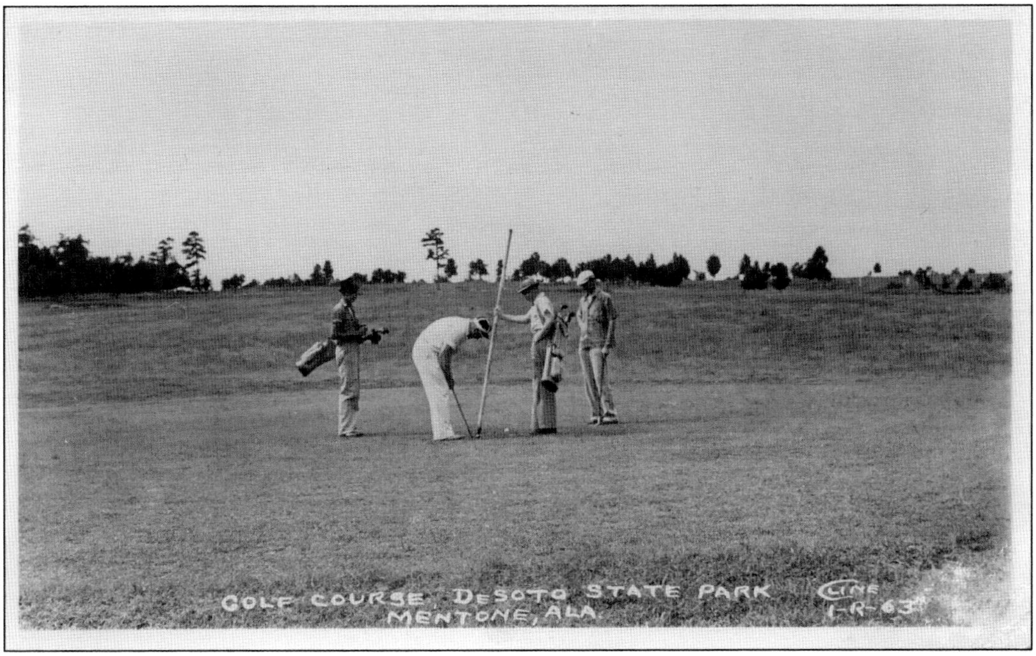

This Cline card from the early 1940s shows golfers in action at DeSoto Golf Course at DeSoto State Park. During the World War II war years, the golf course fell into disrepair and was closed and never reopened. In fact, the course is woodlands today, but remnants of the golf course can still be found. Hikers can tell where the greens were due to the perfectly level spots, and one of the cups was found recently, still embedded in the ground. (Courtesy of Collins Kirby.)

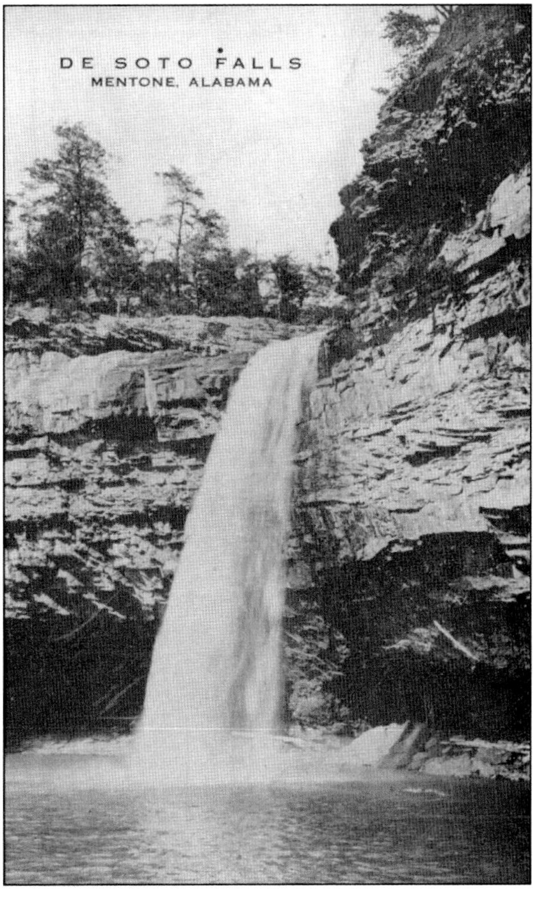

This view of DeSoto Falls is from the basin and gives a better sense of the elevation. This printed card from the early 1920s predates the construction of the 20-foot hydroelectric dam built by A.A. Miller, which opened in 1923. Miller sold his business to Alabama Power in 1928. A square concrete base still marks the spot where electricity for Fort Payne and Mentone was generated. (Courtesy of Collins Kirby.)

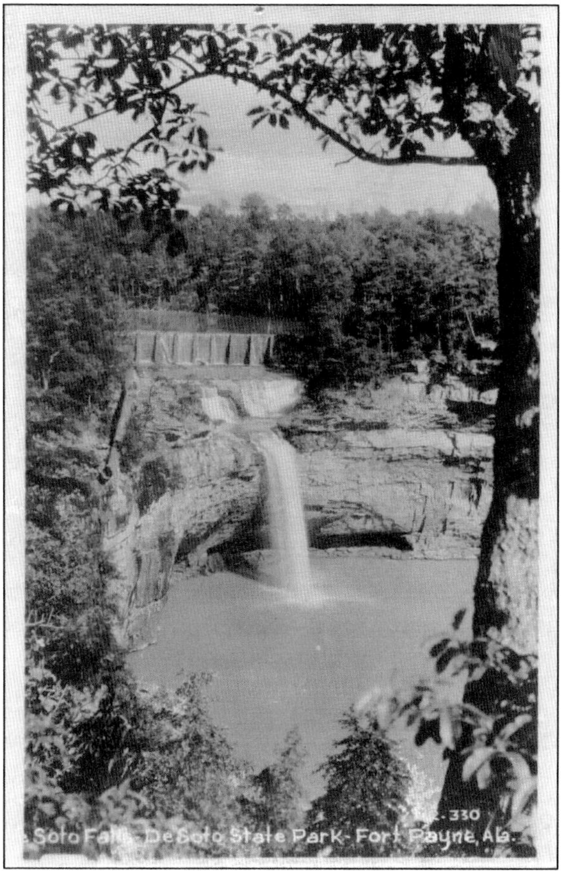

This Cline real-photo postcard is from the early 1940s and shows the falls from a distance. (Courtesy of Collins Kirby.)

DeSoto State Park lodge is pictured here. Like many state and national parks that were built and opened in the 1930s and early 1940s, DeSoto was constructed by the Civilian Conservation Corps (CCC). This massive undertaking by Franklin Roosevelt helped pull millions of families out of the Great Depression by giving them jobs building parks, roads, walls, and dams. When World War II began, the CCC camps were closed since anyone who wanted to work during the massive military construction and development projects for the war effort had a job. After World War II ended in 1945, the economy boomed. (Courtesy of Collins Kirby.)

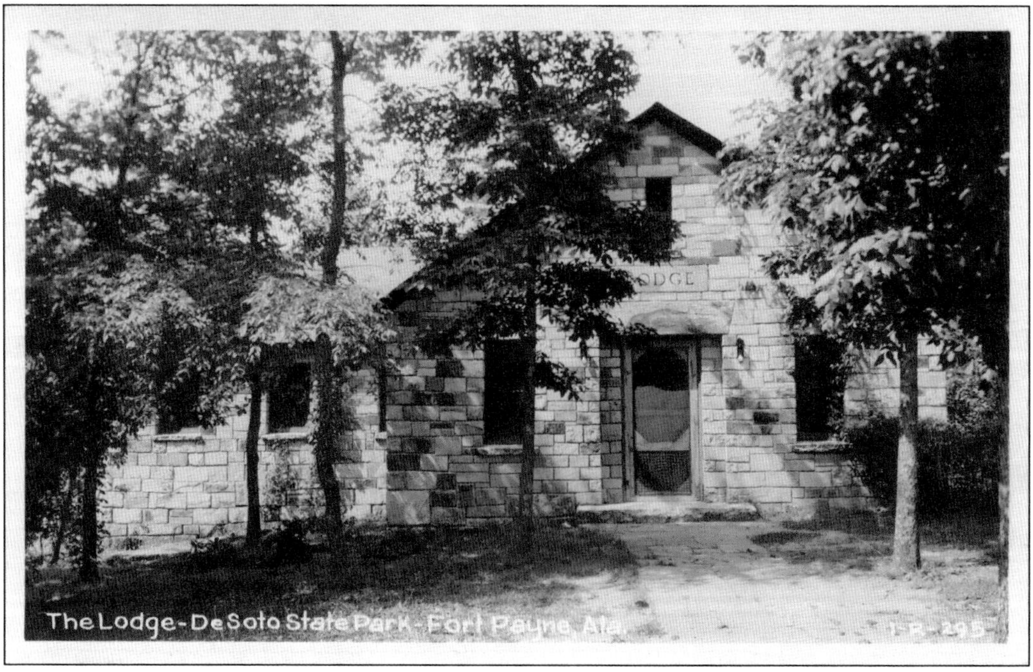

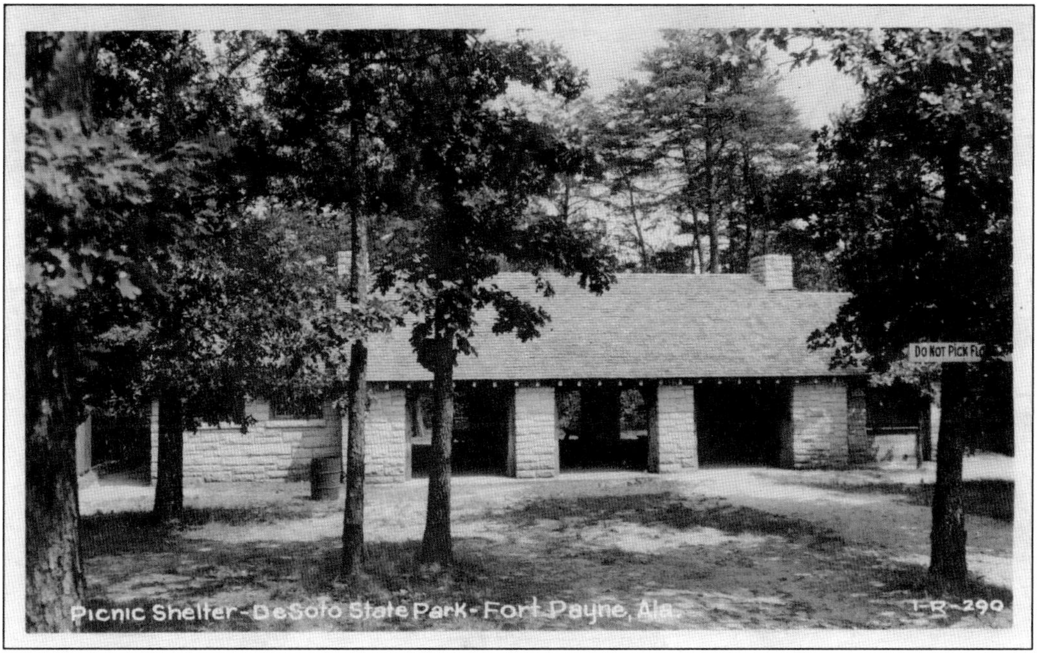

This postcard by Walter Cline from the same era shows the magnificent stonework of the CCC. This picnic shelter, along with most of the work of the CCC, is still in use on a daily basis at DeSoto State Park. In fact, this view looks almost identical today. In 2013, the original stone entry building to DeSoto State Park was made into a CCC museum and serves as a great reminder of the wonderful CCC work done all around this park and in other parks nationwide. (Courtesy of Collins Kirby.)

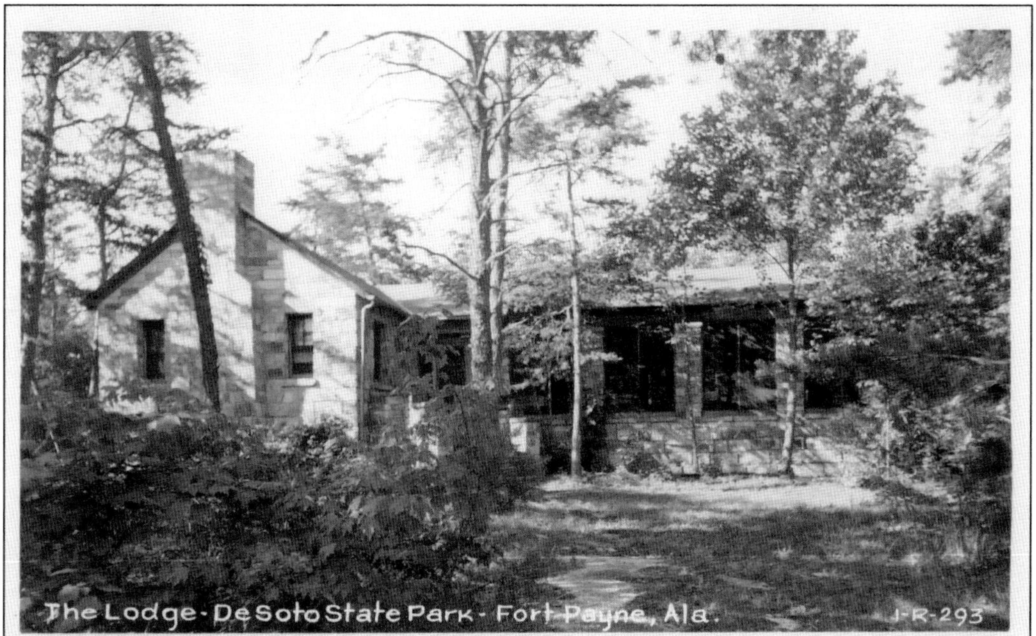

This Walter Cline postcard shows a different view of the lodge, probably taken the same day as others in this sequence. (Courtesy of Collins Kirby.)

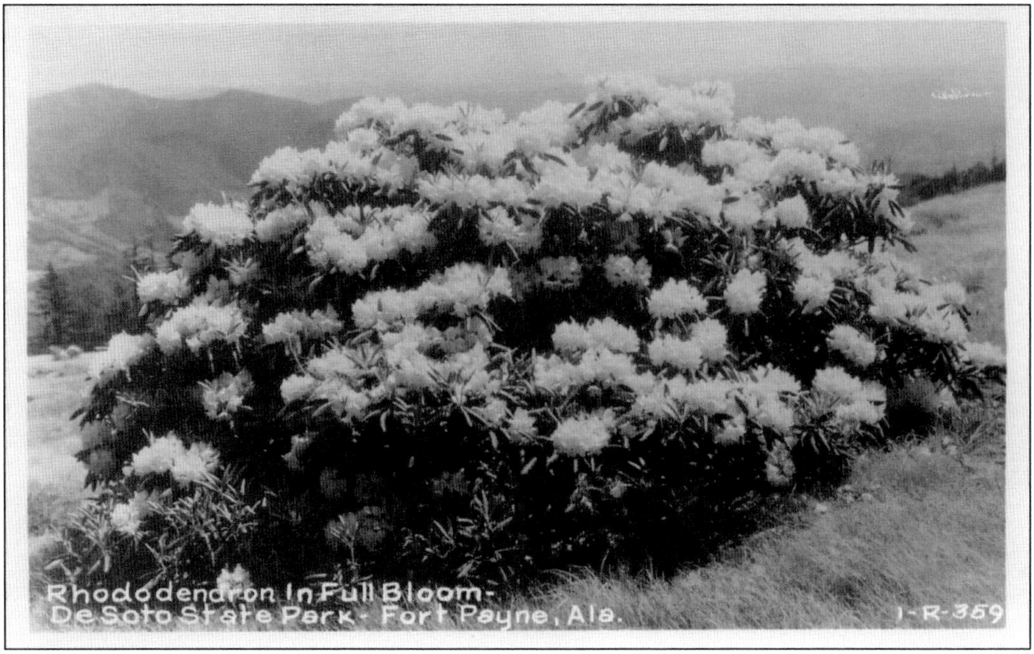

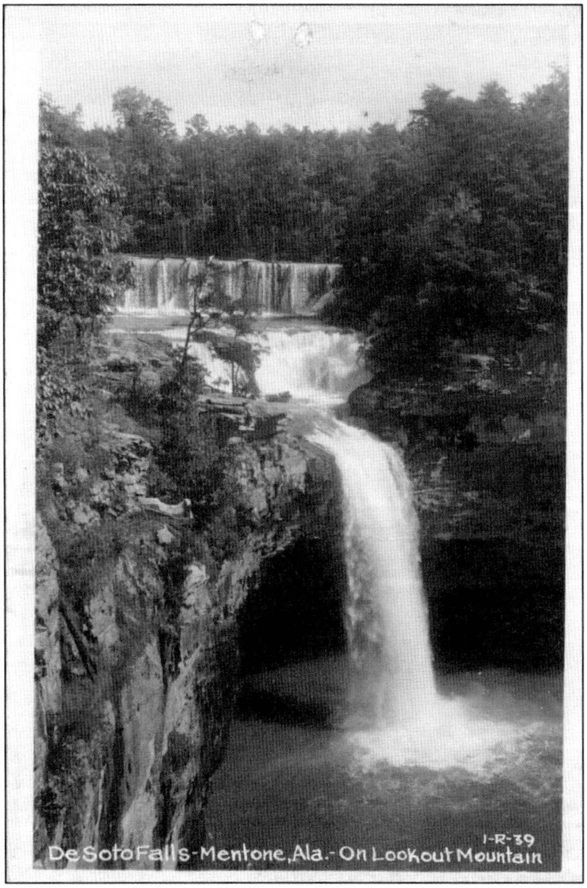

Rhododendron blooming near DeSoto State Park on Lookout Mountain is pictured in 1957. The interesting thing here is the view behind the plant. This was taken along the brow of the mountain with a clear view of the valley below. Like other photographs from the era, it shows a landscape less heavily covered with trees than today. (Courtesy of Collins Kirby.)

DeSoto Falls was captured by Cline Photo Company. This 1940s real-photo postcard is from an angle that looks out over the bluff to the water. New vegetation and tree coverage over the years alter the available lookout points. (Courtesy of Collins Kirby.)

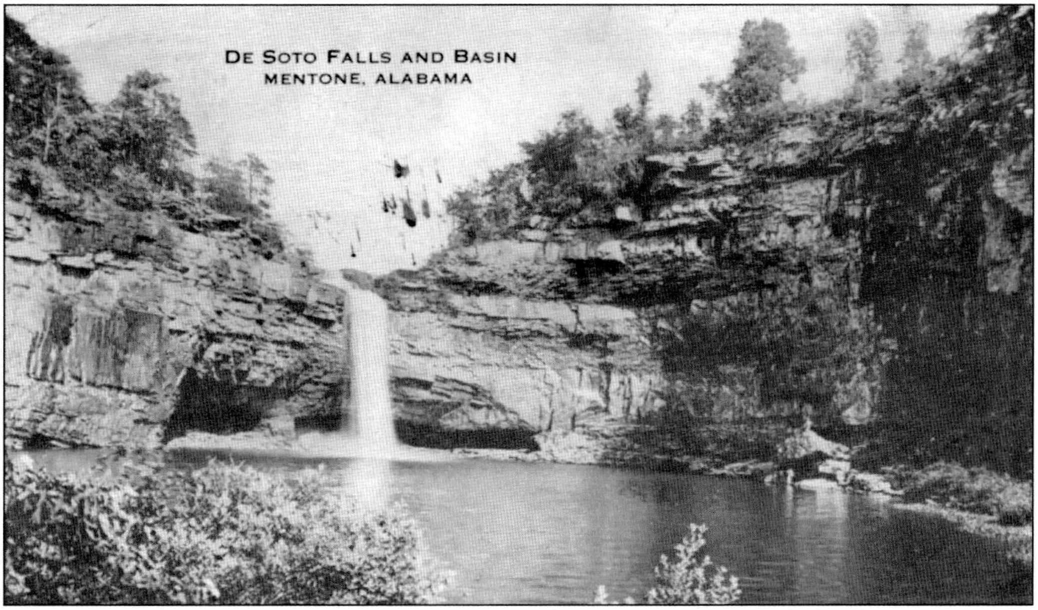

DeSoto Falls and its basin are pictured on this commercially printed card from the 1930s. Most pictures of DeSoto Falls are taken from the bluffs above. Access to this point is limited and takes quite a bit of hiking and climbing. (Courtesy of Collins Kirby.)

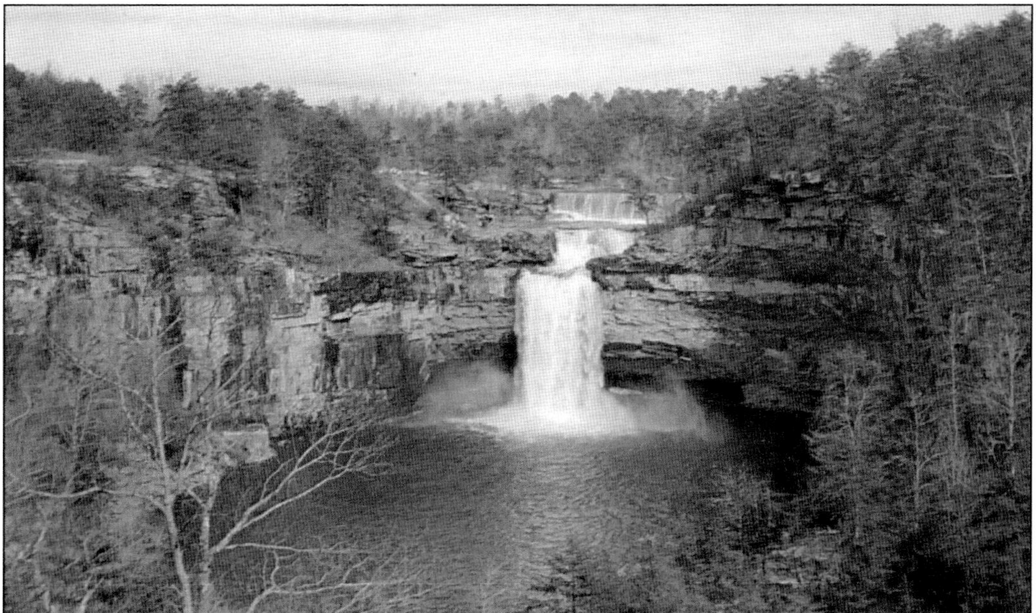

Here is a 1950s Kodachrome postcard. The photographer used Kodak Kodachrome film and then commercially printed the card to look like the Kodachrome original. Most of these cards were printed on line-textured card stock to improve their appearance. (Courtesy of Collins Kirby.)

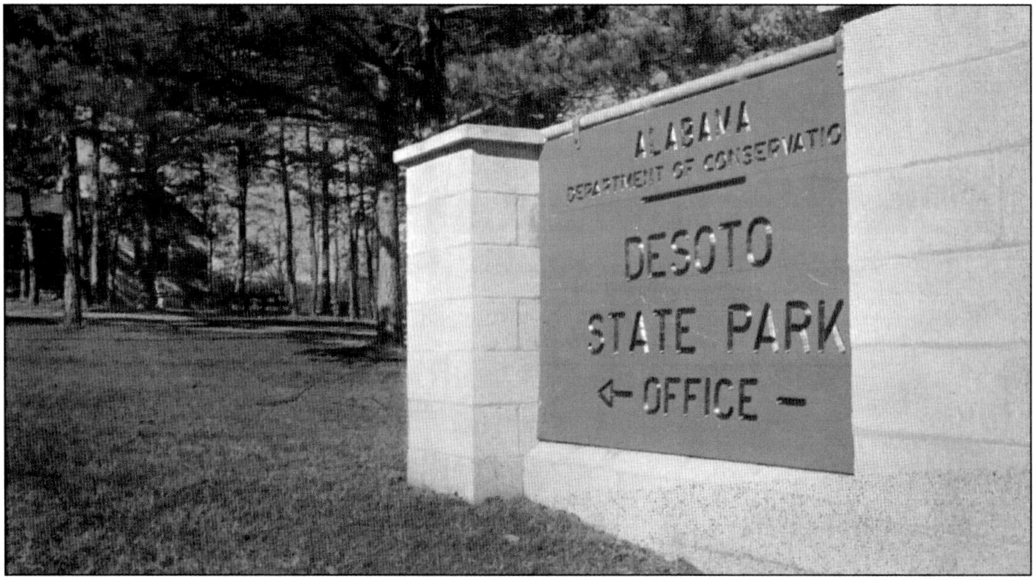

This commercially printed card from the 1960s shows one of DeSoto State Park's signs. Most state park systems around the country use the same look on all their signs. DeSoto Sate Park has a lodge, restaurant, rental cabins, and two campgrounds, with one being primitive and the other with full water, electric, and sewer hookups. There are wonderful trails, playgrounds, and picnic shelters. The West Fork of the Little River flows through the park, and some of the trails follow it. (Courtesy of Collins Kirby.)

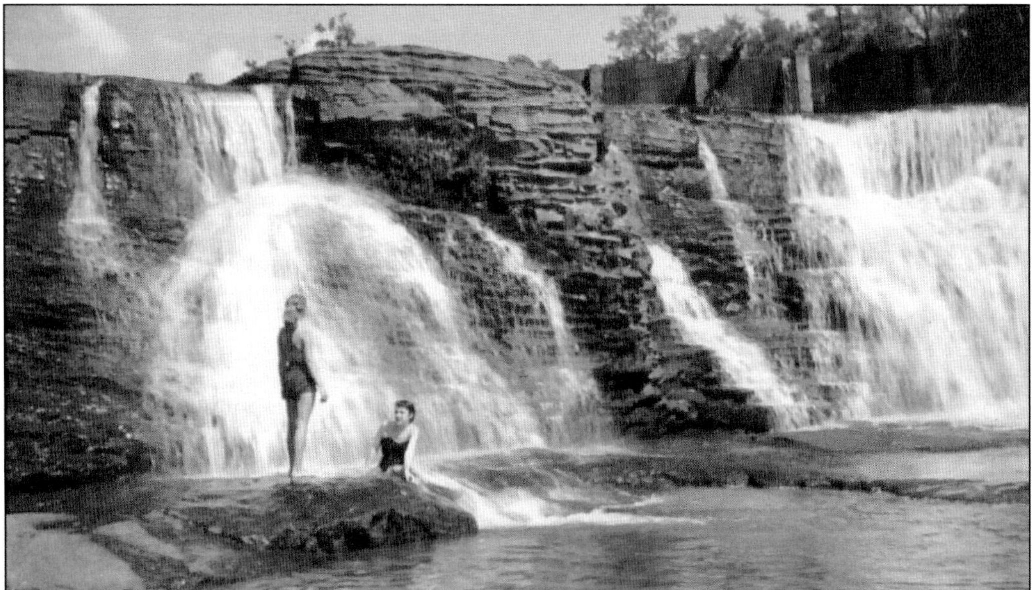

DeSoto State Park and DeSoto Falls have been an extremely popular tourist attraction since the park opened in 1939. This 1950s postcard shows young women enjoying the water below the first part of the double waterfalls that make up DeSoto Falls. Lookout Mountain enjoys highly developed tourism. It has many parks and public lands and privately owned attractions, bed-and-breakfasts, campgrounds, rental cabins, restaurants, and artisans across the nearly 100-mile-long mountain. (Courtesy of Collins Kirby.)

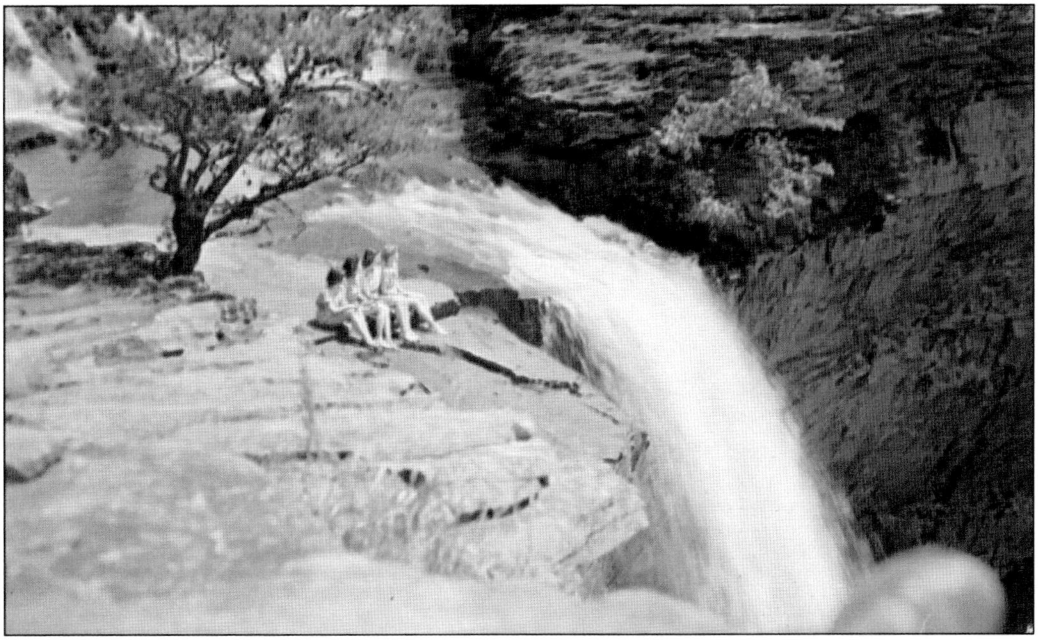

Lookout Mountain is full of summer boys' and girls' camps. There are eight in the area near Fort Payne and Mentone on Lookout Mountain. Many people who attend these summer camps take vacation time with their parents on weekends prior to camp beginning or after camp ends. These summer camp families fill the lodging and attractions each summer season. Here, in the 1960s, young ladies are enjoying the sun at DeSoto Falls. (Courtesy of Collins Kirby.)

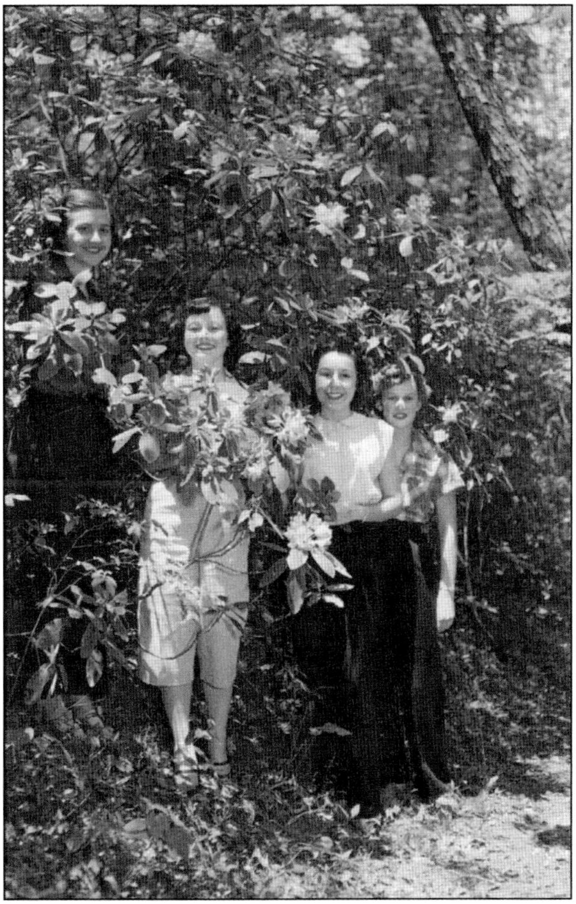

All along the top of Lookout Mountain are native rhododendron, wild azalea, and mountain laurel. All are part of the heath family of woody shrubs and bushes. These plants are typically associated with points farther north in the Appalachians, but they flourish here on Lookout Mountain in the southern region of the Appalachian Mountains and foothills. This 1950s postcard shows girls from one of the mountain's many summer camps posing with a rhododendron. (Courtesy of Collins Kirby.)

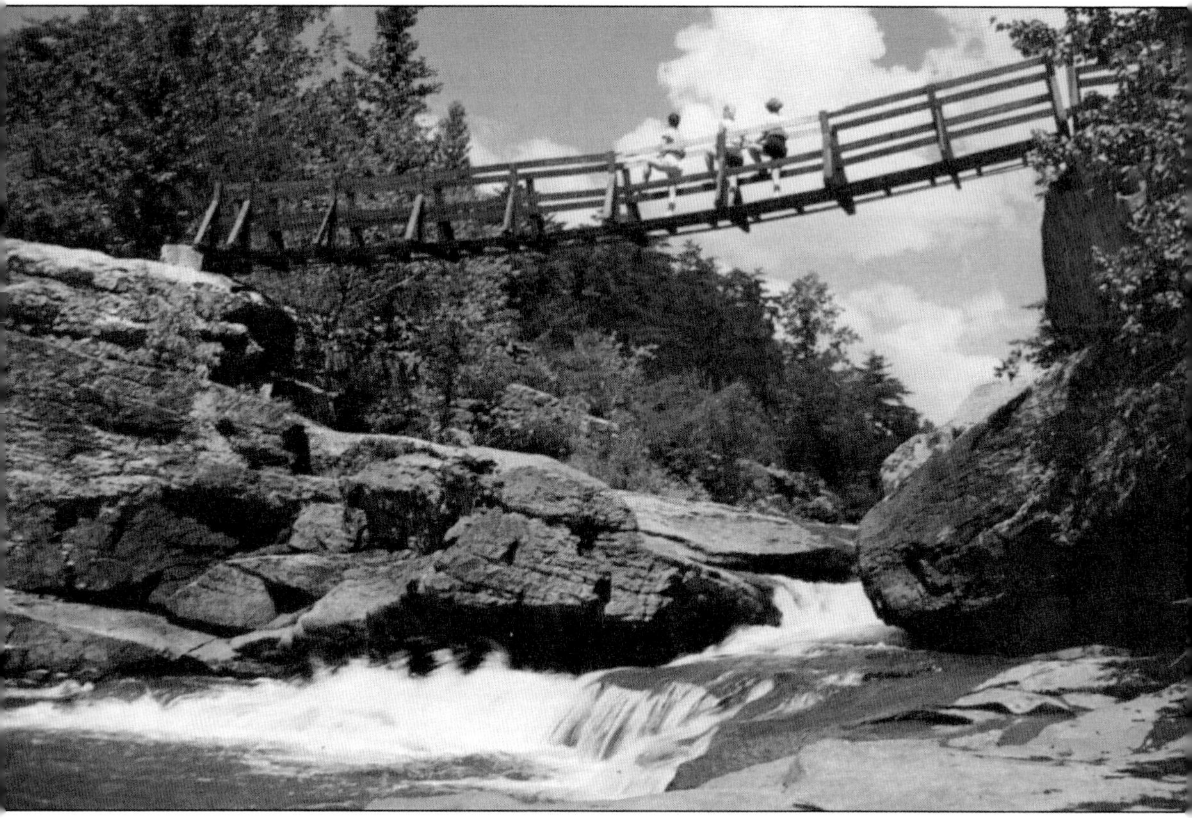

Colonel Howard, who built Howard's Chapel, also constructed a nearby tourist attraction called Alpine. This suspended walking bridge was part of this development project, which included a resort lodge. This 350-acre parcel of woodland paradise on Lookout Mountain is now Alpine Camp for Boys, which opened in 1959. The lodge is still used on this property as part of the camp. The Christian-based camp is a summer retreat that provides learning experiences with a strong outdoor content to get boys unplugged and back to nature with horseback riding, archery, water sports, mountain biking, golf, wilderness camping, music, art, and other wholesome activities. (Courtesy of Collin Kirby.)

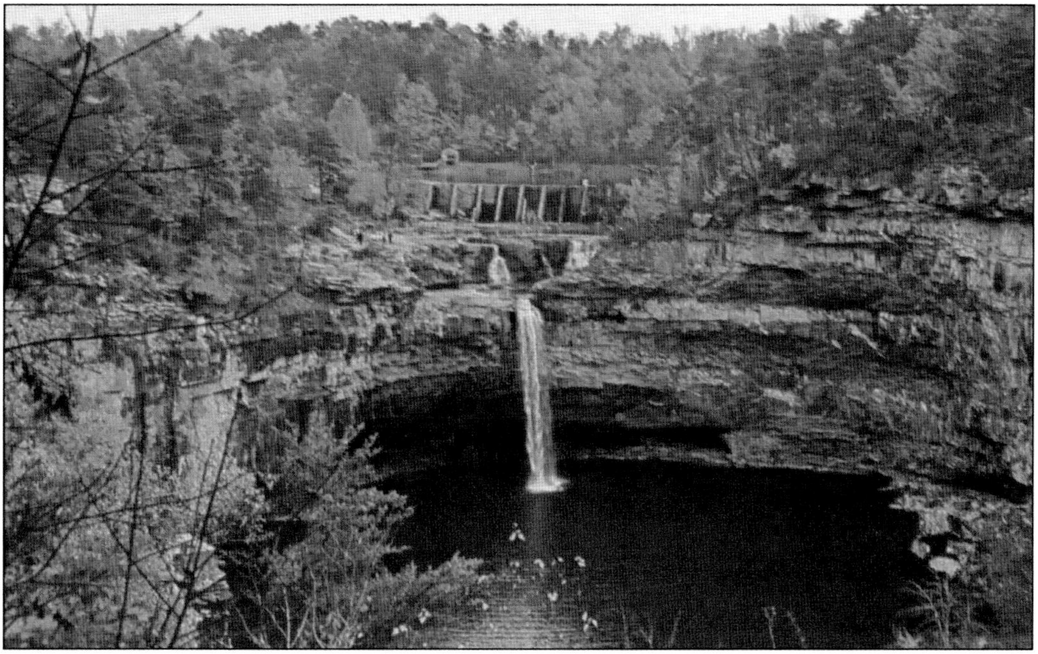

DeSoto Falls is seen from the bluffs above. This 1970s fall image shows less water coming over the falls. Usually October and early November are the driest months of the year in this area. Water levels go down, but the falls never go dry. (Courtesy of Collins Kirby.)

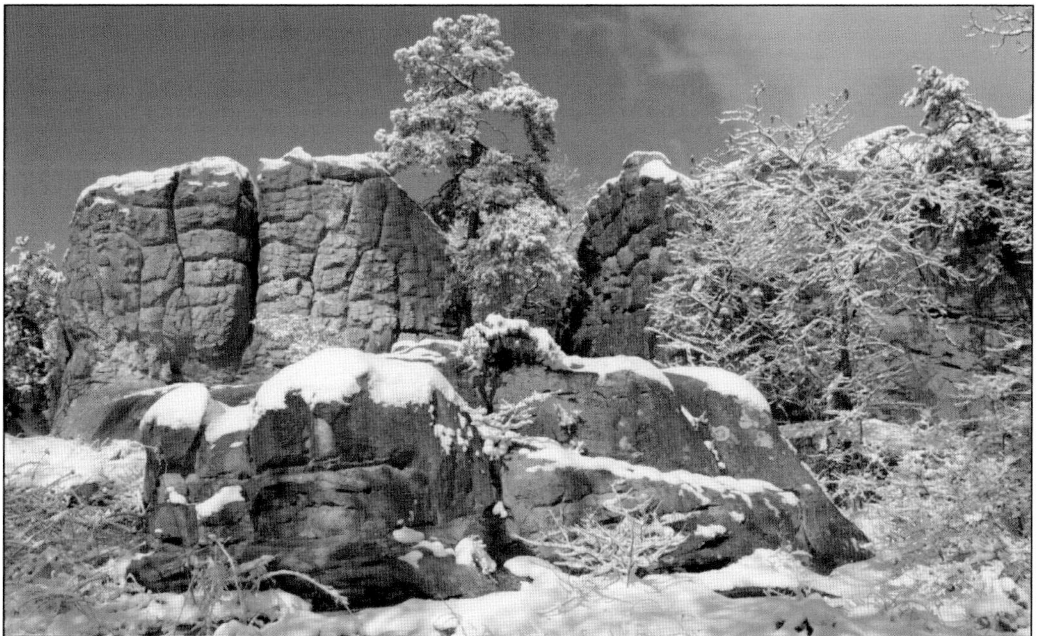

This February 2014 photograph shows major rock outcrops on Lookout Mountain. Lookout Mountain extends from Chattanooga through a corner of Northwest Georgia, but with most of it in Alabama and ending in Gadsden. The mountain is covered in public lands and great scenery. This rock outcrop, three stories in height, is similar to many seen along the entire length of this nearly 100-mile-long mountain. (Author photograph.)

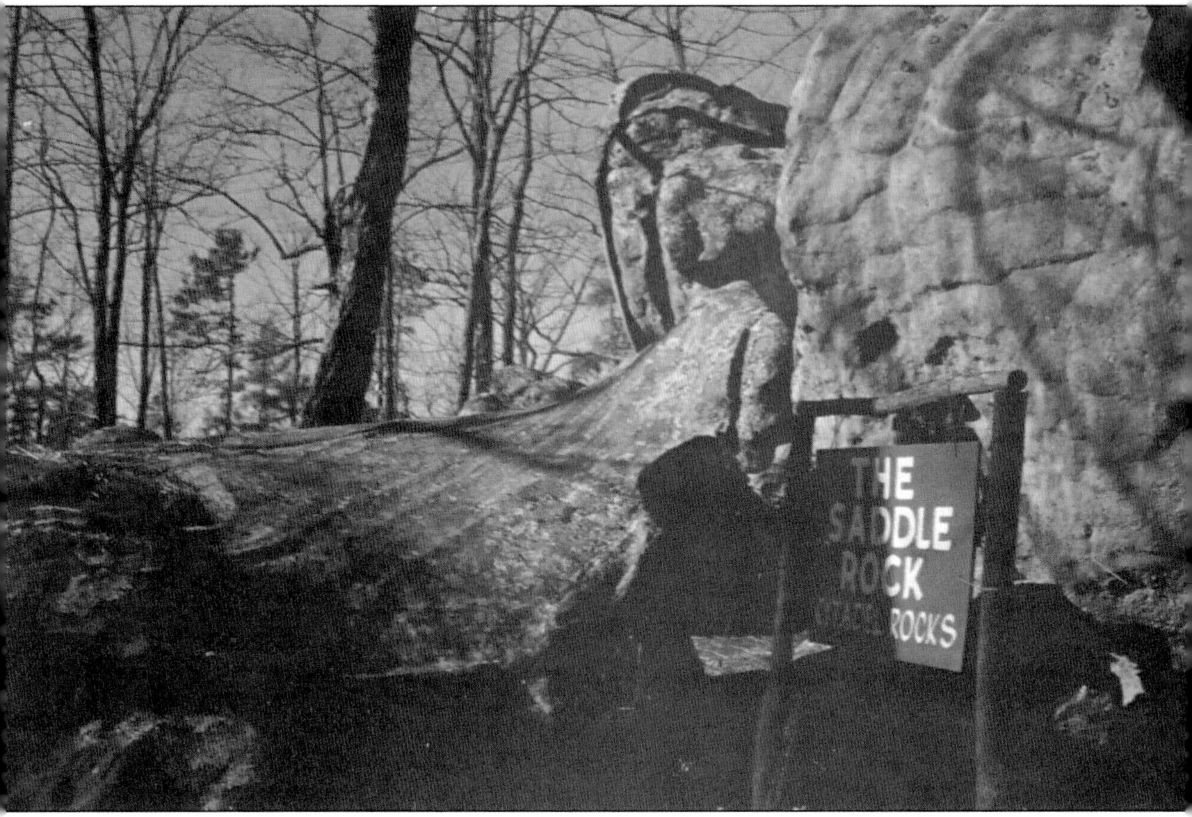

Once a very popular tourist attraction, Citadel Rocks lies on the western brow of Lookout Mountain above Fort Payne and near DeSoto State Park. At one time, it had a concession stand and significant infrastructure to help visitors see and climb these giant rock outcrops. (Courtesy of Collins Kirby.)

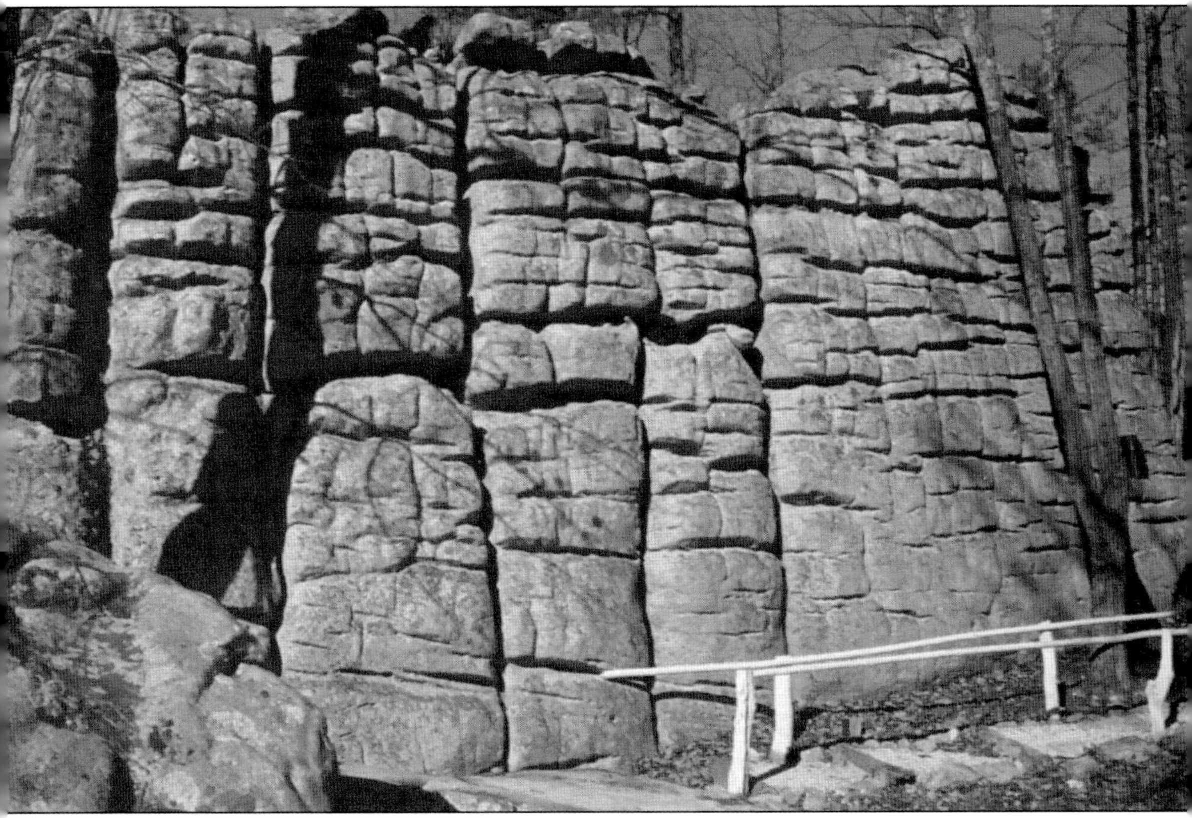

This card from the mid-1960s shows some of the features of the rocky outcrops and supporting signs and walkways. The location has been in private ownership for many years and has never been redeveloped. (Courtesy of Collins Kirby.)

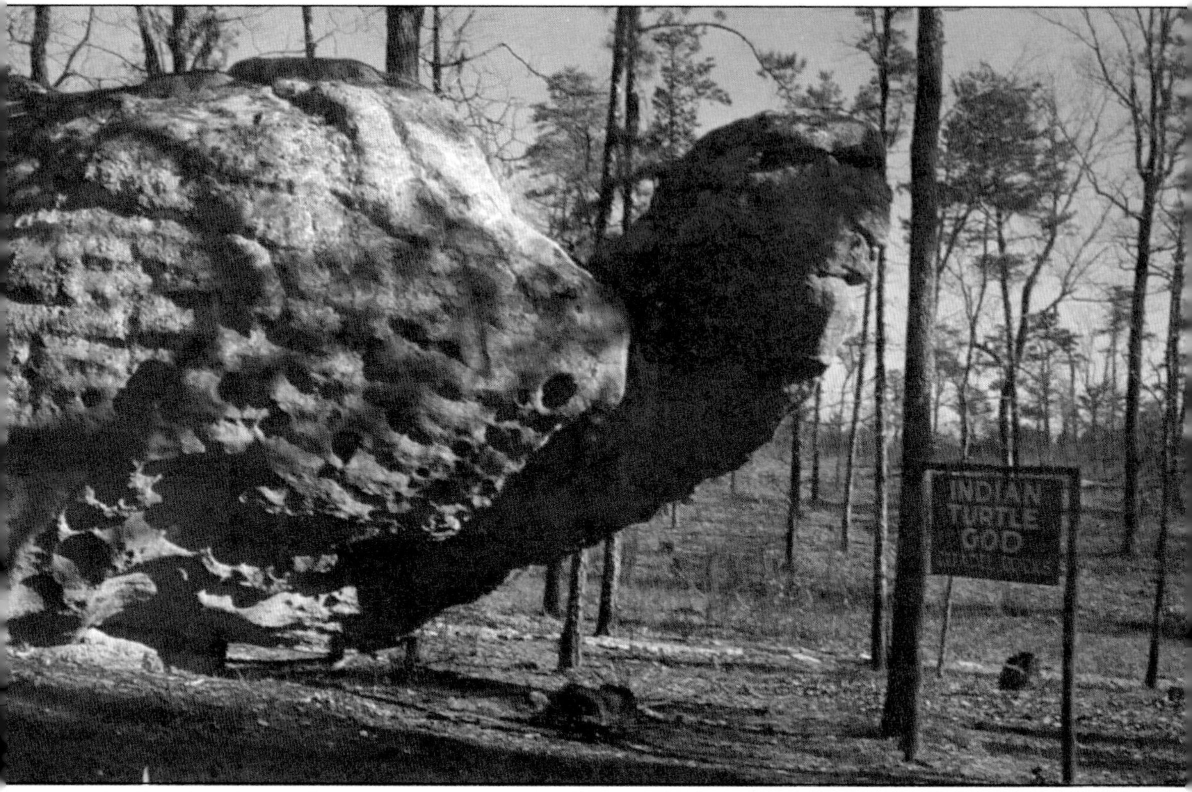

Indian Turtle Rock is seen here. Many of the rock formations on Lookout Mountain have been named over the years by owners and visitors who see faces and shapes of animals in the magnificent rocks. (Courtesy of Collins Kirby.)

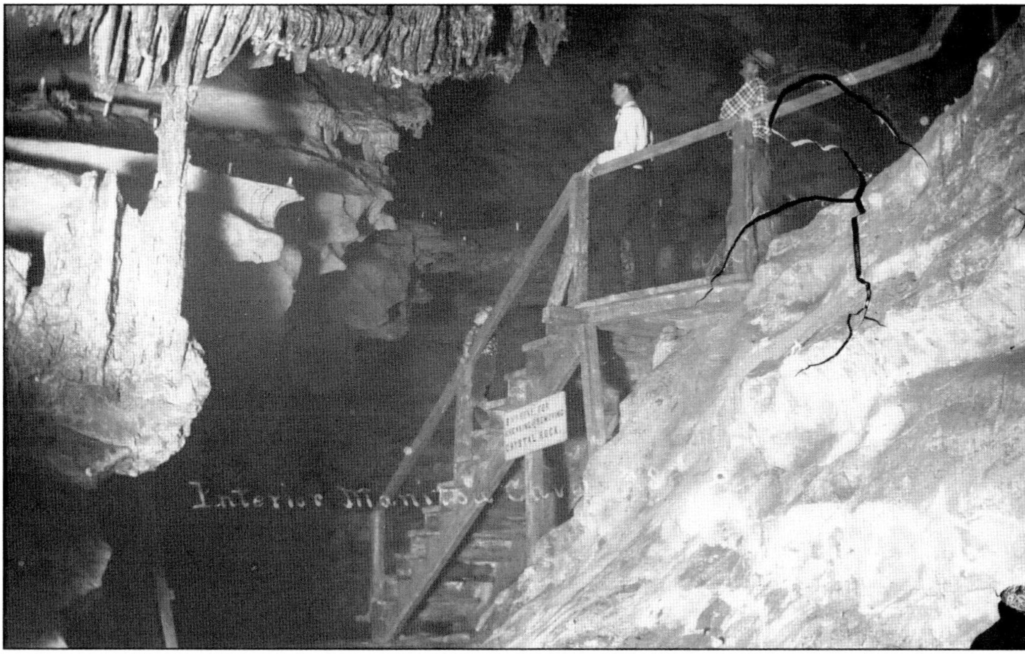

Dating back to the boom days of the late 1880s, Manitou Cave in Fort Payne was one of Alabama's first public tourist attractions. Prior to the advent of white settlers in the area, the cave was used by many generations of Cherokee and Woodland Indians. Cherokee Sequoyah, who invented the Cherokee alphabet called the Syllabary in 1821, lived in Fort Payne part of his life when it was called Willstown. There is some old writing in the cave using the Cherokee Syllabary, but it is unknown if it was written by Sequoyah. (Courtesy of Dr. Stephen Brewer.)

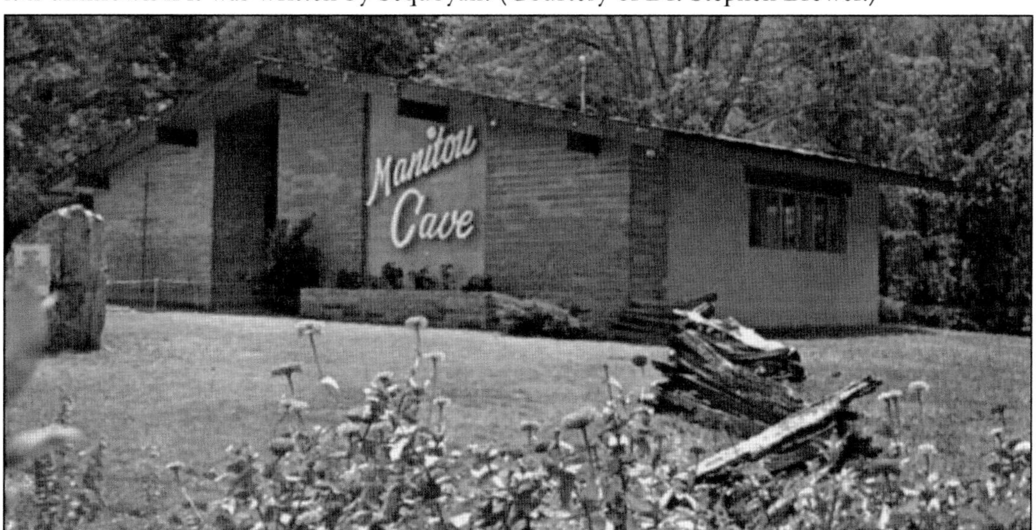

This 1960s commercially printed postcard shows the building at Manitou Cave used as the gift shop and ticket counter. Visitors would enter here and hike a short trail partway up the side of Lookout Mountain to enter the cave. This was a very popular attraction for many years. It was owned much of the time by the Raymond family, who came from New York and purchased the assets of the Fort Payne Coal and Iron Company at the end of the boom days. Much of the assets were in land, which included Manitou Cave. (Author's collection.)

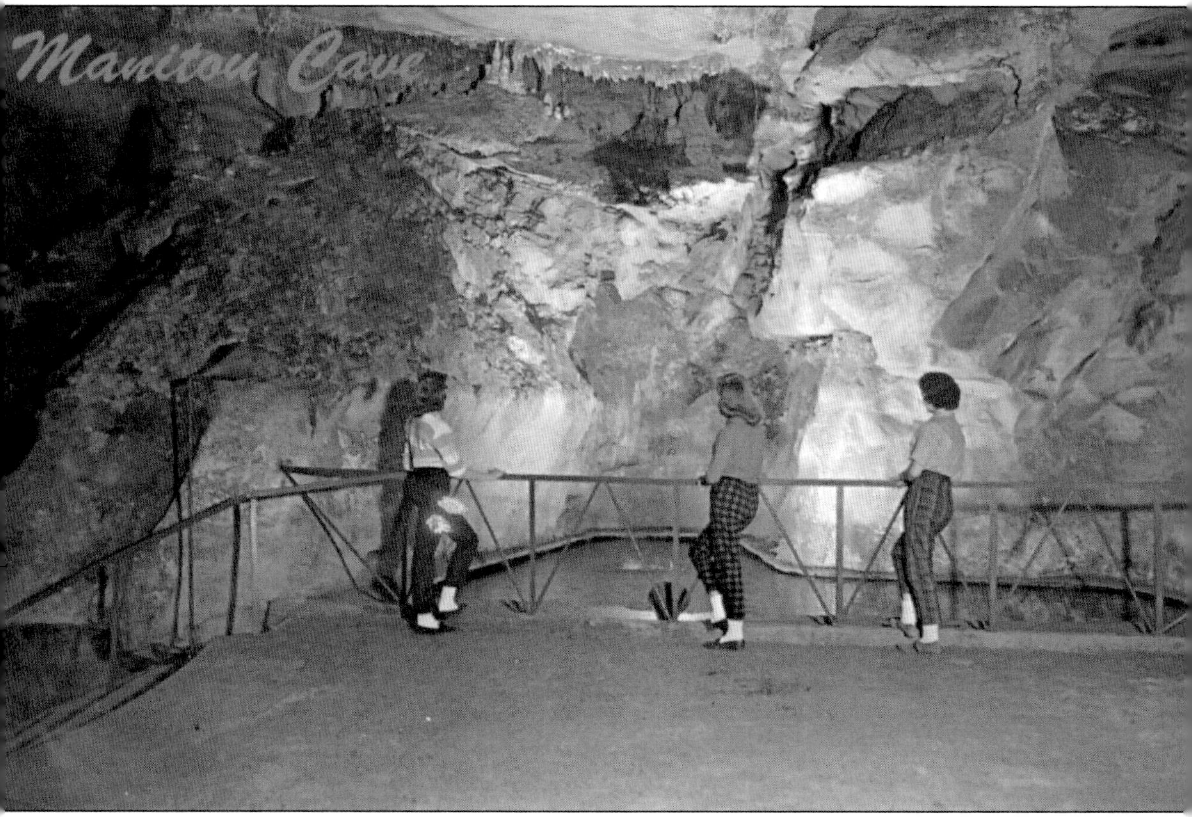

Manitou remained vital until Interstate 59 opened on the outskirts of Fort Payne in the 1960s. The new road took travelers off US Route 11, which the cave was near. Due to the speed of travel on the interstate and a changing culture of not stopping much along the way, Manitou Cave and hundreds of attractions on the entire Route 11 from north to south began closing. (Courtesy of Dr. Stephen Brewer.)

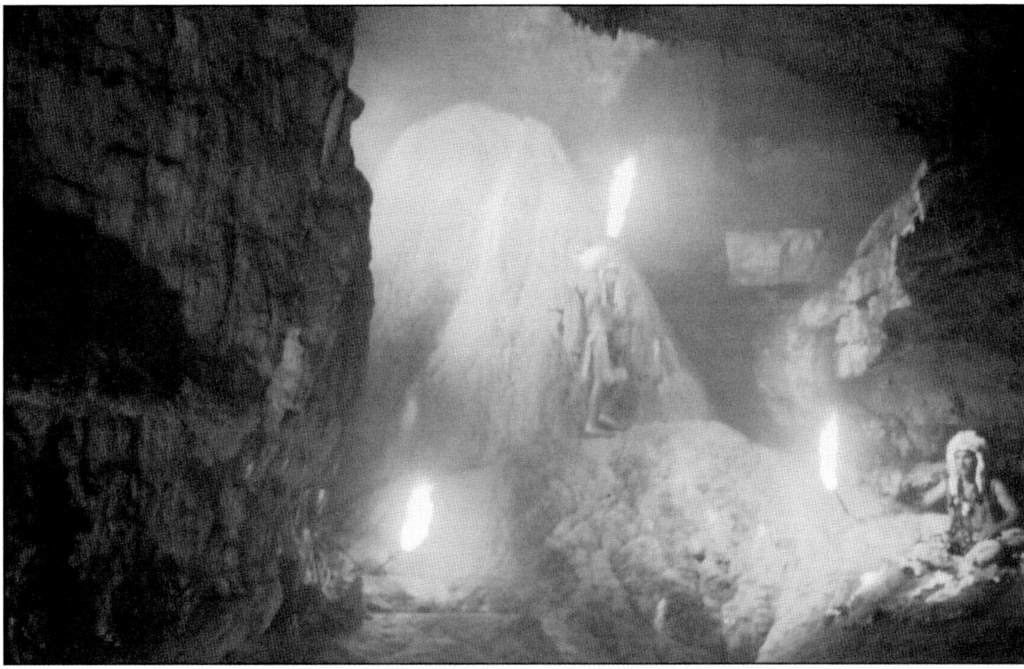

In the early 1970s, a young dentist named Stephen Brewer bought Manitou Cave, and ran the business through much of the decade. In the late 1970s, the visitor traffic was not enough to keep it going. It has never reopened to the public but has been used or leased by spelunkers and deep cave explorers. Much of the infrastructure inside the cave, including railing and walkways, dates back to the boom days. (Courtesy of Dr. Stephen Brewer.)

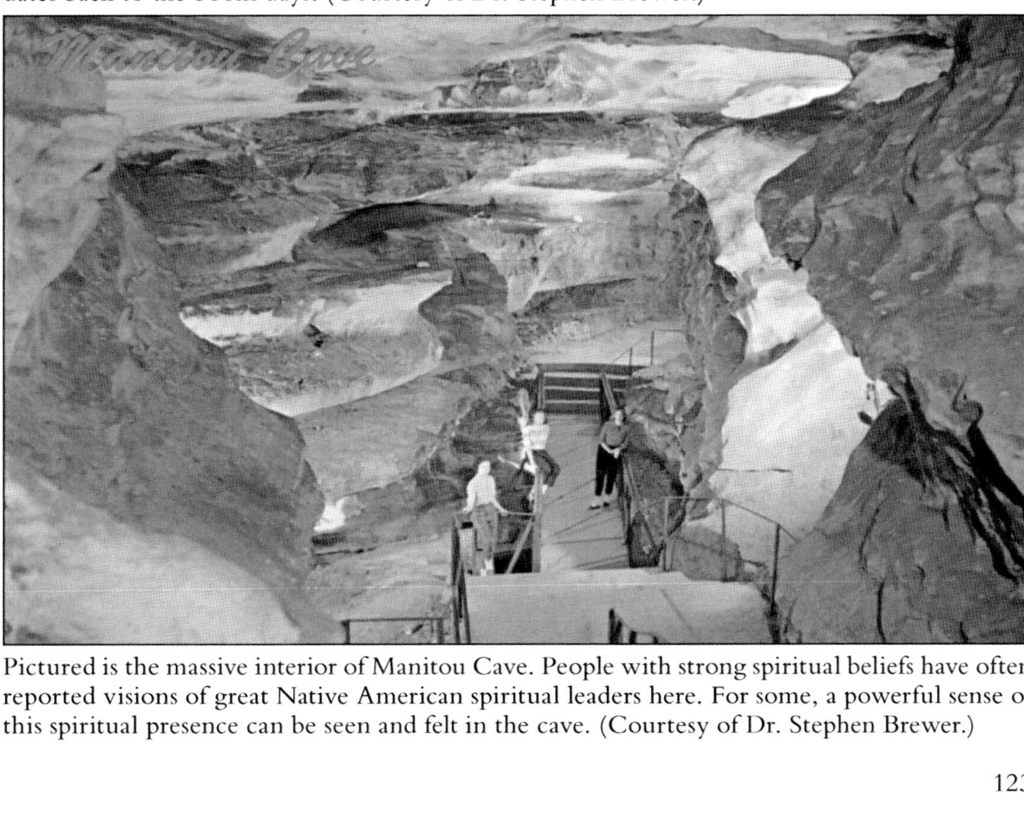

Pictured is the massive interior of Manitou Cave. People with strong spiritual beliefs have often reported visions of great Native American spiritual leaders here. For some, a powerful sense of this spiritual presence can be seen and felt in the cave. (Courtesy of Dr. Stephen Brewer.)

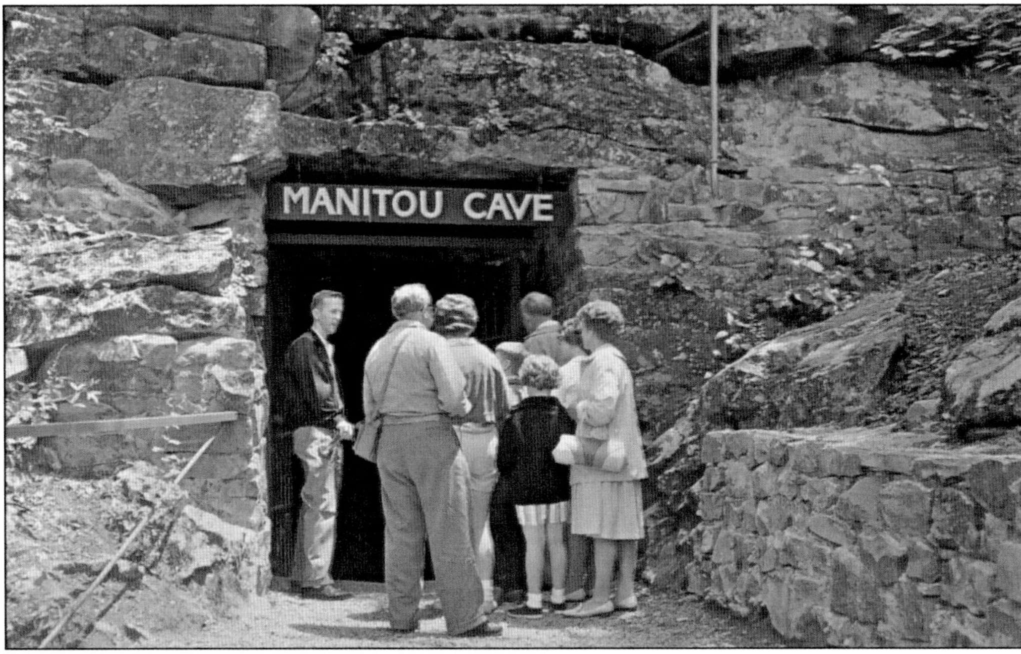

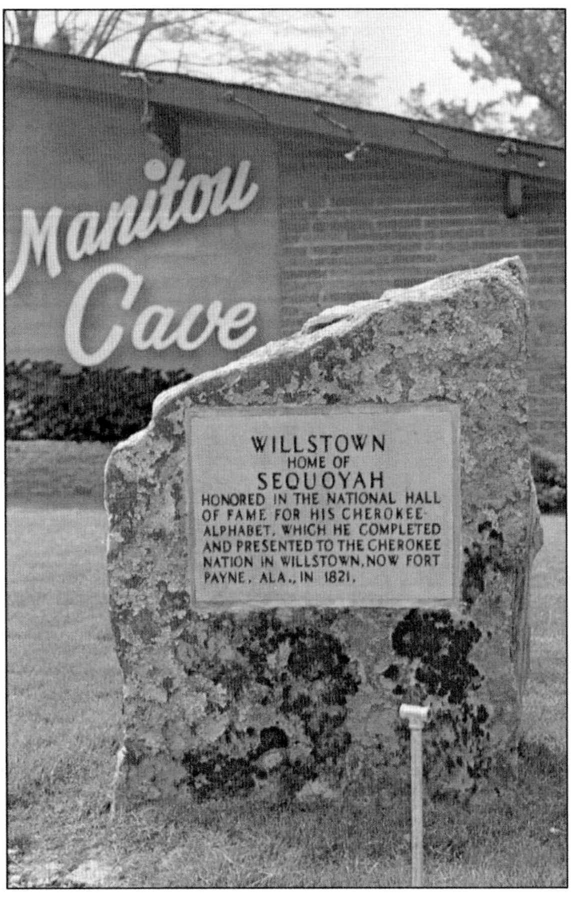

Visiting caves has long been popular. It has only been in the last couple of decades that cultural interests in what to do on vacation have changed and left many caves fighting for survival. Entertainment tourism featuring live action, computer programming, and lots of music and activity have replaced some of the culture of sightseeing at caves and other static historic locations. (Courtesy of Dr. Stephen Brewer.)

This sign outside the Manitou Cave gift shop honors Sequoyah, inventor of the Cherokee Alphabet. (Courtesy of Dr. Stephen Brewer.)

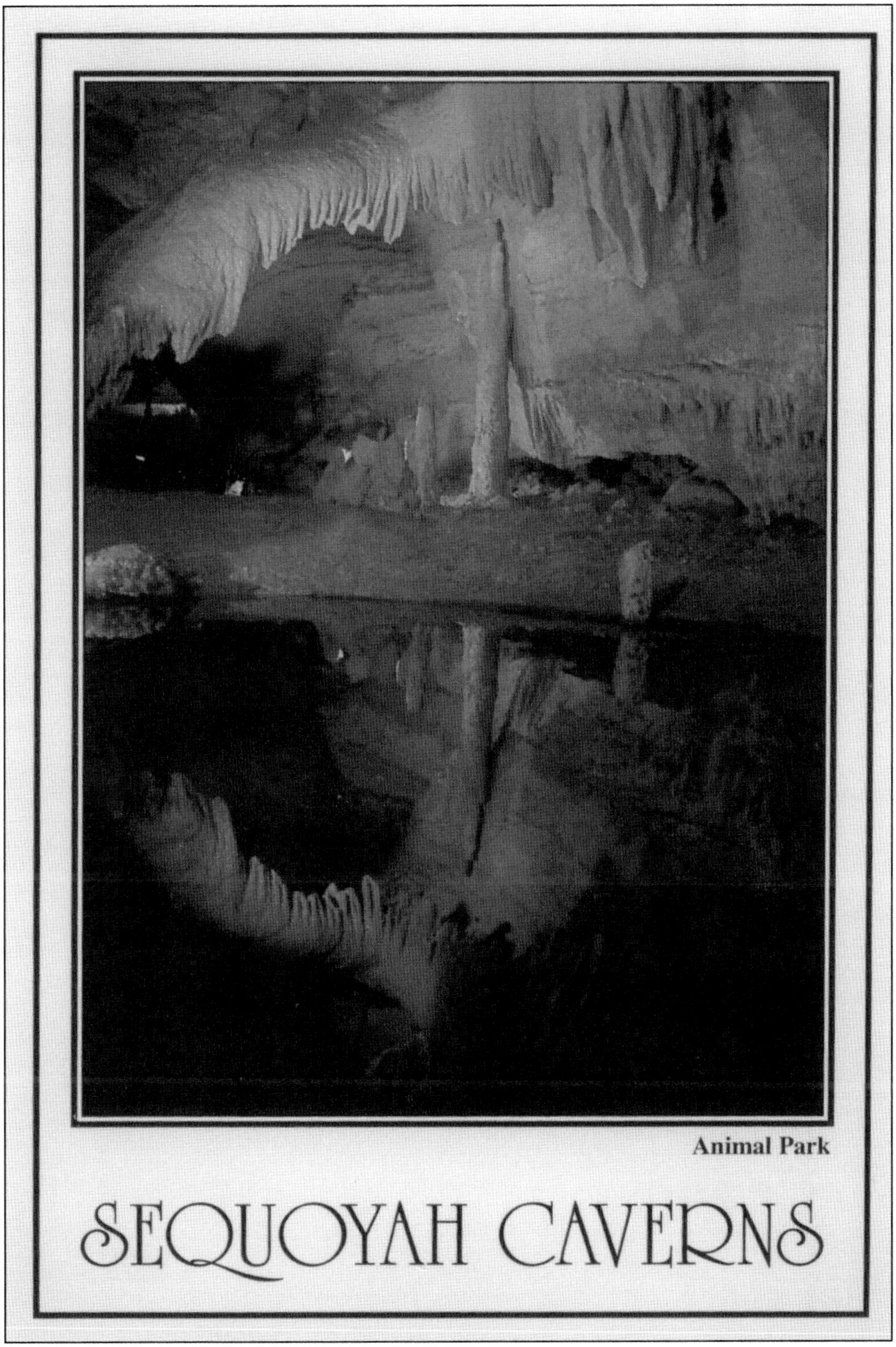

Sequoyah Caverns, located near Fort Payne in Wills Valley, has been owned by the same family since 1841. The cave, which is at the foot of Sand Mountain, was a popular tourist attraction open from 1964 through Labor Day 2013, when it was closed by the owners, the Jones family. The more than 1,000 acres of beautiful Wills Valley land is now used for farming, specifically strawberries. (Courtesy of John and Roy Jones.)

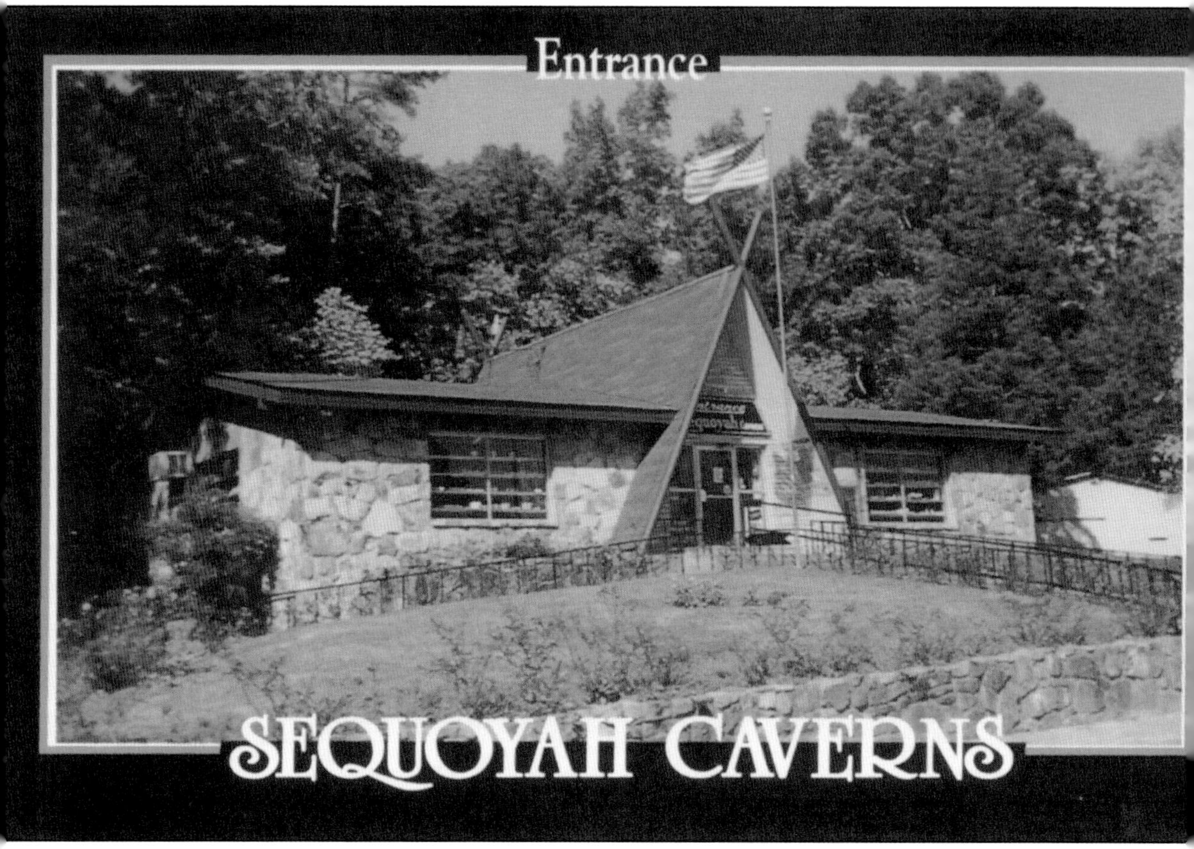

Does the building look familiar? Yes, Sequoyah Caverns had a campground with the familiar KOA branding and the recognizable building. This beautiful property had spring and fall festivals, a picnic area, camping, and a swimming pool. The official name was Sequoyah Caverns and Ellis Homestead. It is the Ellis family that the Jones family descended from. On the property are historic log cabins used by descendants. (Courtesy of John and Roy Jones.)

Sequoyah Caverns is known for it famous reflecting pools. The water is so still, dark, and clear that the pools work to form a perfect mirror image of those viewing it. It is truly a beautiful cave with outstanding formations and has been very well maintained over the years. This postcard of Rainbow Falls in Sequoyah Caverns provides a beautiful view of the interior. (Courtesy of John and Roy Jones.)

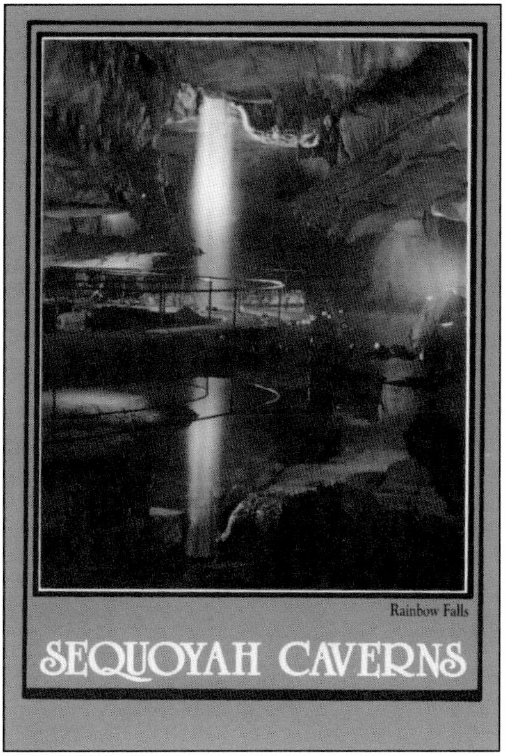

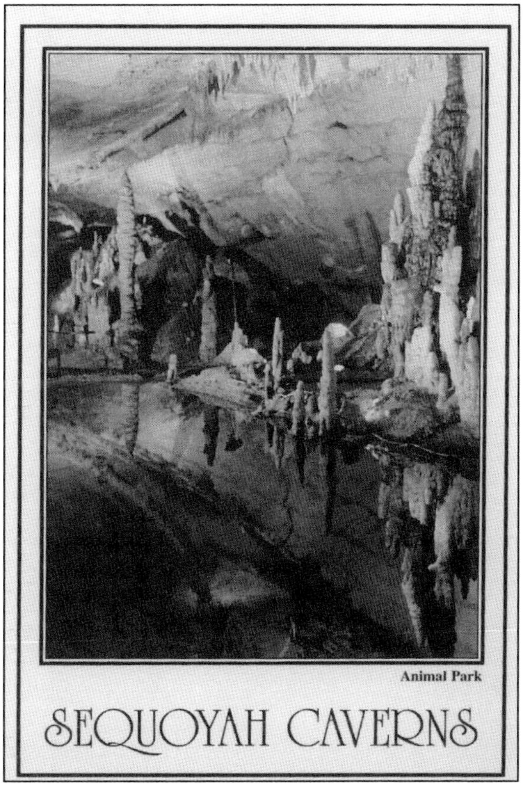

These fantastic formations took thousands of years to create. One formation is named Animal Park due to the interesting animal-like shapes it takes on when looked at from particular angles. (Courtesy of John and Roy Jones.)